Bloomsbury CPD Library: Research-Informed Practice

Jennifer Ludgate

BLOOMSBURY EDUCATION

LONDON   OXFORD   NEW YORK   NEW DELHI   SYDNEY

BLOOMSBURY EDUCATION
Bloomsbury Publishing Plc
50 Bedford Square, London, WC1B 3DP, UK

BLOOMSBURY, BLOOMSBURY EDUCATION and the Diana logo
are trademarks of Bloomsbury Publishing Plc

First published in Great Britain by Bloomsbury Education

Typeset by Integra Software Services Pvt. Ltd.
Printed and bound in the UK by CPI Group (UK) Ltd, Croydon CR0 4YY

To find out more about our authors and books visit www.bloomsbury.com and
sign up for our newsletters.

Contents

Acknowledgements

Firstly, a huge thanks to the team at Bloomsbury Education for believing this book would help those like me who, a few years ago, didn't know where to start in this seemingly new landscape – in particular, my editors Holly Gardner, whose kindness, knowledge and gentle persuasion have always left me feeling more capable than before, and Hannah Marston for supporting us at TLT, for thinking of me and for providing clarity and understanding.

The book is simply a bringing-together of all the sources, people and inspiration that have allowed me to embark on my own research-informed practice. All of them are named in some way in the following chapters and I hope that I will be research-savvy for my whole career thanks to their encouragement. Thanks also to Alex Quigley for his support when I started writing and to all those who have contributed to the book through sharing their classroom practice through case studies.

I would like to thank my colleagues and the senior leadership team at The Mountbatten School for supporting my career and quest to apply and embed research-informed practice. Thank you in particular to Ian Dunn for providing direction whenever I get lost and to Siân Cumming for making the research-informed dream a reality through her creativeness and perseverance.

Finally, thank you to those family members and friends who have supported this project regardless of my ridiculous timing. Thank you to my husband Simon Fountain for his endless support and patience. Thank you also to Lesley and Phil Ludgate for their unfaltering belief in everything we do.

How to use this book

The Bloomsbury CPD Library provides primary and secondary teachers with affordable, comprehensive and accessible 'do-it-yourself' continuing professional development. This book focuses on how to begin your journey to becoming a research-informed practitioner.

The book is split into two halves: Part 1 Teach yourself and Part 2 Train others.

Part 1: Teach yourself

This part of the book includes everything you need to know to help you engage with research, join the debate and consider how to apply this knowledge, thus becoming a research-informed practitioner.

Stage 1: Assess

In stage 1, reflect on what it means for you and your school to become research informed. Consider how much you know about research in education, including what has influenced your decision to explore what it means to be research informed in education.

Stage 2: Improve

In stage 2, learn about the key sources you should engage with if you wish to become, and remain, research informed. Begin to think about your own practice and a particular issue you want to solve in the longer term. Explore the wide range of sources that will keep you up to date with new research ideas and findings. Consider sharing your practice with others and read about interventions that you could adapt and apply to your own classroom.

Stage 3: Evaluate

In stage 3, take your time to evaluate the reading, engagement and development you have done so far, reflect upon the efforts that you have put in, and identify further needs and requirements. Make an action plan for your next steps to secure changes in your own teaching and to move forward by working more closely with others.

Stage 4: Excel

In stage 4, ultimately consider creating an action research question or statement that will encourage you to use your research-informed knowledge to find solutions to your self-identified issue or problem. Work at embedding your ideas, remembering at all times that changes should be introduced carefully and consciously.

At the end of each chapter you will find teaching tips, recommendations for sharing ideas and practice, a reading recommendation or title for discussion at a CPD reading group, a link to useful blog posts, and a 'to do' list to help your planning. I encourage you to use these to the full – they provide the depth, detail and opinion necessary if you hope to fully engage, in the long term, with the variety of views and arguments revolving around this developing teaching and learning movement.

By the end of part 1 you will have assessed, improved and considered the application of your own research-informed practice.

Part 2: Train others

Now that you are immersed in research-informed thought and practice, it's time to train others in your school! External training can be expensive and in-house training is hugely valuable as it can be made relevant to your context – the teachers and students in your school. Whether it is a quick 15-minute training session, a series of twilight sessions or use of a whole-day INSET, you will find advice and training plans in this section, including:

- advice for running good CPD
- training plans for introducing research to all staff
- twilight training sessions to develop engagement and discussion
- training plans for running quick 15-minute CPD sessions
- training plans for middle leaders

- training plans to encourage and implement action research
- a whole-school INSET day training plan.

See page 186 for an overview of the training plans.

Online resources

For templates, questionnaires and PowerPoints from the book please visit:
www.bloomsbury.com/CPD-library-research-informed-practice

Good luck with teaching yourself and training others! Keep us updated on your progress by tweeting using #BloomsCPD.

Part 1

Teach yourself

1

What's it all about?

In teaching, research-informed practice means reading, reflecting, discussing and applying the available scientific research about how students learn and how we choose to teach. The purpose of engaging with research to inform your practice is not to become a researcher yourself, but to become aware of the science behind teaching and learning – thus allowing teachers to make research-informed decisions instead of best guesses. Becoming research informed, I believe, invites us to take a different, sometimes less well-trodden, route towards solutions to often perpetual problems we experience in our classrooms.

Although far from new, research-informed practice is an approach that is becoming ever more prevalent, and arguably necessary, in a world in which we are constantly exposed to facts without being provided with evidence to support them. I have been lucky enough to observe and discuss teaching strategies and practices with many excellent practitioners but haven't always understood why they do what they do, and I believe that sometimes they haven't known why they made certain choices either. Early in my career, I used many suggested strategies without knowing why I was doing so. I remember using a plethora of exciting assessment for learning techniques when being observed but hardly ever acted on the findings – simply knowing and believing it would tick a box but without a real understanding or reason as to why these strategies were popular or what I was supposed to do to make them effective. Many of my decisions were made because it seemed like the right thing to do. Nothing more and nothing less. I often focused on *what* I was doing; it never occurred to me to consider *why*. Seeing as other people did this too I didn't stop to question it.

Up until recently, the vast majority of my discussions with colleagues about their choice of pedagogical approach have either begun or ended with an anecdote. They do what they do, often brilliantly, because 'that's the way it has always been done or because it worked once upon a time', even if that was in 1991, in a grammar school, with a small group of boys who liked rugby and nothing else – it worked then so surely it would work now. In particular, post-observation discussions have often left me wanting to ask:

- Why did you/I do X?
- Why did it work?
- How do you/I know it worked?
- Can you/I be sure it will work again?
- Why did you/I choose to do X over Y?

Whenever I have asked these questions of others or myself, more often than not, there is no clear focus to the answer. A research-informed teacher should be able to respond to these questions without referring to anecdotes or best guesses. Instead, they would be able to explain the problem they had, the inquiry they began, the evidence they reflected upon, the approach they used and the application of this in their own classroom.

Becoming a research-informed practitioner should allow us more confidence in solving our own problems and provide us with ownership over the day-to-day decisions made in classrooms that directly affect student outcomes.

The aim of this book is to highlight key areas of educational research to help us ask better questions of ourselves and to enhance our ability to think proactively about our decision-making processes before we apply strategies to the teaching and learning taking place in our classrooms.

It is understandable that you can be both confused and excited about the ever-changing and expanding world in education of which research-informed practice plays a part. It has started to become part of our professional dialogue and this book aims to make the first steps to becoming a research-informed practitioner simpler and more accessible to either those at the beginning of their journey or those looking to take the next steps in training others to do the same.

What is research?

The word research is derived from the old French term '*recerchier*', which is related to the French '*chercher*' meaning to search. It is this aspect of the word that we too often ignore; we presume research will tell us the answers but do not always appreciate that, often, the part of the process that can be the most beneficial for our practice is the thinking about the question posed and the 'searching' for more questions.

Oxford Dictionaries (2010) defines 'research' as the studying of a subject in detail in order to discover new information or how it will result in new conclusions. Interestingly, many of the examples given in the dictionary relate to the medical field. It is true that research is an area we expect to hear about in relation to modern-day medicine. On a weekly basis, there are stories in the newspapers about new scientific advances or findings from a new piece of research that will impact many people currently suffering from X, Y and Z. Many of us also know not to take these headlines at face value – a lesson we can apply to educational research too.

In a 2008 paper discussing the challenges of evidence-based medicine, medical experts from the University of Sarajevo stated that: 'Today, in almost all western countries doctors apply EBM [evidence-based medicine] in treatment for every patient with the support of the governments of these countries, the ministries of health and pharmaceutical industry.' (Masic et al., 2008) This understanding that EBM is necessary seems commonly accepted (although it's not without its issues) whereas using evidence in classrooms is widely debated. Understandably, there are a wide variety of factors at play in classrooms and I hope that nothing in this book suggests that becoming research informed is the only thing that matters as a teacher, nor suggests that knowledge of research and the ability to implement research-informed practice will solve all of education's ills. I hope that it does suggest, however, that research is something we could all consider a little more. Being part of the debate about whether or not teachers should or shouldn't be research informed matters. Many of the sources and references in this book will lead you to find out more about these debates and perhaps how to become involved in them. At conferences run by organisations such as 'ResearchEd' (a teacher-led organisation set up in 2013 to discuss and disseminate educational research), you will often hear discussions about the concerns and limitations of teachers' use of research. The debate continues as to how much engagement there should be, if any, with research in the classroom; not everyone believes there is a need for a research-informed profession.

What does research-informed practice in education look like?

There are many different possible answers to this question. Depending on your perspective, whether you are a teacher, scientist, researcher or academic, you will have a different response. For the purpose of this book, research-informed practice means to consider the empirical evidence to inform our decisions about the methods we use and the interventions we instigate. We might use this research to inform, challenge or support our decision-making and we should use it alongside our professional knowledge of our own context, reminding ourselves when reading research that every student in every classroom in every school across the world is different; therefore what works in one situation may not work in another.

Whilst reading, consider that although I identify key papers and possible strategies to use based on research, you must critically evaluate, ask questions and decide how trustworthy the source is, how relevant it is to your context and what other evidence you are provided with in order to make your next decision. We will look at how to do this in more detail in Chapter 3, page 49.

Reflection questions

Consider the following:

- What was the last big decision you made about your teaching practice?
- How quickly did you come to this decision?
- Who or what did you or would you turn to when making a decision about your practice?
- Did you feel confident in your decision-making process?

What is the attitude of your school towards research?

Considering your school's values as well as your own will make the process of engaging with research more valuable; becoming research informed as an individual has its benefits but we know that working with and alongside others is beneficial when encouraging change. As with any element of pedagogy and practice, schools vary greatly in their engagement with educational research and this can again be due to a wide range of factors, from funding, to stability of teachers, to the school's individual priorities for improvement, which may be deemed more important or relevant.

It is an easy judgement to make that your school is not research-savvy when decision-making and research is not discussed often or openly with staff. That does not mean that research is not being read, reviewed or engaged with to make important decisions, but perhaps it has not yet become part of the norm in conversations, discussions and practice. It is important to consider the question from an individual point of view and then to go away and investigate a little further in order to have a fully rounded perspective. Chapter 2's self-assessment guide (page 11) will aid you in doing this in depth and is helpful in working out the next steps in your own individual or your whole school's journey.

This is not to say that simply becoming a research-informed teacher and having a better understanding of key research will transform your school but it is a method of improving your own practice, as you will need a clear sense of direction and preferably one that sits comfortably with your own and your school's ethos and values. To consider this further, reflect upon the following features of teachers and schools willing to become more research informed. These are useful to assess your own attitude towards research as well as that of your current school.

Features of a teacher willing to become further research informed	Features of a school willing to become further research informed
Willing to ask questions about new strategies and ideas.	Leaders and managers are open to discussion and alternative interpretations.
Willing to read further and question summaries and overviews.	Collaboration is part of the ethos of the school (at all levels – departments and leadership).
Considers a new strategy or technique before implementing it in the classroom.	Evaluative language is used when implementing policies or strategies.
Conscious that their decision-making will have a complex impact on others.	Policies and strategies are evaluated as routine and adapted as necessary.
Open to changing their practice if necessary.	Teachers at all levels contribute towards the school's improvement plan and are aware of its goals and ambitions.

As teachers and schools, we must be open to the questions rather than simply the answers that being research informed can bring. Many of the statements relate to a willingness to share, collaborate and be open about what we don't know even more than with what we do know. Research-informed practice is, if used badly, in danger of becoming a way in which we justify new strategies or approaches to others above how we continually question and improve our practice. Although becoming repetitive, we must pause to remember that becoming more aware of key research will not mean we have all the answers and that we can then run our classroom or school in a particular way for years to come without asking any further questions.

One reason that we don't and can't have all the answers is because more research needs to take place; it might also be that the research isn't readily available to school leaders or teachers, or often that someone simply hasn't asked that question before, as until fairly recently a lot of educational research was not based on the needs or questions of teachers in the classroom. By becoming more research informed as a profession, this is something we can seek to improve.

Chapter 1 takeaway

Teaching tip
Consider your options
Take the time to consider what led you to be interested in research in education. You should consider how long you have been teaching and

why you wish to look at this now. Being aware of what brought you to think about research does matter as it might help you in deciding on your application of research in the classroom. Consider your values as a teacher at this point – what do you believe in? Are there certain theories of teaching you would align yourself with? Why?

There will be an internal struggle as you proceed, as research might cause you to query what you thought to be true. It might also throw up some challenges between you and others. Consider what tensions might be caused both internally and externally and then think about what you can do to address these as you read on. Don't underestimate the importance of time to consider these issues fully.

Pass it on
Make a cuppa
Talking to others about their values and questions they have about using research to inform their teaching is a good place to air your own views. It is best to do this informally at first – try to gauge what others around you know and whether or not they can be of any support. You may wish to do this off the back of a decision that has recently been made in your school, department or classroom. Having an understanding of the views of those around you and the knowledge you might gain from them or can share with them is an important place to start – especially if you are hoping to eventually get them on board.

CPD book club recommendation
It is worth reading this report from Teach First but it is long and might leave you with more questions than answers! The introduction and pages 8–12 are very valuable when starting out on your journey: Rose and Eriksson-Lee (2017), available at www.teachfirst.org.uk/sites/default/files/2017-10/Putting_Evidence_to_work_2017.pdf.

Bloggers' corner
'Breaking beyond our old ideas' by Alex Quigley. A blog post on the stages of finding new ideas and the benefit of evidence in doing so.

Link: www.theconfidentteacher.com/2016/03/escaping-the-tyranny-of-our-old-ideas

TO DO LIST:

- ❑ Define your own values and which theories of teaching you best agree with.
- ❑ Define your school's current values so that you can consider how your journey will work in your current setting.
- ❑ Answer the questions in the reflection box on page 6 and discuss them with a colleague.
- ❑ Talk to school leaders and colleagues about their experiences of research-informed practice.
- ❑ Read Alex Quigley's short blog post on changes to old habits.

2 Self-assessment

Considering where you and your school currently are in relation to research-informed practice, as discussed in Chapter 1, is the important first step towards moving forward in your understanding and engagement with educational research, yet it can be challenging.

Depending on your experience, role and confidence in your own teaching and/or your leadership of others, it can be difficult to take a step back and rationally, fairly and accurately assess your current position in contrast to where you would like to be. In order to create a sustainable and future-proof action plan that will carry you forward successfully, we must know where to begin.

This is where the self-assessment section of the book comes into play. This chapter will provide you with a starting point and will help you avoid the panic gap-filling that so often happens if we jump right into a new way of working without full consideration.

How to complete the self-assessment questionnaire

In this chapter you will find a self-assessment questionnaire to encourage you to start the 'teach yourself' process by thinking very carefully about your current understanding and use of educational research before you jump into trying to improve your practice using it.

There is more than one way to approach reviewing your current practice in order to form a clear view of where you are now and what the next steps will be, and your approach will depend on you as a person. For some people, it is useful to go with your gut and listen to the first thing that comes into your mind – your instinctual answer. For others, it is better to spend a good amount of time really considering the self-assessment questions slowly and in more detail.

Quick response approach

If your preference for the self-assessment is to go with your gut, then focus on filling in the quick response section for each question. Do not mull over the question too long; simply read carefully and answer. This approach will give you an overview of your current understanding and practice of using educational research in your decision-making processes and will take relatively little time. Just make sure you are uninterrupted, in a quiet place and able to complete the questionnaire in one sitting with no distractions so that you get focused and honest answers.

Considered response approach

If you choose to take a more reflective and detailed approach, then you can leave the quick response section blank and go straight on to reading the further guidance section under each question. This guidance provides prompt questions and ideas to get you thinking in detail about the question being asked and is designed to open up a wider scope in your answer. It will also enable you to look at your experience and pull examples into your answer to back up your statements. You may want to complete it a few questions at a time and take breaks, or you may be prepared to simply sit and work through the questions all in one sitting to ensure you remain focused. This approach does take longer, but it can lead to a more in-depth understanding of your current practice, and you will gain much more from the process than from the quick response alone.

Combined approach

A thorough approach, and one I recommend, would be to use both approaches together regardless of personal preference. This involves firstly answering the quick response questions by briefly noting down your instinctual answers for all questions. The next step would be to return to the start of the self-assessment, read the further guidance and then answer the questions once more, slowly and in detail,

• I have done this self-assessment before. • I only want a surface-level overview of my current understanding and practice. • I work better when I work at speed. • I don't have much time.	**Quick**
• I have never done this self-assessment before. • I want a deeper understanding of my current understanding and practice. • I work better when I take my time and really think things over. • I have some time to do this self-assessment.	**Considered**
• I have never done this self-assessment before. • I have done this self-assessment before. • I want a comprehensive and full understanding of my current understanding and practice and want to compare that to what I thought before taking the self-assessment. • I have a decent amount of time to dedicate to completing this self-assessment.	**Combined**

Fig. 1 How should I approach the self-evaluation questionnaire?

forming more of a narrative around each question and pulling in examples from your own experience. Following this, you would need to read over both responses and form a comprehensive and honest summary in your mind of your answers and a final view of where you feel you stand right now in your use of educational research to support decision-making regarding your teaching and learning.

This is the longest of the three approaches to this questionnaire but will give you a comprehensive and full understanding of your current practice, thoughts and feelings in relation to research-informed practice being used in schools. You will be surprised at the difference you see between the quick response and the considered response answers to the same questions. It can be very illuminating.

Rate yourself

The final part of the self-assessment is to rate yourself. This section will ask you to rate your confidence and happiness in each area that has been covered in the questionnaire, with a view to working on these areas for improvement throughout the course of the book. The table below shows how the scale works: the higher the number you allocate yourself, the better you feel you are performing in that area.

Rating	Definition
1	Not at all. I don't. None at all. Not happy. Not confident at all.
2	Rarely. Barely. Very little. Very unconfident.
3	Not often at all. Not much. Quite unconfident.
4	Not particularly. Not really. Not a lot. Mildly unconfident.
5	Neutral. Unsure. Don't know. Indifferent.
6	Sometimes. At times. Moderately. A little bit. Mildly confident.
7	Quite often. A fair bit. Some. A little confident.
8	Most of the time. More often than not. Quite a lot. Quite confident.
9	The majority of the time. A lot. Very confident.
10	Completely. Very much so. A huge amount. Extremely happy. Extremely confident.

Fig. 2 Rate yourself definitions

Top tip

Self-assessment is a vital skill for self-reflection and progression in your professional life. It is important that we are honest, kind and constructive when it comes to self-assessing. As trainee teachers we are often asked to consider our own practice but often, after this point, as our career progresses, we become too busy to do so. As a result, habits become ingrained and it becomes harder to step back, reflect and make changes.

It can be easy to be too harsh on yourself when you self-assess and allow your insecurities to cloud your judgement. Being objective and honest about your practice is a hard thing to do and it takes practice. Before you begin self-assessing, carefully consider the criteria you are using to assess yourself and focus on that at first without thinking about yourself. Feeling comfortable with what you are assessing will lead to a more accurate assessment. If you jump in and self-assess too early, before you have considered the assessment criteria, you may well have a clouded judgement and be unable to learn as much from the process. Don't rush it – it is too important.

Research-informed practice self-assessment questionnaire

QUESTION 1: How happy are you about the decision-making process you use to choose which pedagogical approaches or strategies to use in your classroom?

Quick response:

_____

_____

_____

_____

Questions for consideration

- Do you have a 'go-to' resource, text or colleague you consult when looking for new ways forward?
- Do you consider a wide variety of sources before deciding on an approach for teaching and learning?
- Do you always consider an approach or strategy fully before embarking on it?
- What approaches or strategies have you trialled successfully in the past? Why were they successful?

Considered response:

_____

_____

_____

_____

_____

Rate yourself

QUESTION 1: How happy are you about the decision-making process you use to choose which pedagogical approaches or strategies to use in your classroom?

1   2   3   4   5   6   7   8   9   10

QUESTION 2: How effective are new pedagogical approaches or strategies that you implement in the classroom?

Quick response:

_____

_____

_____

_____

_____

_____

Questions for consideration

- Consider an approach or strategy you have implemented in your classroom. Do you implement it immediately upon hearing or reading about it or after some time?
- Do you feel confident when implementing a new strategy?
- Do you discuss the approach or strategy with others before, during or after?
- Do they work in the long term?

Considered response:

_____

_____

_____

_____

_____

_____

Rate yourself

QUESTION 2: How successful are new pedagogical approaches or strategies that you implement in the classroom?

| 1 | 2 | 3 | 4 | 5 | 6 | 7 | 8 | 9 | 10 |

QUESTION 3: What factors would trigger you to change an approach to your practice that you have been using for an extended period of time?

Quick response:

_____

_____

_____

_____

_____

_____

Questions for consideration

- Are there any strategies or approaches you either use or endorse but you are not sure why?
- Do you find yourself influenced by others' views of your teaching?
- How important are the opinions of others in your own practice?
- Has there ever been a time when you have reconsidered a strategy that has worked in previous scenarios, schools or situations?

Considered response:

_____

_____

_____

_____

_____

_____

Rate yourself

QUESTION 3: How confident are you in adapting or changing a long-term approach to your practice?

1	2	3	4	5	6	7	8	9	10

QUESTION 4: How happy do you feel about your current response to new initiatives or strategies put in place in your school?

Quick response:

_____

_____

_____

_____

_____

Questions for consideration

- When a new initiative is suggested, what is your automatic response?
- Would you consider yourself someone who enjoys change or avoids change?
- Why do you respond in this particular way to new initiatives?
- As a leader, how would you prefer your team to respond to new initiatives or strategies?

Considered response:

_____

_____

_____

_____

_____

Rate yourself

QUESTION 4: How happy do you feel about your current response to new initiatives or strategies put in place in your school?

1   2   3   4   5   6   7   8   9   10

QUESTION 5: To what extent are your decisions in the classroom affected by your own personal experience; the views of students and/or parents; school data; and performance figures or educational research (as described in Chapter 3, page 37)?

Quick response:

_____

_____

_____

_____

_____

_____

Questions for consideration

- How confident are you in using your current professional experience in your decision-making process?
- Do you ever consult or consider student voice?
- When making decisions about your pedagogical approach, how often do you consider the impact on results and data?
- Would you consider consulting research sources before implementing a new idea?

Considered response:

_____

_____

_____

_____

_____

Rate yourself

QUESTION 5: How confident do you feel in your decision-making processes?

| 1 | 2 | 3 | 4 | 5 | 6 | 7 | 8 | 9 | 10 |

QUESTION 6: Do you have an awareness of your school's current level of engagement with research-informed practice?

Quick response:

_____

_____

_____

_____

_____

Questions for consideration

- Do you know whether your school's leadership and management currently engage with educational research? How do you know?
- What type of decisions do you believe are currently influenced by educational research in your school?
- Do you contribute to or attend CPD opportunities provided in your school currently?
- Do these CPD sessions make explicit reference to educational research?

Considered response:

_____

_____

_____

_____

_____

Rate yourself

QUESTION 6: Do you feel confident in judging your school's current level of engagement with research-informed practice?

1   2   3   4   5   6   7   8   9   10

QUESTION 7: Do you understand your department or phase team's level of research-informed practice?

Quick response:

_____

_____

_____

_____

_____

_____

Questions for consideration

- Do you ever discuss research-informed practice in a formal setting with your department or team?
- Do the team share knowledge, work and resources regularly?
- Do the people in your department or team question the strategies and approaches they use?
- Do you consider yourself separate or integral to discussions about best practice?

Considered response:

_____

_____

_____

_____

_____

_____

Rate yourself

QUESTION 7: Do you feel confident in assessing your department or phase team's level of research-informed practice?

1	2	3	4	5	6	7	8	9	10

QUESTION 8: What impact does educational research currently have on your practice?

Quick response:

_____

_____

_____

_____

_____

_____

Questions for consideration

- Can you think of a time when a decision you made about your practice was directly influenced by evidence from a research base?
- How did you acquire this information and what did you do with it initially?
- Have you adapted your practice based on research evidence that was explained to you but that you did not fully understand?
- What impact have you seen on your students' work based on any changes you have made that were heavily influenced by research?
- How do you measure the impact on your students' work? Have you ever carried out any surveys or comparisons between outcomes before and after changing your practice?

Considered response:

_____

_____

_____

_____

_____

_____

Rate yourself

QUESTION 8: How much of an impact does educational research currently have on your practice?

1 2 3 4 5 6 7 8 9 10

QUESTION 9: How confident do you feel about knowing how and where to access educational literature findings or summaries?

Quick response:

_____

_____

_____

_____

_____

Questions for consideration

- What sources do you have to hand that you would use to access up-to-date educational ideas?
- How often do you access and read research?
- Do you have access to a CPD library or online journal access?
- What type of document would you prefer to access – the full research paper or a paraphrased overview?
- Do you know your way around the Education Endowment Foundation's Teaching and Learning Toolkit? How often do you access this?
- Are you subscribed to any newsletters that give you an overview of current educational research?

Considered response:

_____

_____

_____

_____

_____

Rate yourself

QUESTION 9: How confident do you feel about knowing how and where to access educational literature findings or summaries?

1   2   3   4   5   6   7   8   9   10

QUESTION 10: What educational research, theories or studies do you know about and use to inform your teaching practice or leadership decisions day to day?

Quick response:

_____

_____

_____

_____

_____

_____

Questions for consideration

- Do you have any knowledge of key and/or current educational research studies and findings? What studies do you know already and use to inform your practice?
- What has stopped you from looking further into research to inform your teaching, e.g. time constraints or lack of accessibility, or has it never been discussed at your school?
- Do you pride yourself on being aware of current studies or findings?
- If so, how do you ensure you keep up to date?

Considered response:

_____

_____

_____

_____

_____

_____

Rate yourself

QUESTION 10: How happy are you with the amount of educational research, theories or studies you know about and use to inform your teaching practice or leadership decisions day to day?

1	2	3	4	5	6	7	8	9	10

QUESTION 11: Do you currently discuss educational research findings with colleagues in the staff room or in informal situations?

Quick response:

_____

_____

_____

_____

_____

_____

Questions for consideration

- How confident are you in identifying and sharing educational research with others?
- Who would you approach first to share and discuss educational research with?
- What barriers are there to sharing educational research in your department, phase or school?
- If you already feel confident in this area, how do you suppose others receive your input?

Considered response:

_____

_____

_____

_____

_____

_____

Rate yourself

QUESTION 11: How confident are you when discussing educational research findings with colleagues in the staff room or in informal situations?

1   2   3   4   5   6   7   8   9   10

QUESTION 12: Do you have a network of colleagues outside of your school, either in local schools or online, with whom you can discuss educational research?

Quick response:

_____

_____

_____

_____

_____

_____

Questions for consideration

- Who would you usually call upon to discuss pedagogy and practice?
- Whose opinion outside your school do you value the most with regard to teaching and learning strategies?
- Do you use social media in a professional capacity?
- How do you feel about discussing your ideas and practice with strangers?

Considered response:

_____

_____

_____

_____

_____

_____

Rate yourself

QUESTION 12: How happy are you with the network of contacts you have for discussing and keeping up to date with educational research?

| 1 | 2 | 3 | 4 | 5 | 6 | 7 | 8 | 9 | 10 |

QUESTION 13: How do you quality-assure and evaluate a strategy that you have purposefully implemented in your classroom?

Quick response:

_____

_____

_____

_____

_____

_____

Questions for consideration

- What evidence could you collate to compare outcomes before and after using a new strategy?
- For what purpose do you use observations in your school?
- Whose responsibility is it to ensure the approach to teaching and learning in your classroom is evaluated?
- Can you use your tracking and assessment systems to reflect upon the strategies you have implemented?

Considered response:

_____

_____

_____

_____

_____

_____

Rate yourself

QUESTION 13: Can you confidently quality-assure and evaluate a strategy that you have purposefully implemented in your classroom?

1   2   3   4   5   6   7   8   9   10

QUESTION 14: How confident are you that you understand the benefits and drawbacks of research-informed practice?

Quick response:

_____

_____

_____

_____

_____

_____

Questions for consideration

- Do you consider yourself to have an understanding of what would be deemed good practice in the classroom at your school?
- Does your school's specific context push you towards research-led practice or does it seem unappealing in your circumstances?
- What do you believe is an appropriate relationship between research and teaching? Do you consider them to be separate entities?
- In your opinion, should research only inform teaching or can teaching inform research?
- Does the thought of research influencing your day-to-day work seem overwhelming or difficult? Why?

Considered response:

_____

_____

_____

_____

_____

Rate yourself

QUESTION 14: How confident are you that you understand the benefits and drawbacks of research-informed practice?

1   2   3   4   5   6   7   8   9   10

QUESTION 15: Do you know how to assess the reliability of a research paper or findings report?

Quick response:

_____

_____

_____

_____

_____

_____

Questions for consideration

- When you read a research paper or summary (perhaps an article or blog), how confident are you in its reliability? Where would you look to find out who carried out the research and when?
- What sources do you trust and why?
- What reasons might there be for you discounting the evidence presented to you?

Considered response:

_____

_____

_____

_____

_____

_____

Rate yourself

QUESTION 15: How confident do you feel about assessing the reliability of a research or findings report?

1	2	3	4	5	6	7	8	9	10

QUESTION 16: In general, how confident do you feel about choosing, implementing and evaluating a research-informed approach in the classroom?

Quick response:

_____

_____

_____

_____

_____

_____

Questions for consideration

- What makes you feel prepared and confident before teaching using a particular approach?
- How confident are you in trying new things?
- What tools do you feel you need before implementing a new strategy?
- Do you feel you have enough time to devote to this process?

Considered response:

_____

_____

_____

_____

_____

_____

Rate yourself

QUESTION 16: In general, how confident do you feel about choosing, implementing and evaluating a research-informed approach in the classroom?

1   2   3   4   5   6   7   8   9   10

The results

Now that you have completed the self-assessment and considered where you currently see yourself with regard to your knowledge, understanding and use of research-informed practice, it is time to consider what the next steps are. How can you become well informed in the latest thinking and arm yourself with the ability to gain access to, question and respond to research? It is important to remember that educational research is a fast-moving area and what comes next is not the end of your journey but only the beginning. The reflection questions asked you to consider many areas relating to your expertise, the expertise and attitudes of those you work with, the possibility of change and how well informed you consider yourself to be. Some of the questions were no doubt difficult to answer because they require us to take a step (perhaps a leap) back and look as objectively as possible at our own performance: this can be very difficult to do so ensure you take the time to let the self-assessment responses sink in.

When you have done this, take a look at how you rated your answers for each question in the questionnaire and compare your ratings with the chart below. The guidance will help you form a plan for how to become a research-informed practitioner.

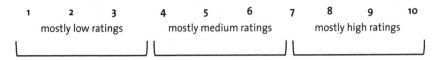

Fig. 3 How did you rate yourself?

Mostly low ratings

You are aware that research might have a positive impact on your decision-making and therefore your approach to teaching and learning, but are unsure where to begin. Read through where to begin, the overviews of key researchers and easy access to research in Chapters 3, 4 and 5. Take the steps slowly and consider how the research could be adapted and implemented in your teaching context. Your aim is to become research literate so that you can question and critique new research as it emerges.

Mostly medium ratings

You are aware of educational research and have engaged with it in your own teaching context with some success. Begin by building a network of colleagues using the approach in the chapters that follow to discuss, argue and work on building your engagement with research as a wider group. Be prepared to ask as many questions as you get answers. Work towards having a clear understanding of the most up-to-date research and widen your network to become involved in important discussions.

Mostly high ratings

You are in a strong position to move towards leading on using educational research in your own context in the near future. Work to fill in the gaps in your knowledge and experience and start to think about whom you could train in your school (for example trainees, subject leads or teaching and learning teams). Consider which new platforms you might use to grow the current knowledge and accessibility to research for your team, department or school.

Now what?

The results are in. So now what? You have a full and detailed self-reflection on your use and understanding of research-informed practice. It is important that you now make the most of it. Take the time to develop an action plan as a result of the answers you have given and the conclusions you have drawn. This can be adapted and worked on throughout the process but it is a good place to start. Don't make this simply another bit of paperwork you have completed. Use it to really open your eyes as to where you are, where you need to be and how to get there. Prioritise what you want to work on and get started.

Chapter 2 takeaway

Teaching tip
Be kind to yourself
Research in education might not be new but it hasn't been high on the agenda for everyone. In teacher training programmes it is not commonly touched upon and therefore generations of teachers will feel the same. Therefore, do not be surprised or worried or feel threatened in any way if you feel as though the self-assessment questions have led you to think in a particular way. Remember, teachers have a vast set of skills that the self-assessment has not measured and the point of completing it is to help you to work out how to add the knowledge required to refine your skills further. It is not a stick to beat yourself with!

Pass it on

Set the agenda

Consider asking to set or setting the agenda in a forthcoming meeting so that it includes a brief discussion of your colleagues' understanding and views of educational research. It might be that they have more knowledge and interest than you think and you can share this journey with them or use them as a sounding board for your own interests and thoughts. It may be that they are in a very similar position, in which case talk about why you are interested in research-informed practice and how you would like to consider it in your practice moving forward.

Share and tweet

Revisit some of the questions you found of most interest and perhaps most challenging. Gain others' perspectives by tweeting out the question or exploring your concerns with it. If you have a clear understanding of the possible answers, use the voting tool on Twitter to get a more definitive response.

CPD book club recommendation

In order to gain an understanding of what a practical yet research-informed classroom might look like, read *Making Every Lesson Count: Six principles to support great teaching and learning* by Shaun Allison and Andy Tharby (2015).

Bloggers' corner

David Didau has a good selection of blogs relating to his talks at ResearchEd conferences, and in particular he is in favour of research-informed practice: https://learningspy.co.uk/research/research-vs-evidence.

TO DO LIST:

☐ Identify the specific areas that you feel you need to build on to become more research informed using the self-assessment questions.
☐ Reflect on your written responses and consider what they suggest to you about your current practice.

❏ Look at your confidence ratings and work out where they are high and where they are low – think about whether or not there are any patterns and what you need to increase your confidence in some areas. Tweet out any questions that you considered interesting in the self-assessment and don't forget to tag me.

❏ Read *Making Every Lesson Count: Six principles to support great teaching and learning* by Shaun Allison and Andy Tharby (2015).

3 Engaging with research

Before writing a reading list as long as your arm and embarking on some form of action research based on newspaper headlines alone, a great place to start is to consider the current resources out there to guide you in becoming research informed. Where can you find support and information to assist you along your journey towards making research-informed decisions suitable for your specific context?

There have been many attempts to create resources, institutions and organisations that support schools in engaging with and using educational research; however very few have had a positive impact on classroom teachers' practice and some are already defunct despite vast funding from central government. It seems odd that despite investment and drive from key stakeholders in educational improvement over many years, discussion of research in staff rooms and on teacher training courses continues to be either dismissed or disliked.

It would seem that much of the current movement towards research-informed practice is being driven by teachers themselves, with the belief that it is vital for teachers to expand their knowledge and understanding of relevant research, rather than attempting to become the researchers themselves. Although conducting your own research trials might be your intention in the long term, the majority of teachers are not trained researchers, nor do many have the time to become experts in this field. Therefore, we should look to become more aware, engaged and interested in the findings and summaries of trained researchers, aiming to work alongside them, to utilise their expertise in order to expand our own knowledge and drive improvement in our classrooms.

This chapter will give an overview of the steps you can take to become more engaged in research debates, which will in turn lead you to getting to grips with the most useful research sources (see Chapter 4, page 53), before considering whether the big ideas currently discussed in educational research can help you and your students to improve (see Chapter 5, page 72). At the end of this chapter I'll also give you a step-by-step guide for how you can assess whether the research you are reading is credible and encourage you to start thinking about an area of focus for your first research-informed intervention.

Before we begin

Research studies cannot provide us with precise and exact answers for every pedagogical question we ask, yet it can, I believe, provide us with a signpost pointing towards a less contrived route and help us avoid ineffective practice.

The work of Dr Gary Jones is key in this area. He has created a distinction in his work between *research*-based practice and *evidence*-based practice. In his handbook for teachers and school leaders, *Evidence-Based Practice*, Jones (2016) clarifies that when he talks about *evidence-based* practice he could be referring to 'information, facts or data' and that this 'may be based on numbers or it may be qualitative or descriptive'. In one chapter, Jones explores what types of evidence should be considered by school leaders in any decision-making process and names 'educational and other research' as one of four areas that should be taken into account. Jones makes a valuable and crucial argument that research is not the only area we should consider when making decisions and highlights how important it is to critically assess research before using it. In other words, research should not be used lightly or on its own. Jones describes how if something is evidence-based it encompasses a variety of elements. Below I will summarise these different elements according to Jones. However, in the chapters to follow, I will focus on how best to engage with research alone as I believe that the other three areas (professional experience, your school's data and how decisions are received) are either instinctive or covered through internal professional development opportunities.

What is an evidence base?

Jones states in his handbook that there are four areas to focus on when making evidence-informed decisions, including 'stakeholder values and concerns', which he describes as considering how those who will be affected by the decision being made will react. This could be from students to governors and beyond. In terms of decision-making in the classroom, this might mean we should consider student voice or parental concerns on a particular topic before taking the next step. I perceive this to be the moment where you pause to consider how a decision will be received by those it will inevitably affect. I have reworked Jones's four areas into the diagram on page 38 to show their interrelationships and equal importance in our practice.

All of the elements we need to consider can influence each other and need to be taken into consideration when making decisions. I believe that due to the very nature of teaching as both a vocation and a profession, we rely predominantly on our own professional experience (however short) or that of others as the first port of call when trying to find a solution to a problem.

Secondly, we instinctively think about the possible ways in which a decision will be received by the different stakeholders and whether or not the decision is likely to impact them in a positive or more negative way, be it students, parents

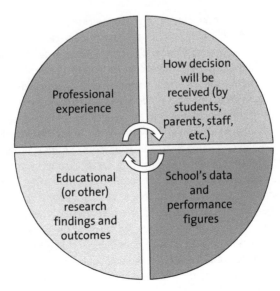

Fig. 4 The four different areas to focus on when making evidence-informed decisions according to Jones (2016)

or colleagues. Sometimes, we focus very strongly on this area, for example when making leadership decisions, whereas at other times we avoid focusing on this area, especially when it can make us uncomfortable, for example when implementing change.

The next area we instinctively rely on, particularly when in a managerial or leadership role, is the class or school's data or a variety of performance figures. This might be large, finite data, such as SATs results or A level results, or more temporary data, such as the results of the most recent class test, number of absences in a given period or forecast grades. We often use this data to make decisions about the future. Lots of questions should be asked when we do this as we know only too well how data cannot give us the full picture, let alone make decisions for us. Decisions made purely on the data alone without considering the current situation, the possible changes that have occurred (from year group to year group for example) and the impact on what Jones calls 'stakeholders' might lead to some rather unfavourable outcomes.

The processes we go through every day when making simple decisions are in themselves complex – we often don't even consider what is influencing our decision-making. The outcomes and consequences of these decisions are often even more complicated. Research provides us with a more explicit and overt decision-making tool to add to make up our professional judgement. Jones states that we must consider all evidence just like 'in a court of law where evidence is presented in a variety of forms'.

As a starting point, this book encourages you to begin first with understanding the impact research might have on these decisions. All practitioners who wish to make decisions that they can honestly say are well thought-through and considered should begin to embrace the outcomes and findings of educational research and in order to do so you need to know where to find it, when to question it and how to apply it. There are some people who do this currently and share their knowledge with others through various platforms (Twitter, blogging, writing articles, speaking at conferences, etc.) and it is worth engaging with them as soon as possible.

Follow the new leaders

Historically, education research has been an area safeguarded for debate and discussion by university researchers and academics alone. Within a school environment, more often than not, research as a form of evidence is passed over when talking about teaching and learning strategies and approaches. Although teachers have access to documents published by the Department for Education (DfE), which often cite key research, not many of them will have the time to pick it apart or find the original sources to enquire further. In addition, with more on-the-job teacher training than ever before, the exposure to high-quality and rigorous research, summaries or reviews is often variable depending on the ethos and priorities of the school in which teachers train. Some more traditional training routes such as a PGCE barely touch upon the use of educational research to inform teaching practice and others refer to methods and strategies that have long been disproven. There is, no doubt, a wide variety of exposure and level of discussion in this area but it does seem to be increasing through the efforts of a number of individuals and organisations – many of whom are listed on page 41.

Another impeding factor is that research on teaching and learning approaches carried out in higher education is not always passed down to those who require it in an accessible format – or at all. However, we now have a plethora of leading educational figures who work tirelessly to bridge the gap between researchers, their findings and those of us working in the classroom day to day.

The work of leading teachers, bloggers and writers such as Alex Quigley, Carl Hendrick, Robin Macpherson and The Learning Scientists (a small yet influential collection of cognitive psychological scientists interested in research on education, see http://www.learningscientists.org/) among many others has led to an emergence of accessible and relevant research, presented predominantly in the form of resources, blogs and summaries. This has made it much easier for busy teachers to consider the findings without feeling overwhelmed or put off by difficulties in accessing the information.

Engaging with the work, opinions and debates sparked by some of these current leaders in research-informed practice is a great starting point. It will give you an insight into the variety and relevance of their writing to your context. From topics such as mixed-ability setting and revision methods to motivation in the classroom, you will find relevant research contextualised and summarised into bite-sized chunks for your consumption, without the requirement of a PhD in cognitive science, a dictionary on standby or a large glass of wine.

How to engage with those in the know

A simple way to get started is to join in with conversations in a professional capacity from the comfort of your own home via Twitter, or similar social media networks and forums. Twitter has a great capacity to quickly increase your network of professionals you can learn from and discuss ideas with.

Here are some tips for using Twitter to build your network:

- Be open-minded and follow a variety of professionals including teachers, researchers, organisations, politicians and social movements.
- Use the bookmark tool to save relevant and interesting tweets – particularly those referring to evidence.
- Set aside time for reading links, evidence and blogs posted in Twitter threads.
- Following the @ResearchEd1 account, which aims to raise 'research literacy in the teaching profession', is a useful and speedy way to find out where events are taking place that you can attend in person as well as to simply see what is being retweeted.
- Follow #UKEdResChat by typing it into the search bar and take part or simply observe a weekly chat. It is a great way of getting to grips with some of the current issues in educational research.

How and why to get started on Twitter

- Read Erin Miller's guide to getting started on Twitter and heed her advice to 'be a radiator, not a drain'. See: www.theguardian.com/teacher-network/2017/apr/20/teachers-on-twitter-why-join-get-started-social-media.

Where to find the new research leaders on Twitter

- Alex Quigley @HuntingEnglish
- Carl Hendrick @C_Hendrick
- Impact Wales @ImpactWales
- UKEdResChat @UKEdResChat
- Robin Macpherson @robin_macp
- The Learning Scientists @AceThatTest
- Tom Bennett @tombennett71
- Rebecca Foster @TLPMsF
- Greg Ashman @greg_ashman
- Amy Forrester @amymayforrester
- Deep Singh Ghataura @DSGhataura
- Phil Naylor @pna1977
- Daniel Muijs @ProfDanielMuijs
- David Didau @DavidDidau

Building a network

Part of becoming a research-informed teacher is about becoming more connected – whether that's with individuals in your school or with organisations that are leading the movement in creating a research-informed profession.

Building a network of individuals you can talk to about current and relevant research studies and how to understand and use them is a vital next step in moving forward in your professional development. To start with, identify and ask your teaching and learning (T&L) lead for some time to discuss with them what's going on in your school in terms of research-informed practice, and whether there are any other teachers they recommend you should connect with face to face. It might be that you already have a T&L library or that there are reading groups that you could take part in. Building a network that 'normalises' discussing research is key to success, but it is important to remember that this will take time. Later in the book, I will explain a range of ways to increase your exposure to and the sharing of your practice with others through the training plans. Working alongside others on a particular endeavour can be quite an overwhelming task at first, but it is an important stage. You must reach out for both support and discussion, but also so that your own ideas are constantly questioned, as this will ensure you are on the right track for you and your students.

As mentioned earlier in this chapter, getting involved in conversations online is a great first step (and a valuable strand of the network that will support you in becoming research literate); however, it's important not to miss the opportunities already in front of you. Conversations in the staff room are likely to be more powerful than the ones you might have online as they are the most relevant to your context and your students and this is where we all hope to make a positive change.

National networks

There are numerous national organisations that have sought to bridge the gap between research and classroom practice. Some have been moderately successful and there are some that are on the up and seem to be making a real mark on policy and practice. In Chapter 4, page 57, I will look in more detail at research sources and where to go to read summaries, articles and infographics that will allow you to access and question educational evidence before engaging with it further. In particular, the Chartered College of Teaching and the Research Schools Network are worth gaining access to and exploring further to enhance your development in becoming research informed.

There are now a number of schools, known as Research Schools, that specialise in using and sharing their research-informed practice with others and with whom it would be a good idea to connect when beginning your research-informed journey and considering the elements of your teaching you wish to improve through learning more about what the evidence says.

The Research Schools Network is a 'collaboration between the Education Endowment Foundation (EEF) and the Institute for Effective Education (IEE)' creating a 'network of schools that will support the use of evidence to improve teaching practice' (Research Schools Network, 2016). You can find out more about these schools at https://researchschool.org.uk/about.

Research Schools are schools that have been awarded status and funding to allow them to share their best practice and support schools, particularly those local to them, wishing to learn more about research-informed practice. There are currently just over 20 Research Schools spread across England. Finding a Research

School local to you and becoming involved in events that they run is a brilliant place to start if you are looking for advice or informative courses to help you on your research journey. Many run courses on how to become a Research Lead in your school as well as more bespoke courses on themes such as metacognition, making the best use of teaching assistants and subject-specific CPD. The Research Schools newsletter provides an abundance of information in easy-to-understand, bite-sized chunks that have been carefully considered, before being passed on to teachers.

The aim of the network is to lead the way in research-informed practice by sharing knowledge, expertise and training with other schools in the local area to help build a more research-savvy approach to teaching and learning. Identifying, contacting and engaging with a local Research School is one considered approach to improve your own understanding of educational research and, vitally, how to apply it in the classroom. Moreover, it should encourage you to discuss your thoughts with like-minded teachers.

Visiting some of these Research Schools myself left me very impressed by their dedication to using research thoughtfully and raising its profile amongst other schools. It is in itself a huge commitment to take on and means that they have steadily and carefully, over many years, changed the thought processes and procedures within their own schools and teaching staff to encompass a wider range of evidence on which to make decisions and move forward. I highly recommend a visit.

How to find a Research School near you

Simply, you can access The Research Schools Network online via their website: www.researchschool.org.uk.

Research Schools span the length and breadth of the country and hold a wide variety of events. These events are often twilight sessions taking place over a number of weeks, meaning you can attend them easily after school without the need for cover if you are local, or one- or two-day events, which might require a small amount of funding from your school in order for you to attend, whereas the shorter courses are often free. Currently, there are many Research Schools in the north of England, spreading from Merseyside to the Yorkshire Coast, but the network is seeking to increase its provision on the South Coast in particular, which will mean there are Research Schools within reasonable reach of all in the UK in the next few years.

It is also worth considering visiting a Research School on a less formal basis if you simply want to discuss what they do and why they do it. Research Schools have Research Leads who work to implement and embed research-informed practice in their school, as well as sharing this practice with schools in their local area. There are a variety of primary and secondary schools so you are sure to find one willing to let you visit for a few hours or a day if you are able to get the time to do so.

If you do decide to visit a Research School (or any school for that matter) with the intention of finding out more about how they work and the decisions they make, I would recommend completing and considering the following in advance of the day:

1. Do your very own 'research' on the school beforehand: If you visit a school vastly different to your own you can definitely take away a huge amount; however, it depends entirely on your aims. These are questions you should ask or investigate before your visit:

- Do you know about the context of their school?
- How does it compare to your school? Consider the age and size of the school, student demographic, results and leadership style.
- Why and when did the school become a Research School?

2. Contact the Research Lead directly: My top tip is to use their school email address – social media can be a great way to make contact but for a formal visit ensure you treat it as a professional conversation.

3. Consider an area of focus: Share with your contact the areas in which you are interested in advance. It is difficult to create a programme of observations and discussions when you aren't sure what the intended recipient needs from their day. Do you want to see a particular subject or a strategy in practice or discuss a particular training need? Let them know.

4. Consider your timings carefully: Half a day or a full day might sound like a long time but it is almost impossible to see everything let alone discuss your thoughts and feelings immediately. Remember, the school you visit will be as busy as your own and although Research Schools might be used to visitors, they still have their everyday jobs to do. Therefore, ensure you don't ask for too much. Pick two or three areas to focus on and leave it at that – if you love it, I'm sure you can return!

5. Write down your questions: But don't always ask them. As you go throughout the day, you will have lots of questions regarding the practice you see or hear about. Let them sink in and return to them later.

6. Write to say thank you: Do this soon after your visit. It takes a lot to organise visits especially during school time. Make sure you thank the person who has taken the time out of their day to do this for you. It is part of building your professional network.

7. Return to your notes: After 24 hours consider looking at your notes – give everything time to sink in first. Can you find links between your ideas on the day, and why do you think particular areas stood out to you? It is worth highlighting in red, amber and green which areas are most relevant to your current practice (green), which you would like to know more about (amber) and which you are interested in but don't suit your current context (red).

8. Consider how to feed back: Do ensure you feed back to those in your current context via an informal discussion. Anything more formal than this should really wait until you have had time to consider, discuss and embed new ideas. Do not do this immediately after your visit and don't let anyone tell you that you have to do so. Let things sink in then feed back on what you found and consider your next steps.

Research Schools' websites to visit

- Kyra Teaching School based at Mount Street Academy, Lincoln: kyra. researchschool.org.uk
- Huntington Research School, York: huntington.researchschool.org.uk
- Durrington Research School, West Sussex: durrington. researchschool.org.uk
- Sandringham Research School, Hertfordshire: sandringham. researchschool.org.uk

Engaging with research through action research

This chapter has given you an introduction to how you can start getting involved in research-informed practice through widening your awareness and network. The next chapters will look at key resources you can use, key pieces of research you could consider to get started and examples of how to translate them into research-informed practice.

Before we move on to these chapters, it is important you consider how the information they contain might impact your everyday practice in a practical way. Therefore, no matter how you fared in the self-assessment, I encourage you to decide now upon a research focus, which will eventually be turned into a statement or question that will allow you to consider the following chapters in a more strategic and therefore more effective manner. Your research question will vary hugely depending on your experience, context and understanding of research methodology.

Context is vital when it comes to becoming an effective research-informed practitioner, and the point of creating your own research question is to encourage you to remain research engaged and informed rather than as a means to rigorously research a particular strategy. This is an area of great debate, as being research informed does not mean you have to be engaged in your own research. However, according to Julie Nelson and Clare O'Beirne's (2014) report published by the NFER (National Foundation for Educational Research), 'Evidence suggests that teachers engaging in their own research or enquiry are best served when they also engage with external evidence, as this reinforces the relevance of their work.' This book suggests you do engage with external evidence before deciding on your own research enquiry and, in doing so, ensure you are fully aware that your enquiry is not comparable in rigour or validity to those you read about from external sources, but is there to allow you to consider the evidence in your own context and make judgements on the best way forward regarding your teaching alone.

Unless you have developed the sophisticated skills required to carry out complex research studies (which you may if you were perhaps completing a Master's in education and required to set up and run randomised control trials), then the point of developing a research question or deciding upon a general area of reading is not to complete a perfectly controlled and valid experiment on your own, but to engage with research in a practical and manageable way rather than dismiss it due to its seeming irrelevance to your classroom. I believe that this engagement is better than no engagement and perhaps can lead over time to a more disciplined enquiry when you have gained the adequate knowledge on which to base your own research.

Choosing an area of focus

At this stage, I want you to consider whittling down an area of focus, based on your self-assessment results in Chapter 2, page 31, and your current practice, to have in the back of your mind as you teach and read through the book. Perhaps give yourself a half term to really consider what you might end up looking at. The following chapters then summarise how to become more involved in research-informed discussions, what research to read and some strategies you could use to address your problem area. It is worth taking the time to complete the steps outlined in this section so that you have an area to focus on as you read, but do remember that this can adapt and develop until you decide more precisely on your research focus in Chapter 8, page 160 – where I will suggest a method of doing so. This is because, as you read through the following chapters, you may gain further ideas about the strategy you wish to trial. Consequently, when you reach Chapter 8, you should have a better idea of the best way forward and I will provide you with a more rigid framework as to how to create your statement, with the aim of embedding your strategy and trialling your practice in the classroom.

Teachers are often told to be reflective practitioners; before making any changes it is important to pause and ensure you have completed the self-assessment questionnaire in Chapter 2, page 15. Spend a few weeks before you embark on your journey towards implementing research-informed strategies in the classroom considering what you already do and read around the best strategies and methodologies, which can be found in the remainder of the book.

In essence, I am asking you to consider how you might use an area of focus to begin making changes in your own practice. I would like you to consider beginning an informal and individual action research project that will encourage you to engage with, embed and evaluate research for the benefit of your knowledge and your students' outcomes. Action research is a key element of embedding any new strategy or practice and should be undertaken on a low-scale, individual level to begin with. Action research is the process of implementing a new strategy in your classroom, with the intention of analysing the outcomes and evaluating both the impact and success of the trial before considering whether or not it will be a permanent change. This leaves the option open to revert back to a previous strategy or to continue to find something new. It is the opposite of being a magpie and taking what looks like a good idea and implementing it without thought or guidance in a context in which it may not work. It is the key to embedding new strategies in a considered manner.

Action research, however, is often implemented badly if not enough time and thought is given to the process of preparing for the use of a new strategy, conducting the trial and evaluating the whole process. The rest of the book will help you to avoid these pitfalls.

Engaging with research through an area of focus

Eventually, you are going to create a statement, known as a PICO statement, in which you summarise your area of focus to serve as a reminder and an anchor for your focus when using research-informed practice in your classroom.

The term 'PICO statement' is widely used in medical evidence-informed practice but was adapted for education by Dr Gary Jones, whose work in this area was first mentioned on page 37. I have used this style of question to better define and understand my own use of research-informed practice and have adapted it to create 'PIO statements' (yes, the C is missing here), which are now widely used by all teachers at my school and in particular those in the early years of their career.

You can read more about Dr Gary Jones's use of this style of question on his blog about the role of a school research lead. See http://evidencebasededucationalleadership.blogspot.com/2015/01/the-school-research-lead-and-asking.html.

PIO or PICO statements

A PIO or PICO statement (the subtle difference is explored in Chapter 8, page 162) is a focus statement to create precision in your research-informed practice and is made up of the following elements:

P – Problem with pedagogy: Specify which group of students you will focus on.

I – Intervention or strategy: What intervention are you going to trial after considerable thought and reading?

C – Comparison (not always needed to begin with): Which class or group will you compare your outcomes to?

O – Outcome: What would you like the outcome to look like if the intervention is successful?

So, a final PICO statement might say:

I want to improve the use of peer assessment with Year 9 by using Ron Berger's peer critique compared to a class using WWW and EBI in order to ensure students can successfully and accurately critique their own and each other's work.

A PIO or PICO statement is not something you need to create straight away and the process of creating, adapting and using the statement to drive your practice forward is further outlined in Chapter 8, page 162. It will prove most useful once you have considered the relevant research resources, read some of the evidence provided and considered the best strategies – jumping straight in at this point would mean you haven't been informed by the research at all but have perhaps simply gone with your gut instinct.

Once you've got an area of practice in mind, start to actively review your current methods. To do so purposefully, you could:

- Keep a note of your routines in this area as you plan your lessons. Do you even plan for this focus? Does your approach vary? What strategy might you currently be using and why?
- Ask a trusted colleague to pop into a lesson to give their view of your current practice. This does not need to be a formal lesson observation and certainly in no way graded!
- Deliberately give yourself ten minutes at the end of the day to consider what you did and whether or not you made any conscious decisions about your practice in this area.
- Find out what is happening in the rest of your school – outside your classroom and outside your year group or department and mostly in relation to your proposed area of focus. Avoid making incorrect presumptions based on what you think is happening rather than what is truly happening.

As you continue reading the book, you will be given guidance on when to consider your area for development. Action research is far from all it takes to become research informed but it plays a part in engaging yourself fully in the process and, having trialled research-informed strategies for yourself freely and deliberately, you set yourself up as a more credible voice when wishing to share your views on what works and what is unlikely to.

Considering the evidence

With a plethora of information bombarding us every day via email, newspapers and notifications, it is difficult to know what to use, who to trust and what questions to ask of the evidence we are faced with. Often, in a summarised format such as a headline, we are fooled into believing and, worse still, using or denouncing an idea or strategy without delving deeper into the facts. Summaries and systematic reviews, in general, are vital in making educational research relevant, understandable and accessible but we must be wary of some that seem too good to be true or simply antagonistic! In Chapter 4, page 57, I provide further information on some recent and reliable sources that can be used to determine the validity of many of the statements we read on a day-to-day basis about what works and what doesn't.

Much like the approach suggested for determining whether or not we are reading 'fake news', we should consider a number of factors when approaching educational research summaries and descriptions to ensure we are fully informed before buying into any particular approach or concept. As those leading learning in the classroom, the validity and details of any evidence must be examined before taking any further steps that might impact students' outcomes.

The ability to judge evidence as valid or invalid becomes an area of real complexity as it is likely that you will often be able to compare the evidence you have identified with further evidence that contradicts or disputes the thesis. As long as we remain aware of the differences between the evidence and ask questions of it, then I believe this is a good thing as it leads us to think harder and more than we did before.

As professionals, it should become part of our job to engage with the research available to us in order to make us better thinkers, questioners and decision-makers. Knowing how to identify and read research is only one step towards becoming research informed and, alone, it will make little or no difference to your practice or drive students' improvement; it is the act of knowing what and how to digest that matters before developing the outcomes of the research in your own context, with an understanding that you have been through a more rigorous decision-making process than you would have without the access to research.

Check your sources

When considering the validity and therefore possible impact of research you have identified or that has been given to you as evidence for a decision that has been made, it is important to ask some key questions:

1. **Where did it come from?**

   - Can you trust the source that provided the research or evidence?
   - How well known is the source? Are they regarded as trustworthy?
   - Do they have a conscious or unconscious bias that you are aware of?
   - Who wrote the summary? When?
   - Who was involved in the original research study or studies? For example, was the study financed by a particular business or group?
   - When and where was the original evidence collated?

2. **Why is it relevant to you today?**

   - Has the research only just been published or has it resurfaced? If so, why now?
   - Why is this research relevant to you and your students today?
   - Why is it being reported on in such a way – is it in a headline in national newspapers? Is it only being discussed in certain forums? Is it linked to a different agenda?
   - Why are you searching for answers on this particular issue or topic? What else have you found and what other evidence would you consider alongside this research?

3. How did it come about?

- How was the evidence compiled and the research undertaken?
- How many studies took place and who was involved?
- How long did the study take place for (a week, a month, a year)?
- How many participants were there and why?
- How are the participants similar or different to those in your context?
- Who funded the original study and what might their vested interest be?

When reading research (perhaps in relation to your area of focus) it is important to keep these questions in mind or even print them off as a handy reminder! This is particularly true when reading original reports but also blogs and summaries by teachers who might not have considered these questions in advance. It might take a bit of digging to answer 'How did it come about?' However, if you wish to contact the researchers directly then you can usually do so via their institutional email addresses, which can be found via the study. Many are keen to share their research or you can look at the abstract of the study to find out more.

As much as possible, it is important to maintain a critical voice in your head that asks these questions of the research that you find and that others might pass to you. This will prove useful when identifying the research you wish to read and take account of before you embark on a new intervention as part of your research project.

Chapter 3 takeaway

Teaching tip
Play devil's advocate
The term 'devil's advocate' is perfect for someone who wishes to be research savvy and informed. When given a particular point of view or when research is placed in front of you (particularly if it is being sold as a panacea for all educational ills), then play the role to its full extent and, for the sake of debate and discussion, consider the alterative point of view so that you fully evaluate the research before taking any next steps.

Pass it on
Debate with colleagues
Next time an appropriate opportunity arises, however formal or informal, to discuss pedagogy or practice in the classroom and a new strategy or innovation is suggested, use some of the questions in the

'Check your sources' section, page 50, to gain clarity on the approach. Be careful to do this in a supportive and considered manner. It is important to seize the opportunity to question and discuss with others but, depending on the situation, you may wish to leave some time between the initial conversation and your questioning. Furthermore, I would avoid questioning colleagues via any electronic medium – your supportive tone may not seem so supportive in a list of bullet points! Remember, in doing so, you are not intending to simply disagree but to increase discussion and debate around why we take the steps we choose to.

CPD book club recommendation

Evidence-Based Practice: A handbook for teachers and school leaders by Gary Jones (2016).

Not strictly a book, this is a free PDF download from Dr Gary Jones's website: www.evidencebasededucationalleadership.blogspot.com/2016/02/evidence-based-practice-handbook-for.html

Bloggers' corner

Mark Enser has some great posts on being informed, from subject knowledge to how we approach 'fads' in the classroom. 'In defense of being informed' is a particular favourite post of mine.

Link: www.teachreal.wordpress.com/2017/11/26/in-defense-of-being-informed

TO DO LIST:

- ☐ Build your network by following some of the key voices on Twitter.
- ☐ Read Chapters 1 to 4 of Gary Jones's handbook on evidence-based practice.
- ☐ Go to the Research Schools website to identify a school near you.
- ☐ Consider contacting the Research Lead at an appropriate Research School and organise a visit.
- ☐ Identify an area you wish to improve.
- ☐ Spend time actively reflecting on this area.
- ☐ Organise for a colleague to pop into your classroom to look at your current area for development – try not to change anything! Use evidence from students' books, prior work and planning to discuss what you have done up until now and why.
- ☐ Read Mark Enser's blog.

4 Research starter toolkit

Once you have embarked upon the journey of becoming further research informed, you will find that there are many contradictory sources and discussions taking place. It can become a complicated and often infuriating world, which might make you wonder why you started and make you consider buying a Magic 8 Ball to decide the best course of action instead.

In education, you will always find alternative opinions and methods and although you may read of academics who worry about the way in which research might be misconstrued or manipulated to fit a particular process or agenda, I believe that, on an individual level or as an establishment, shying away from educational research altogether due to its complexity is more concerning than engaging with it and making a few mistakes on the way.

That is not to dismiss the complexities of educational research or research in general. It is a difficult field of study, the history of which is well detailed in Chapter 2, 'Science and belief', of Daniel T. Willingham's (2012) book *When Can You Trust the Experts?*, which is well worth reading after considering and exploring the sources suggested below and in advance of making any grand research-informed decisions. Willingham's book questions and explores our propensity to believe in authority figures and their claims, and provides a step-by-step process to use when making difficult decisions that will lead to a change in teaching practice. It is particularly helpful if you are in the position of being approached by companies or organisations wishing to sell their products to improve teaching and learning – ranging from resources to intervention programmes.

In this chapter, I will outline some key resources for you to begin looking at in order to broaden your engagement with research, and, perhaps more importantly, those that will encourage you to engage with research in the long term. They have been chosen thanks to their clarity, accessibility and explicit sense of purpose. There are many sources available, but these resources and sources are arguably key to sparking my interest and maintaining my engagement in educational research. Moreover, the ease of use provides a stepping stone to make further connections and build a network with those who are leading the way in engaging our profession in research-informed practice.

So, as you continue your research journey, steer gently through the melee of claims and take your time to engage with the many helpful resources that have been created to engage and help teachers navigate through such a complicated field, all whilst doing (and hopefully improving) their day job. The resources I have chosen will allow you to:

- directly identify findings, issues and outcomes
- become better informed and therefore begin making research-informed decisions yourself

- better understand those decisions made by others that directly influence your classroom practice and your students' outcomes.

Experts on putting research into practice

Before we talk about specific sources and ways in which you can practically apply research-informed strategies and learning techniques to your classroom, I want to mention a number of people who do offer this advice frequently through their online platforms. Keeping up to date with the latest thinking not only requires reading documents such as those you'll find in Chapter 5, page 73, but also using a mix of resources (such as those listed later in this chapter) and following blogs from teachers who are often Research Leads or those who work directly in institutions involved in educational research – these connections are an accessible and time-saving way to stay up to date. If you attempt to stay up to date with the latest findings by reading the original sources or large documents all of the time you will soon become weary and likely struggle to understand the research findings, which could put you off implementing changes that would be beneficial to both you and your students.

Keep up to date with the latest thinking and debates by signing up for regular updates from the following evidence-engaged writers and bloggers.

Research-into-practice experts

Alex Quigley

Website: www.theconfidentteacher.com

Alex Quigley is a teacher (previously Director of Huntington Research School) and author who now works at the EEF. He has a vibrant and resource-filled blog specialising in evidence-informed practice and Alex's specialist subject: how to improve and teach vocabulary to enhance students' academic and life chances.

Dawn Cox

Website: www.missdcoxblog.wordpress.com/author/missdcox

Dawn is a fan of cognitive science and, in particular, using practice-testing to improve memory. As a secondary RE teacher, Dawn writes about classroom practice and shares resources freely with others. Her strategies are easily adapted to other age groups and subjects.

Harry Fletcher-Wood

Website: www.improvingteaching.co.uk

Harry previously worked as a history teacher and is now an educational researcher for the Institute of Teaching. His posts are based in his research and have a real clarity to them. They range from discussing feedback to teacher confidence, and are regularly updated.

Clare Sealy

Website: www.primarytimery.com

Clare has been writing her blog since 2015 and shares her thoughts and strategies online through her blog posts and Twitter. Clare is a primary headteacher in London who believes in research-informed practice and who often discusses how we can see past our differences and disagreements in approaches to education.

Key considerations

When deciding upon which resources and texts to share in this section of the book, I applied similar criteria to those that I used when deciding whether or not to engage with them in the first place. I considered:

- **Accessibility:** Many research journals are closed access, meaning you cannot read their articles without paying or being part of a particular institution such as a university. Although I do recommend that certain sources are worth signing up to due to the access they then give you, many of the resources and later the research shared are open access. Many people are working hard to encourage more educational research to be shared openly and freely so I hope this will be less of an issue over time.

- **Clarity:** Some journals, websites and publications are very difficult to digest particularly when you don't have much time to do so. I have tried to choose resources that are easy to navigate and engage with no matter how much time or inclination you have to do so.

- **Purpose:** When considering the purpose of a particular resource, just as with research itself, there are questions you can ask. I consider whether it is clear who has created and contributed towards the resource. Is their purpose explained and does it sit comfortably with my personal values? Can I happily say that I used this as a platform to develop my decision-making or would I be worried about explaining where I found the information?

For each of the suggested resources that follow, I will outline the key elements to be aware of, how to use the resource and anything to be wary of. Using such resources should not be considered cheating or bypassing any particular system. If we want teachers who are often time-poor to engage with research, then there must be resources that make it easier to do so.

A final thing to say is that by explaining how to access these resources and the best ways to use them I am not necessarily endorsing all of the approaches or strategies they suggest. Instead, I am suggesting them as a great starting point. Hopefully some of them will allow you to create your own set of tools that you can then adapt and use within your own context.

A research-informed teacher's toolkit

The Education Endowment Foundation's Teaching and Learning Toolkit

How to access the resource:

Go to the website at www.educationendowmentfoundation.org.uk.

What is it?

The Education Endowment Foundation (EEF) is an independent charity that was established in 2011 by The Sutton Trust. It was originally established thanks to a substantial government grant with the aim of providing guidance to schools on how to use research to improve the attainment of disadvantaged students. The original Sutton Trust Pupil Premium Toolkit is now managed by the EEF. More recently, the EEF has developed as an online database with guidance and research-based recommendations for teachers of all students, ranging from Early Years to secondary school. The Teaching and Learning Toolkit is one strand of the EEF's website that provides 'an accessible summary of the international evidence on teaching 5–16 year olds'. In other words, the Toolkit specifically brings together the research so that you don't have to and provides you with a clear, understandable summary that you can digest quickly and investigate further should you wish.

Where to begin

Begin by exploring the Teaching and Learning Toolkit, which is neatly organised into key areas of pedagogy. You could start by looking at areas related to the focus you identified at the end of Chapter 3. The Toolkit is carefully constructed into strands of evidence summaries, ranging from arts participation to performance-related pay. This allows you to pick a strand related to your area of interest easily. Each strand has an infographic explaining the impact on cost, quantity of evidence and impact on attainment.

- **Cost:** The cost ratings consider any resources, training or activities that might be required should a strategy be put in place. They are rated between a single £ (very low) to £££££ (very high). This value is significant considering that the purpose of the Toolkit is to improve decision-making that will impact the most disadvantaged students, and often this includes considering how a student's Pupil Premium money is spent. A cost rating of a single £ sign indicates less than £80 per student whereas five £ signs means a cost of over £1,200 per student.

- **Evidence strength:** The quantity, type and consistency of the studies used to inform the evidence summary is represented through a padlock sign on the Toolkit's website. The strength of the sources reviewed in the evidence summary is indicated through the number of padlocks assigned. Any evidence summary with a single padlock is likely to be a single study based on observational data, perhaps run by teachers in schools rather than by researchers. As the padlocks grow in number the studies become more rigorous, and include meta-analyses as well as using developed methodological practice such as randomised controlled trials. Five padlocks implies a secure set of studies were reviewed; a summary with five padlocks would therefore include research evidence based on a large number of studies carried out in the past three years and in a school setting.

- **Impact (months):** The number of months of progress made due to the intervention in comparison to those who did not take part in it is then identified as the last image on the Toolkit. This is simply given as the number of additional months of progress that would be made on average by calculating, mostly, the effect sizes stated in any of the research evaluated, which are then translated into a number of months. It is important to note that a negative figure does not mean that students have regressed due to the intervention but that they have made less progress than would be expected without it.

What else to consider when using this resource

The high-quality interface and easily accessible nature of the Toolkit sits well with teachers who are looking for further information regarding a specific area. It is important to note that the EEF strongly state that the 'aim of the Toolkit is not to provide definitive claims as to what will work to bring about improvement in a new context. Rather it is an attempt to provide the best possible estimate of what is likely to be beneficial based on the existing evidence.'

Therefore, as with any resource providing us with a route into the research or evidence to inform our decisions, we must be aware that it is providing us with a framework rather than a set of answers.

The Toolkit can sometimes feel like it creates more questions than answers but I do not think this is a cause for concern. It won't necessarily point you in the direction of a specific strategy but it will give you some understanding and guidelines. At the end of each evidence summary, the Toolkit poses some areas to consider and questions to answer before your next steps. For example, if you are looking to implement new behaviour strategies, the summary provides you with information in which to frame your thinking such as: 'Have you considered what training and professional development is required for any programmes you plan to adopt?' (EEF, 2018b). Depending on your area of focus and personal CPD requirements, this might be a key question to consider before deciding upon a strategy or intervention to tackle your problem. With further knowledge and information, you can then investigate the studies looked at by the EEF (these can be found in the full report under the resources section of each strand) and proceed in a more informed manner.

Institute for Effective Education's Best Evidence in Brief newsletter

How to access the resource: Go to the website at www.the-iee.org.uk/what-we-do/best-evidence-in-brief and sign up using the form or email your details to the institution directly.

What is it?

The Institute for Effective Education (IEE) is an independent charity based at the University of York that is dedicated to making research accessible for teachers as well as commissioning new studies and working closely with the Research Schools Network. The Best Evidence in Brief newsletter is a fortnightly publication sent directly to your inbox, summarising key studies and recent findings from both the University of York and the Centre for Research and Reform in Education at Johns Hopkins University in Maryland, USA.

Where to begin

The IEE Best Evidence in Brief newsletter arrives in my inbox fortnightly on a Tuesday lunchtime (at the time of writing). I don't always sit and read the newsletter straight away, but I do file it in a folder titled 'IEE Newsletter'. I do this so that I know I can come back to it later without having accidentally sent it to the abyss that is 'deleted items'.

- A quick scroll through the headlines provides me with a glimpse into the topics and strategies discussed.
- Each newsletter includes four to six reviews of key studies, with details about where the study took place, where the information was reported and the key findings.
- Some of the reviews are studies commissioned by the IEE whereas others are based on reports in educational journals or from American or British universities.
- The newsletter provides a short summary (around 400 words) of the findings and links to the relevant sources.
- The quick links tab on each newsletter also allows you to find previous editions of the newsletter, which is useful when you did forget to file it properly!

The newsletter is useful as a starting point because it is brief. Although it may not provide a stack of answers it will certainly create questions and has a very up-to-date feel. It is easily accessible and extraordinarily clear and the links to relevant sources make further reading easy to source, explore and question. The variation in content matter and the fact that it is the product of two institutions make it a great starting point for those keen to increase their reading base and evidence-based knowledge without being overwhelming or intimidating.

What else to consider when using this resource

The resource is great for increasing awareness of international studies. This is a great benefit, although it is important that you consider the findings, outcomes and implications based on our own specific context. Some of the information may seem unfamiliar; however, this does not mean it is irrelevant. Use the 'check your sources' questions from Chapter 3, page 50, when looking at a study for the first time, in particular considering: where did it come from? Why is it relevant to you today? How did it come about?

If you don't fancy signing up for a fortnightly newsletter, then all of the previous articles can be found on the Best Evidence in Brief website, which is easy to search because each article is tagged with key words such as 'behaviour' or 'wellbeing'.

The IEE's main website also links to a number of other useful features. For those in leadership positions or in the position of investigating educational programmes to buy to support students, there is an easy-to-navigate Best Evidence Encyclopaedia where UK programmes from a variety of companies are independently reviewed. This feature might prove useful when looking at new programmes to invest in.

All documents can be downloaded in a PDF format, thereby saving time collating reviews. The Best Evidence Encyclopaedia can be found at: www.bestevidence.org.uk.

The Teacher Tapp app

How to access the resource: You can download the app straight to your phone via your app store for free. Once you have the app, sign up with your school email address and provide the name of your school and postcode. If you don't currently work in a school but want to see what's going on you can still sign up.

What is it?

An app created by Professor Becky Allen from UCL Institute of Education alongside educational journalist Laura McInerney, with technical support from Sam Sims and Alex Weatherall. The idea is that you answer three multiple-choice questions a day and in return are provided with a little snippet of CPD in a convenient and simple format.

The app was created in order to act as a conduit of information that might help teachers who are struggling with similar problems to those around the country but simply aren't aware of what others are thinking. In allowing teachers to see how others are currently thinking and approaching teaching elsewhere in the UK, Professor Becky Allen hopes to empower teachers by allowing them access to each other's opinions in a simple process that could be completed every day.

Where to begin

Once you have signed up, you should receive a notification at 3.30 pm every day (at the time of writing). I would suggest that answering the questions immediately at 3.30 pm is not always the wisest choice as your answers may be affected by the afternoon you have just had; however, it is a great time for a reminder and often the wording of the questions can brighten up a rainy Thursday afternoon!

The app will fire three multiple-choice questions to you. Usually the questions are related, but not always. On completion of the three questions, you are given yesterday's results, which you can scan through to see the percentage of people who gave each answer to yesterday's questions. This gives you an immediate insight into the current feeling of thousands of teachers across the country. Sometimes the data is surprising, but often it is simply affirming your own thoughts. Many of the questions indicate a wide demographic, which I think of as a real positive as it suggests that despite teaching in schools that are worlds apart in some ways, there are often consistencies in beliefs and values that many would like to have you believe do not exist.

When you have read through yesterday's qualitative findings, you are encouraged to read 'Today's Tip'. This is, I think, the most useful part of Teacher Tapp. You are provided with an article, blog, infographic or video that is related to yesterday's questions, alongside a suggested reading or watching time. Most are around three to five minutes long and you can always open the link and save it to read or watch later.

What else to consider when using this resource

The questions are very simple to answer and often Teacher Tapp will tell you who is asking the questions and why. For example, questions may be sent in by an individual or be created in response to a news article published that week or a declaration from the DfE. The transparency of the questions and responses is one reason that this app is a useful tool.

When reading the articles, bear in mind that they are not necessarily evidence or research based. They may be opinion articles in response to a recent idea but this does not devalue them as they often link you to further sources that you can then evaluate as to their credibility and once again ask the key questions of the evidence you have stumbled across.

Although this is not strictly a research resource, it is incredibly useful to get you feeling part of the conversation surrounding education research. It will lead you to read and consider opinions that you may not have come across without it and this is key to building your network and moulding your own opinions on key ideas, which in turn, combined with research, can lead you to making better decisions for you and your students.

The Learning Scientists website

How to access the resource: Go to the website at www.learningscientists.org.

What is it?

Two cognitive psychological scientists based in the US set up The Learning Scientists in a bid to improve communication between experts in the education field. Megan Sumeracki PhD and Yana Weinstein PhD originally set up the hashtag #AceThatTest to give worried students advice, via Twitter, in advance of a test or exam. They have brought together their own continual studies on learning with those of other experts to help both teachers and students approach testing, providing research-informed, effective study strategies that will benefit them at every stage of education.

The website is an Aladdin's cave of resources, clear explanations, discussion and debate. You can also find The Learning Scientists on Twitter at @AceThatTest and read their book *Understanding How We Learn* (Weinstein and Sumeracki, 2018), which is beautifully illustrated by Oliver Caviglioli.

Where to begin

The best place to start is the downloadable materials section. Here you'll find tangible and helpful research-informed resources. The research used to inform the strategies and resources can be read about in the blog section of the website. There is often discussion about whether or not cognitive psychology should be applied to the practical classroom. In their book *Understanding How We Learn,* Weinstein and Sumeracki (2018) crucially warn that 'if evidence supports the effectiveness of a strategy, then we should by all means adopt it, but continue to be flexible as the science evolves'. They argue that they are fully aware that not all findings from cognitive psychology are relevant and that in the past many have been misinterpreted or falsely advertised, often creating ineffective fads based on evidence that has later been disproved. It is valuable to remember that both authors teach and have tested their findings out in their own classrooms as well as considering what happens in the lab.

If you do purchase their book, you can use it neatly alongside the online resources; however, this is certainly not necessary. Online, the downloadable materials include a range of resources supporting six effective learning strategies focused on improving memory and retention, and are differentiated for use by teachers or students. Clearly and vitally, The Learning Scientists state that 'the materials are intended to teach about principles of learning and to provide teachers and students with flexible guiding principles to guide learning and studying. However, they are not intended to fix all problems within education.'

The six strategies were chosen not only because they were backed by research (some more than others) but also because they were often missed out in previous teacher training literature, and therefore The Learning Scientists felt that teachers and students needed more exposure to them.

The six strategies suggested to help students study effectively are:

1. spaced practice
2. retrieval practice
3. elaboration
4. interleaving

5. concrete examples
6. dual coding.

At no point does the website suggest that these six principles are all we need to know about teaching students how to study effectively, but they do provide a great way in to understanding further and applying such ideas to your own teaching without overwhelming or misunderstanding the process. To help you on your way, for each principle you can download either a poster that summarises the approach or a PowerPoint that further explains the ideas and is very helpful when explaining to students or colleagues about the process required to use the strategy effectively. Moreover, each strategy comes with a strategy bookmark and YouTube video to add to the ways in which you and your students can digest the information. Resources are clearly labelled and accessible to all. In the next chapter, I will focus on two of the most research-informed strategies (spaced practice and interleaving) that are mentioned as effective in The Learning Scientists' downloadable materials.

What else to consider when using this resource

One mistake that you might make when first approaching these resources is trying to use them all at once and without proper consideration. Once again, it is important to question not only the original evidence itself but also any strategies or ideas that come from them. In this case, I would suggest considering your own context carefully – what issues are you having with your students regarding testing? What type of testing are you currently concerned about? Is the test internal or external (i.e. under your control or not)? What is the purpose of the test? Once you have considered these factors, you could consider which strategy to focus on first. There is, by The Learning Scientists' own admission, a lot of overlap in these strategies and therefore, whilst they support each other well and a range of strategies are required both as teachers and for students, it could become rather confusing if you try to understand let alone implement them all at once.

The Learning Scientists reference a number of reasons for collating these particular strategies, including the impact of a report called 'What every new teacher needs to know' by the National Council on Teacher Quality (Pomerance et al., 2016), who reviewed the textbooks used to train teachers in the US and claimed that important theory about how students learn effectively was not being adequately referenced in teacher training books, thus requiring many teachers to learn about these strategies through trial and error alone. The Learning Scientists chose these specific strategies based on the gaps identified and therefore we should be aware that there are of course others and the list is not exhaustive.

An additional element to be aware of on the website is The Learning Scientists' podcast, which can be found on their website at: www.learningscientists.org/podcast-episodes.

These podcasts are rooted in research-informed learning and take place in the form of 30-minute explanations by Megan or Yana about their core strategies or more recent discussions with a range of experts in education from a wide variety of institutions from across the world.

The Chartered College of Teaching's magazine: *Impact*

How to access the resource: To gain a printed copy of the magazine you do need to be a member of the Chartered College of Teaching (more details below). However, there are open-access articles that can be found online at www.impact.chartered.college/category/open-access.

What is it?

The Chartered College of Teaching (CCT) was established in 2017 in a move to develop the previous College of Teaching, which has held the Royal Charter for teachers since 1849. The CCT aims to connect teachers to one another and to build a network of teachers' voices, to create further accessibility to research, to inspire teachers through events and to create opportunities through accreditation. To gain full access to the resources available, either you or your institution need to become a member. There is an annual subscription fee for the full host of resources, access to a research database and a printed copy of the magazine. The best resource is the termly magazine *Impact*, which contains beautifully presented, peer-reviewed articles written by teachers and researchers. Each issue has a critical topic such as 'the science of learning' or 'developing effective learners' and the magazine shares experiences from the classroom rather than just from the laboratory.

Where to begin

Stating the obvious... start at page 1. Read through the contributors to the particular edition of *Impact*. I find this helpful as when you go on to read particular articles that are of interest, and if you find yourself with more questions, it is very likely that you could contact the author and they will kindly offer you more advice or information. Generally, if a teacher or researcher is willing to contribute to a magazine that is all about sharing information and findings with others, they will also be keen to help those who engage. This stands true for many researchers too. If you find a report, meta-analysis or research paper that is of interest, then often you can email the author and they will send you more information for free.

The editorial of each edition will also make for an interesting read, as *Impact* always has a guest editor linked to the key theme of that issue. What I also love about this particular educational magazine is the clarity of their references and links. Each article is categorised into subsections with similar articles. This makes it extremely easy to choose where to start. This is not a magazine that I suggest reading through in one go like the *Radio Times* at Christmas. Instead, I would pick a section most relevant to you and your context at the time and work your way through those articles. You may wish to then have a nosy through some of the references used in these articles to dig deeper and further and evaluate the evidence for yourself. This would be the best thing to do before trying to emulate immediately the successes (or failures) of others who have gone before you. Many of the articles highlight an individual's issues and findings based on their own particular research question, and as inspirational as their work might be it is key to still play devil's advocate – to question how or why it might or might not work in your own setting. To check, ask whether this is an area of importance for you right now or whether it is something you could return to at a later date when you have solved problems X, Y and Z.

What else to consider when using this resource

If you sign up to become a member of the CCT, you'll be able to access other areas of the website, giving you access to an excess of academic research and two other resources:

'Members meet'

'Members meet' is an area on the website that includes videos with experts in a range of educational roles – from Ofsted inspectors to teachers to researchers. This can be found under the 'Members insights' tab. Click on 'Members meet' and to start with you will see only a small snippet of the clip, but if you are logged in and open up the video further by clicking 'Read more' you will find the full ten- to 15-minute videos underneath. The videos are in a question-and-answer format and the questions are sent in by members of the CCT. Some of them are more anecdotal than others but they are an interesting way to get an insight into some of the experts and key educational figures you otherwise may not have access to.

Research database and research summaries

As your research journey continues, you might wish to look directly at the studies and references provided for yourself or you may have a burning question that you wish to explore further that you cannot find written about in any of the articles or books you have access to. One benefit of the CCT is that you do have access to their research database, which gives you the ability to search through thousands of research studies and papers. It is simple to use although often less simple to tackle the papers themselves! To help with this, there is also a useful tool called the Document Summary Service run by the University of Bristol, which once again you have access to when you sign up. Rather than signing up to this separately, simply begin searching for the summary you wish to read and enter your individual access code, which will be sent to you when you join the CCT. Do note that this code only allows personal access, and with an institutional subscription to the CCT you do not get this benefit.

The document summaries are usually one to two pages in PDF format and are easy to digest. Further links to information are always given but they are a brilliant starting point when considering studies you wish to look at further. Some are available without subscription to the service or to CCT but these are limited in number. If you do subscribe and can access these documents then you will also find them easy to search, but a 'current' section will give you the most up-to-date summaries.

The Document Summary Service can be through your membership page on the Chartered College of Teaching or directly via the University of Bristol's website: https://edn.bris.ac.uk/dss.

Further sources

A further brilliant source to be aware of is the SUPER network. It includes links to some of the sources mentioned above as well as many others. These links include those to the EEF, Research School websites and many more besides. The links are updated often to ensure they are live, free and accessible and it's definitely worth adding this to your favourites so that you have easy access to the relevant sources. See: https://schooluniversitypartnership.wordpress.com/access-to-research.

If you think the non-technical approach would be a good place to start then I suggest looking up subscriptions to the following publications to add to your research starter toolkit. Many of them have been around for some time and others are more recent but they are all a great way of engaging with evidence-informed writing. I would suggest attempting every now and again putting by some PPA time to sit and read with a cup of tea. Anyone who questions what you are doing in this time because it doesn't involve a laminator or 30 sets of exercise books should be ignored fully – time to read and think should be considered both preparation for teaching and CPD.

- **ResearchED Magazine:** Similar to *Impact* but free, this publication features articles from teachers and educational experts galore, with book recommendations and reviews plus interviews with top researchers. It is also a great way to learn more about ResearchEd conferences.
- **Teach Early Years, Teach Primary** and **Teach Secondary:** These magazines have a lot more opinion articles than *Impact* or *ResearchED Magazine* but they are a great starting point to see what else is going on. The magazines are subscription based but you can sign up as a school or they often do deals for new customers. The magazines are also focused more on specific sectors so might be better tailored to your requirements.

Finally, attending and networking at events such as ResearchEd mentioned above is a fantastic way to learn about how others are putting into practice their knowledge and understanding of research in the classroom. ResearchEd is the best place to start for true grass-roots inspiration. An inspirational pair of teachers, Tom Bennett and Hélène Galdin-O'Shea, created the wonderful movement that inspires thousands of teachers from across the world to use and invest time in research-informed practice. Their conferences are far reaching, full of debate and excitement and are certain to get you thinking about your own classroom in a considered and thoughtful way. I was blown away by the uniqueness of such an event and movement at my first ResearchEd conference in 2015. I wrote about it soon after attending in a blog post (https://littlemisslud.wordpress.com/2015/09/06/last-night-researched-saved-my-life/), in which I recalled fantastic presentations from Daisy Christodoulou, Sara Davidson and Louise Mower, and Sam Freedman, amongst others.

Find out more about events near you via the ResearchED website: https://researched.org.uk/.

What next?

These resources are simply a starting point for becoming more research aware and research literate. I have purposefully chosen a range of resources to encourage thinking and participation with others. The link between them all is how they encourage those who wish to engage further in research to build a network, whether that be simply through answering a few questions a day and better considering the evidence others bring to the fore or whether that means building contacts with writers and researchers who have come before you.

This chapter works as a research starter toolkit, designed to give you an insight into what is out there and what conversations are happening right now. It may be that you feel isolated in your quest to become a more evidence-based teacher, department or school but by engaging with some of the most simple resources you will see that this isn't necessarily the case. They are also simple tools that can be shared with others – more on how to do this successfully in Part 2.

I would suggest working your way through some of the tools a little at a time. If there are some you have used before then perhaps double check the considerations section and see that you haven't missed out on some of the added extras that many provide. If you haven't ever used or engaged with these tools before then just go for it – you have nothing to lose and the majority are free.

Your action research

Now that you have some resources to engage with, you can begin to consider these in relation to the general area you chose to develop in Chapter 3, page 46. Using one area to begin with can help you on your research-informed journey. See this first exploration (if it is that) as a test run. You are using your current area for development to engage with new sources and from that point you can make inroads that will provide you with, eventually, more answers than questions. If you have a clear idea of the area you wish to focus on then you can choose your tools accordingly. For example, if you are sure that memory and recall is an area you want to focus on, then engaging with The Learning Scientists first and foremost makes sense. However, if your area is a little broader than this, for example behaviour management, then you might wish to start with the EEF Toolkit.

If, for any reason, you are still not sure where to start making changes, then reading the magazines suggested and using the IEE Best Evidence in Brief newsletter to look at current issues being addressed in the world of education is a good place to start. Either way, you now have a way into current discussions and through these will be able to find some research to read and strategies to consider. In the following chapter, I provide an overview of the key research-engaged writers and more specifically the key research-informed strategies and outcomes influencing teaching currently.

Chapter 4 takeaway

Teaching tip
Pay attention to your choices
If possible, keep a note of some of the decisions you make each day. This can be done in a journal fashion or jotted down after a few lessons. Your decisions will range in difficulty, perhaps ranging from how you deal with a behaviour management issue to why you sit a student in a particular place. Through paying closer attention to the choices you make, you will be able to better identify the area you want to focus on and therefore which sources you should engage with first. When you note down the decision you had to make then perhaps add reasons why or list the main factors in making that decision.

For example: *Weds P3 – stopped class to check for understanding and retaught metaphors through short quiz – used mini whiteboards for checking responses. Fast, simple and helps to identify misconceptions.*

Pass it on
Saw this and thought of you
One way of building a network within your own school, as well as building your own understanding, is to scan articles or posts that you think may not be relevant to you but may be relevant to someone else. Thanks to our teaching and learning team, most of whom have a penchant for nice stationery, our school's copy of *Impact* or *Teach Secondary* is often littered (beautifully) with sticky notes. As the team read the magazine articles, they identify those that might be relevant to others in the school and often then scan these in to send to the relevant department or teacher. I wouldn't suggest you do this every week but as most publications are termly you could do a 'Saw this and thought of you' email every now and again!

CPD book club recommendation

Read *Understanding How We Learn: A visual guide* (2018) by Yana Weinstein and Megan Sumeracki with Oliver Caviglioli and delight in the simplicity, honesty and clarity of a book that is full of top tips for teachers, students and parents. It is beautifully illustrated by Oliver Caviglioli and turns complicated science into effective strategies for real classrooms.

Bloggers' corner

Written in 2013, but as relevant now as ever, Tim Taylor gives some advice regarding the way in which we approach cognitive psychology in the classroom – a good, quick read that presents the thoughts of many who were subject to teaching certain 'fads' succinctly: www.theguardian. com/teacher-network/teacher-blog/2013/aug/20/cognitive-psychology-classroom-caution

TO DO LIST:

❏ Pick one or two of the resources suggested in this chapter to engage with to begin thinking about new ideas and perspectives.

❏ When choosing what to investigate further, make sure you ask the key questions about how relevant this information is to you at this point in time: use the 'check your sources' questions from Chapter 3.

❏ Remind yourself of your area of focus, which you broadly decided upon at the end of Chapter 3. As you engage further with these sources, consider which ones you might come back to in order to find out more about your specific area for development and to create your PIO/PICO statement.

❏ Share articles or blogs that interest you with others in your school or share anything that interests you on Twitter with a comment about what you found interesting.

❏ Download the Teacher Tapp app to your phone.

❏ Read Tim Taylor's article for the *Guardian* from 2013.

❏ Read articles in recent issues of *ResearchED Magazine, Teach Primary, Teach Secondary* or *Impact*.

5 Getting to grips with the key research

The previous chapter presented a research starter toolkit, including a range of resources that you should use as a starting point to access ideas and research, as well as resources you can turn to when you want to find out what people are currently debating. They will help inform your knowledge of research and point you in the direction of reading around the key area you identified at the end of Chapter 3, page 46, or any future questions you have. When considering making a change to your approach, in the hope for a change in outcome, it is important to consider the research studies that are applicable alongside the evidence you have from your own experience, school and stakeholders, and always remember that the point of engaging with research in this way through practical application in your classroom is to see what works for you rather than to find a definitive approach that can be applied to other classrooms or policy.

In Chapter 8, page 160, we will look more closely at how you can develop your questions to improve your practice in a considered way, but as a starting point, it is important be aware of the influential researchers, the key research-informed writers and the pivotal work that influences both policy and practice. In doing so, you are building yourself a foundation within which you can continue your own individual journey. Also, by understanding the current educational research landscape, you'll become more aware of some of the reasoning behind the decision-making that may be going on around us both in governing bodies such as Ofsted and in our schools. This then puts you in a strong position to start questioning and challenging decisions in a more informed manner.

Key reading

It is difficult to keep up to date with the latest research when you have such a demanding, time-poor job and so the best way to keep informed is to read summaries and blogs and identify the key reading. As mentioned, we must be wary of research that may be up to date but isn't necessarily methodological or accurate or that hasn't been replicated in a variety of situations. That is why literature reviews, research syntheses, blogs and books are a great source of information, as they save you trawling through thousands of studies yourself. Therefore, in this chapter, I have identified a few of the key works (a range of evidence reviews, syntheses and reports) that I suggest you read in advance of creating your own questions and undertaking your own specific reading and research. Some of the key works cover a vast range of educational issues in one individual paper, encompassing many areas of pedagogy in an evidence summary style. They may use meta-analyses or combine qualitative data in their findings and it is important to remember that the suggestions are often based on access to an array of previous studies and are undertaken by trained researchers and scientists. In many ways the suggestions and findings might seem generic. They don't necessarily provide us

Research every teacher should read

	Title	Author(s)	Year of publication	Where to find it	Length	Worth reading if...
1	Improving students' learning with effective learning techniques: promising directions from cognitive and educational psychology	John Dunlosky, Katherine A. Rawson, Elizabeth J. Marsh, Mitchell J. Nathan and Daniel T. Willingham	2013a	www.indiana.edu/~pcl/rgoldsto/courses/dunloskyimprovinglearning.pdf	55 pages (a link to a shorter article summarising this can be found on page 80)	You are interested in the impact of cognitive science on learning and want to know about strategies to improve memory and recall.
2	Principles of instruction: research-based strategies that all teachers should know	Barak Rosenshine	2012	www.aft.org/sites/default/files/periodicals/Rosenshine.pdf	Nine pages in total, summarising a slightly longer original paper linked on page 86	You want to understand why you often do what you do instinctively.
3	Metacognition and self-regulated learning	Alex Quigley, Daniel Muijs and Eleanor Stringer (EEF-commissioned review)	2018	www.educationendowmentfoundation.org.uk/tools/guidance-reports/metacognition-and-self-regulated-learning	32 pages reviewing the EEF's original research (a shorter summary is available)	You want to aid students in understanding their own learning and want to really understand the word of the moment!
4	What makes great teaching?	Rob Coe, Cesare Aloisi, Steve Higgins and Lee Elliot Major	2014	www.suttontrust.com/wp-content/uploads/2014/10/What-Makes-Great-Teaching-REPORT.pdf	57 pages in total with pages 13–22 focusing on good pedagogical practices	You are interested in both your own and others' professional development.
5	A marked improvement? A review of the evidence on written marking	Victoria Elliott, Jo-Anne Baird, Therese N. Hopfenbeck, Jenni Ingram, Ian Thompson, Natalie Usher, Mae Zantout, James Richardson and Robbie Coleman (EEF-commissioned review)	2016	https://educationendowmentfoundation.org.uk/public/files/Presentations/Publications/EEF_Marking_Review_April_2016.pdf	35 pages of clear guidance that summarises different aspects of marking and the research in each area	You are still concerned about the changes in marking policies and maintaining a healthy work-life balance.

with a specific strategy with which to proceed but instead with a set of guidelines and parameters within which to work. It is our job to investigate further by considering our own context and work out what is relevant to us and whether the findings have any implications on our current practice.

There are far too many papers, overviews and books out there that might be considered key reading when beginning to look at educational research. In an attempt to keep it simple and accessible, I have created a table of reference (on page 74) so that you can decide which summary and overview to read first. I do not suggest sitting down to read all of my overviews followed by the whole papers and texts at once!

Each of the papers will be summarised into key points but this does not mean you cannot then go on to read them or investigate further should you wish. This chapter is certainly one you could dip in and out of and many of the ideas explained by the overviews will be discussed further in the next chapter, where case studies and tangible strategies based on the evidence-based ideas shared here can be found. It is a good starting point when considering what strategies you would like to use in your own action research statement, which will help you to further engage with research-informed thinking in a practical sense.

Summaries of key research

1. Improving students' learning with effective learning techniques: promising directions from cognitive and educational psychology (Dunlosky et al., 2013a)

Overview

This document is a monograph (a detailed written study on a specific subject) of effective learning techniques. The study looks at ten common learning techniques and reviews the previous studies, rating them in order of effectiveness based on the evidence available at the time.

The introduction outlines the methodology of the monograph and how the learning techniques were chosen – over 700 studies about the ten most commonly used (not effective) learning techniques were reviewed. The paper explains that some of the choices of learning techniques reviewed were picked due to their perceived effectiveness and popularity with students. The summary states that 'some techniques (e.g., highlighting and rereading) were selected because students report relying heavily on them, which makes it especially important to examine how well they work.' The techniques focused on are those that students are able to implement themselves, therefore excluding more complex techniques that might require technological input or extended teacher input in order for them to be successful. The study therefore outlines some very simple ideas that can easily be transferred and considered in your own context.

As previously discussed, any research (not just in education) has its issues and problems but this is particularly arguable if studies are carried out in a context that is not easily comparable to that of a classroom (i.e. a laboratory). Helpfully, this particular research explicitly identifies the context in which the studies were undertaken and this is further discussed in every subsection three, entitled 'Effects in representative educational contexts'.

The whole text can therefore be easily broken down into individual sections of reading – beginning with the two techniques that are deemed the most robust and effective based on the articles and studies reviewed. Furthermore, the structure of the piece makes it simple to break down into the five subsections, which are: a general description of the technique; how general the effects of this technique are; the effects in representative educational contexts; issues for implementation; and overall assessment. Therefore, this paper is a great piece to use when introducing others to reading research-based materials.

Key ideas to take away

The ten learning techniques reviewed are either used widely by students already (such as highlighting/underlining and rereading), should be used more often (such as practice-testing and distributed or interleaved practice) or should be used more cautiously (such as key word mnemonics or summarisation) according to the authors of this monograph.

The overall findings suggest that of the ten learning techniques explored, only two are deemed to have robust and durable results, and therefore they are the ones that should be recommended to students and teachers as effective learning strategies. They have been judged as effective based on the studies reviewed, which demonstrate they can be used in a range of learning conditions (i.e. they could be used alone or in a group setting) and have what is called 'generalisability', in that the techniques previously explored in individual studies have now been culminated and reviewed through the lens of numerous variables including students' characteristics (age, motivation, prior achievement, etc.) and materials used in study (diagrams, maps, narrative texts, etc.).

At the end of the paper, the study suggests that the two most effective techniques and the only two with high 'utility' ratings are practice-testing and distributed practice – both of which lean heavily on scientific research and theory of long-term memory. This is perhaps of little surprise considering the authors are predominantly cognitive scientists – one of the authors, Daniel Willingham (2009), argues in his book *Why Don't Students Like School?* that evidence from cognitive science can be applied to the classroom and discusses why 'practice improves transfer' of knowledge; in his book, the term practice means 'continuing to work at something you've already mastered'. It is certainly worth reading Willingham's book once you have read the summaries below or the whole Dunlosky et al. paper, in particular Chapters 3 to 6, which focus on the process of gaining knowledge initially then transferring it to the long-term memory so that it can be retrieved via the working memory successfully. The two learning techniques discussed below directly support Willingham's arguments and bringing the ideas together might help you in deciding on how this knowledge will influence your practice.

Practice-testing

Immediately, the authors of this article define practice-testing as low-stakes testing that is separate from summative assessment and explain that it could take a number of forms, varying from immediate verbal recall to answering questions in a textbook at the end of a unit or multiple-choice questions. It also includes testing that students are able to organise themselves without a teacher guiding them through it, for example past paper questions or recalling information from cue cards.

Initially, the authors summarise two theoretical reasons why practical testing should be effective; the paper describes how Carpenter (2009) 'proposed that testing can enhance retention by triggering elaborative retrieval processes'. In other words, whilst trying to recall a specific piece of information, we inadvertently access related information, therefore strengthening the access to that information at a later date. Furthermore, the authors found evidence to suggest that when restudying content along with practice-testing, students performed better than those who simply restudied the content.

The format of practice-testing is further discussed in section 8.2a and the authors argue that, based on the wide range of studies considered, the evidence available at the time suggests that tests that require short answers or recall (verbal or written) are more effective than asking students to respond in a more general way such as completing a fill-in-the-blank exercise. Practice-testing is evidently being extoled as effective but not all practice-testing seems to be created equally. The authors also make reference to the number of studies that have indicated the importance of timing and reoccurrence of testing related to effectiveness. They found that numerous studies support the theory that testing is more effective when completed more than once in advance of a summative test and even more effective when the timing between tests is considered carefully. They state that numerous studies showed that 'Repeated practice-testing produces greater benefits when lags between trials within a session are longer rather than shorter', which links closely to the impact of distributed practice.

Crucially, in the 'Issues for implementation' section on practice-testing, the importance of feedback is mentioned. The authors found that numerous studies demonstrated that when corrective feedback is given in response to practice-testing, students performed better than when simply restudying a topic. The authors noted that the timing of the feedback was not crucial to the improvements, simply that if feedback was given, results improved.

Of course, there are a variety of ways and methods with which we can put practice-testing into, well... practice! What is clear is that if we aren't already, then we should be considering the possible improvements that could be made by students if this strategy was employed in the classroom (through low-stakes or no-stakes testing) or if undertaken by students personally when revising information in advance of a test. Whether a weekly mental maths test or a well-planned end-of-term assessment, it would seem that practice-testing needs to be more explicitly used by all. In Chapter 6, we explore how these learning techniques can be used practically in the classroom and explore some resources that are helpful in doing so.

Distributed practice

The second most effective learning strategy according to the authors of this article is distributed practice – encompassing both spaced effects and lag effects. In summary, they have looked at studies and literature reviews of studies looking at spaced practice, where topics are separated rather than learnt in a single mass before moving on; they have also reviewed those studies that reviewed the advantages of spacing learning episodes over a longer period of time rather than using shorter gaps. Together, they have called these methods of planning learning *distributed practice*.

The authors make it clear that the evidence supporting distributed practice is built on the study of when these learning episodes take place and how far apart they are rather than *what* happens in each particular session. In the most robust of studies, *how* learning takes place was not focused on by the researchers – instead they focused on what knowledge was being looked at again and when it was being looked at. In other words, it does not seem to matter if the learning methods or strategies are slightly different or how learning is presented to students each time; however, it is noted in the article that if the purpose of learning is to be able to recall information then combining practice-testing with distributed practice yields the best outcomes. This does not mean that distributed practice alone (in its various formats) is ineffective.

The authors acknowledge that the majority of studies analysed took place with undergraduates, although students of all ages and abilities have taken part in the research. From three-year-olds to adults, it would seem that distributed practice works for all who are endeavouring to improve their performance, particularly with retrieval practice. One factor that hasn't further been considered yet is students' prior knowledge or motivation – this would be a particularly complicated factor to take into account.

Another interesting aspect of this section on distributed practice is the part that discusses students' own perceptions of how effective such techniques may be. The authors looked at the study habits of students and found that with regular practice-testing, students studied more regularly whereas with spaced testing, occurring less frequently, many saved their studying and completed it in a mass right before the test. Arguably, this is because students are unable to see the benefit of spacing their study over time when there is no immediate incentive to do so. Therefore, the article suggests that students require both clear instruction and evidence (for example doing well in a test where they have used distributed revision) in order to be convinced to use this study method again.

Overall considerations

The authors of this study repeat their multifaceted intent in writing this monograph: to inform teachers of strategies that could be included in their teaching, to train students to use research-informed strategies for learning and to encourage researchers to further investigate under-researched ideas and to do so in what they called 'educationally representative contexts'. The authors argue that although costly and time-consuming, using real representative data from schools as evidence for particular strategies is more likely to lead to recommendations that can have a positive impact on students' learning and improvement, which is why both practice-testing and distributed practice occur at the top of the list – they (along with a few other techniques) have evidence from real-life contexts.

As well as understanding the strategies summarised, the authors' intention was to allow anyone considering using such strategies to both understand and further consider how you can apply them to your own setting (Chapter 6, page 106, will give you further ideas as to how to do this), whether you are a teacher or student. They write that their 'goal was to provide reviews that were extensive enough to allow anyone interested in using a particular technique to judge its utility for his or her own instructional or learning goals'. Therefore, we must do just this when considering any evidence – judge it for ourselves and apply it carefully.

In the conclusion of the study, the authors summarise their ideas and make it clear that the techniques described and reviewed will not aid all students in all contexts. Critically, they mention in most of their suggestions that the techniques 'will benefit only students who are motivated and capable of using them'. It is therefore our job to consider how and why we use such techniques and what we then do to motivate our students and equip with them with the necessary skills to use them effectively.

Further reading

- The study has been neatly and clearly summarised further by the publication *Scientific American Mind* (Dunlosky et al., 2013b) but you do have to purchase it via their website. If you are intending to share this research with colleagues, then I would suggest using the summarised article to do so because it is both clear and engaging in format. It can be found at: www.aft.org/sites/default/files/periodicals/dunlosky.pdf.
- Damian Benney (2016) on how to use spacing in the classroom: www.mrbenney.wordpress.com/2016/11/03/optimal-time-for-spacing-gaps.
- Andy Tharby's (2014) blog on spacing and interleaving and the forgetting curve: www.classteaching.wordpress.com/2014/06/12/spacing-and-interleaving.
- The research article 'Spacing effects in learning' (Cepeda et al., 2008): http://laplab.ucsd.edu/articles/Cepeda%20et%20al%202008_psychsci.pdf.
- Graham Nuthall's (2007) seminal work *The Hidden Lives of Learners* is a powerful book exploring the classroom through research. Chapters 3 and 4 in particular are relevant here.

2. Principles of instruction: research-based strategies that all teachers should know (Rosenshine, 2012)

Overview

Firstly, the format I have linked to is an article from the publication *American Educator* from 2012, which is incredibly easy to access and has great clarity in its presentation. Unlike the previous article, it is adapted from the original publication (Rosenshine, 2010) and suited for a quicker and shorter read. Rosenshine was a professor in educational psychology at the University of Illinois and his beliefs in direct instruction can sometimes come under fire, but this article demonstrates how (even if you do not wholly agree with direct instruction) you can use certain strategies to explicitly teach students information whilst encouraging them to engage with problem solving and applying knowledge.

The teaching suggestions can be used in a number of ways in a classroom and are wide ranging, therefore encouraging us to distinguish between how students learn and how we teach. It is important to be aware of the distinction between research that focuses on how students learn versus evidence that is based on how we teach. It is not always as simple as applying theories of learning to theories of teaching. Often they are spoken of as one and the same yet of course they aren't, and this is something to remain aware of especially in the early years of teaching. In this article, Rosenshine used evidence from a wide range of sources including evidence from teaching observations as well as evidence from studies undertaken by cognitive scientists on learning strategies taught to students.

This short article is worth reading even if you are not completely enamoured with direct instruction. If you are considering using research to influence your practice in any capacity, then this piece provides more than just a list of findings, also giving suggestions as to practical ways these ideas could be used in the classroom. As it says in the introduction to the article, following these principles does not negate engaging activities but, in reference to what Rosenshine calls the 'most effective teachers', he argues that 'Many of these teachers also went on to experiential, hands-on activities, but they always did the experiential activities *after*, not before, the basic material was learned.'

Key ideas to take away

Ten principles are explored, beginning with the research findings in support of the principle and then how it could be applied in the classroom. The ten principles are:

1. Begin a lesson with a short review of previous learning.
2. Present new material in small steps with student practice after each step.
3. Ask a large number of questions and check the responses of all students.
4. Provide models.
5. Guide student practice.
6. Check for student understanding.
7. Obtain a high success rate.
8. Provide scaffolds for difficult tasks.
9. Require and monitor independent practice.
10. Engage students in weekly and monthly reviews.

Some of the suggestions are more complex than others. I love this poster of Rosenshine's principles on the Teaching How2 website, which gives a clear overview of each of the strategies using an image (dual-coding) and summary: https://teachinghow2s.com/blog/principles-of-instruction.

In this section I will expand on three of the principles (numbers 1, 3 and 9) but I recommend that you read the article in order to get to grips with the others. The list of ten principles is not hierarchical, and in many ways principles 1 and 2 link to the evidence previously discussed about practice-testing and distributed practice, but principle 1 has some useful hints that are summarised below.

Rosenshine's principle number 1: begin a lesson with a short review of previous learning

The idea of reviewing learning is not unusual or new, and for the majority of teachers it becomes habitual after a year or two of teaching. But as a new teacher this can be a difficult process. Remember (if it isn't too harrowing) your first few days alone in your classroom – all those eyes staring back at you (or worse, ignoring you). Students waltzing into a room unaware or unprepared for what is to come whilst you hope and pray that you will get through your meticulously planned lesson, which opens with a particularly jazzy starter printed on coloured paper to engage and excite those eager to take part. Such a hyperbolic description is not the case for every newly qualified teacher yet, regardless, one worry is often how you are going to use the first few minutes effectively to set up the rest of the lesson and get students learning. This isn't a concern that disappears after the first few years but something that is often debated in schools and sometimes particular strategies become whole-school policy.

The variety of ways to begin lessons is, of course, endless and depends on a number of factors including the age of students, the subject being taught and all other contextual variants. Some schools insist that lessons begin with ten minutes of silent reading; others believe that you should use a 'hook' to engage students whilst some ask you to begin by writing learning objectives down and underlining them. The variety is understandable but some strategies are deemed better research informed than others. The issue is that often these starters are ineffective in doing anything other than ensuring you can take the register on time and possibly calming down one or two rowdy students who are still bouncing their way around the room thanks to the sugar they consumed at lunchtime. As time has gone on and lessons have moved away from the three-part structure once suggested by Ofsted, so the starter task has matured in purpose. This is where I believe many have turned towards Rosenshine's advice and now often use a review of learning to begin their lessons.

Rosenshine's article clearly summarises the benefits of starting a lesson with a review when you consider the new knowledge you later hope to impart. He states that 'The review of previous learning can help us recall words, concepts, and procedures effortlessly and automatically when we need this material to solve problems or to understand new material.'

The article also suggests that reviewing learning can lead to overlearning, which in turn sees skills (such as addition, multiplication or the learning of vocabulary) become automatic, thereby creating capacity in students' working memories, making it easier to teach new content. It seems logical that recapping knowledge and skills at the start of the lesson will ensure that new content is connected to the old and therefore make it easier to comprehend. Rosenshine states that 'If we do not review previous learning, then we will have to make a special effort to recall old material while learning new material, and this makes it difficult for us to learn the new material.'

There are plenty of ways in which the review of learning can be made varied and engaging for students. Rosenshine mentions how this time can be used to review relevant homework tasks and how in one elementary school, teachers who completed daily review for eight minutes at the start of the lesson had better outcomes than those who didn't.

In Chapter 6, page 114, I will recommend some of the key strategies to approaching daily review and how to make it just as, if not more, engaging but certainly more effective than the jazzy starters we all once designed, used and forgot!

Rosenshine's principle number 3: ask a large number of questions and check the responses of all students

This principle might seem simple and that is likely to be because it is. Based on the three sources reviewed, Rosenshine found that the most successful teachers asked more questions to more students than those deemed to be less successful.

Although one of the most simple techniques we could employ, and one used by all teachers regardless of traditional or progressive approaches, Rosenshine highlights the importance of using questions to engage students actively (due to the different ways in which questions can be asked and answered) and to tell which students had or had not understood the content previously explained. The report lists different types of responses, including choral response, which is often seen as a more old-fashioned or traditional technique but, when used effectively (not necessarily all the time), can prove useful. Helpfully, it suggests that using choral response is only effective if all students start together and that teachers help students to rehearse responses through additional support, examples and explanations.

In the next chapter, I will explore how hinge questions can be used to ensure that not only are we asking enough questions but also that those questions target more students more often. This seems to be the principle argument from Rosenshine – that we need to ask more questions and that we must use these to understand our students' learning rather than simply to ascertain a single right answer.

This principle links well with Rosenshine's principle 6 – check for student understanding. In a similar way to asking more questions, the studies in which teachers did check for student understanding led to improvements for both learner and teacher. For the learner, Rosenshine argues it provides an opportunity for new information to be linked to prior learning in the student's mind, create or strengthen connections and move their learning to their long-term memory. For teachers, it provides a neat opportunity to discover and react to misconceptions that may have been created during the learning process. Both outcomes are incredibly important. Rosenshine leans on cognitive science to explore how students learn by connecting new information to their own prior knowledge, but how in doing so they can make connections that are simply incorrect. This is because the prior knowledge they already have is not relevant at this point or they do not have the prior knowledge we might assume in order to understand a new idea or concept. Granted, these misconceptions can often lead to funny moments in the classroom where students might think they have understood something, but this can also lead to mistakes and errors later on unless you intervene in a timely manner. The hypercorrection effect of feedback at this point can prove powerful, and identifying misconceptions early, argues Rosenshine, is important if students are to improve. In Chapter 6, page 110, one particular questioning strategy is described to aid this early intervention.

Rosenshine's principle number 9: monitor independent practice

Principle 9 is another simple but key reminder for us all about effective teaching. Of course, we monitor students as we are explaining a new idea and topic and many of us will encourage students to take on individual practice or exploration after a concept or idea has been explained, but Rosenshine highlights the fact that this is the point at which misconceptions are most likely to occur. In his summary of this principle, he suggests that as teachers we ensure that:

- The independent practice follows teacher-led instruction and explanation.
- The independent practice allows students to deal with the same knowledge as that which has been previously explored – he allows for a slight variation but we must be careful not to make tenuous links between a topic explained and a topic then being independently explored (this may occur if there are time pressures).
- The independent practice must also encompass teacher input through teachers monitoring the work by circling the room. The report suggests teachers should monitor individual students' work for around 30 seconds or less.
- If a teacher is finding themselves having to intervene with independent practice for longer than 30 seconds, Rosenshine suggests that the students have not sufficiently understood either the topic or task and that it may need to be explained again.

I wish that I had better understood the importance of this principle during my training years. I was certainly told that I could stop students and explain things to them again but I wasn't 100 per cent sure why I should do that if *some* of them seemed to be getting it, even if others didn't – surely they were all just learning at different rates? It takes confidence to stop an entire class from working or to decide that you are going to reteach an element of work. This is particularly the case when it might look like students are working well and are engaged in their learning but on closer inspection you might see that many of them have misunderstood. If I had a better understanding of the science behind learning at that stage, I think I would have identified and reacted to my students' misconceptions a lot sooner and more effectively.

We all know there are numerous strategies we can use, depending on our students' ages and the topics we are teaching, that can engage them in independent practice. Rosenshine highlights that independent practice does not have to be completed in silence and alone but that research demonstrates that cooperative learning – where students explain ideas to each other rather than to the teacher – yields positive outcomes and is particularly beneficial for students who might require another opportunity to rehearse and restudy new ideas.

Overall considerations

Understanding Rosenshine's principles is not difficult, because of the clarity with which the ideas are explained and the sections with strategies for use in the classroom, but it is important to consider that they are fairly generalised and steeped in the argument for explicit teaching (or direct instruction). Therefore, as with any research-informed strategy, the knowledge should be used carefully and in context.

If you were not careful and simply printed off and laminated (obviously) the ten principles and tried to stick to them 100 per cent of the time, I am not convinced you would have the happiest classroom. To turn these ten principles into a ten-point lesson approach would be to miss the point. Rosenshine uses the word 'some' in his introduction, suggesting these aren't the only approaches, and also uses the word 'involves' when defining what education is. This suggests to me that these principles are approaches we must be aware of, that we should experiment with and come to our own conclusions as to how they work with our students in our school. Rosenshine comments on the strategies to engage students and improve engagement on numerous occasions and only we know how to mix these strategies with our own brand of teaching in order to motivate and maintain our students' interest whilst ensuring we are teaching content effectively. If used alongside the knowledge of our students, these principles provide good guidance on how to effectively teach, but if simply used as a list to tick off or, worse, a stick to beat others with then their effectiveness will quickly disappear.

Further reading

- Read *Rosenshine's Principles in Action* by Tom Sherrington (2019), @teacherhead on Twitter, a booklet exploring the possible use of these principles in the classroom.
- The full original pamphlet published by the International Academy of Education in 2010 can be found here: www.ibe.unesco.org/fileadmin/user_upload/Publications/Educational_Practices/EdPractices_21.pdf.
- If you found the ten principles of interest, then Rosenshine's earlier paper from 1997, 'The case for explicit, teacher-led, cognitive strategy instruction', might also be for you. In it, he discusses how and why he decided on pursuing a course of direct instruction despite opposition at the time of writing. You can find it here: http://citeseerx.ist.psu.edu/viewdoc/download?doi=10.1.1.468.1582&rep=rep1&type=pdf.

3. Metacognition and self-regulated learning (Quigley et al., 2018)

Overview

This guidance report from the EEF does not claim to be revealing anything that hasn't been explained in previous research studies. Its aim is to make that information clear and accessible to all. It explains that the term 'metacognition' – now widely used in schools – is complex and, if not understood prior to implementation of metacognitive strategies, might not be as effective as studies suggest it could be. Many schools have embraced 'learning to learn' strategies or schemes that have proved effective in supporting students to achieve; however, the guidance report hints at the possible misconceptions that may occur if the background to metacognition is not fully understood or explained to staff before strategies are used in the classroom.

I would suggest you read and share this report with others who are interested in improving results in the most cost-effective of ways whilst also increasing your knowledge and understanding of a complex subject. As this report is based on a large number of studies and previous reviews of the effects of metacognition, the advice is still generic in some senses. To make it applicable to your classroom, you require both subject-specific knowledge and an understanding of the relevant cognitive skills required in a specific area.

The report provides seven clear and accessible recommendations to making metacognition a part of your teaching or your school's approach to learning to learn. The report states that the recommendations are suitable for those studying between Key Stages 1 and 4 because the majority of studies have taken place within this age range, although it points Early Years teachers to more specific guidance from the Early Years Toolkit.

Key ideas to take away

The seven recommendations understandably overlap in many ways. Some are recommendations for school leaders and others are recommendations for classroom teachers, and all will help to increase your understanding of metacognition so that you can both evaluate what you are undoubtedly already doing in the classroom and then refine your current processes to make it more effective and help students to achieve.

The seven recommendations from the EEF report are:

1. 'Teachers should acquire the professional understanding and skills to develop their pupils' metacognitive knowledge.
2. Explicitly teach pupils metacognitive strategies, including how to plan, monitor, and evaluate their learning.
3. Model your own thinking to help pupils develop their metacognitive and cognitive skills.
4. Set an appropriate level of challenge to develop pupils' self-regulation and metacognition.
5. Promote and develop metacognitive talk in the classroom.
6. Explicitly teach pupils how to organise and effectively manage their learning independently.
7. Schools should support teachers to develop knowledge of these approaches and expect them to be applied appropriately.'

Below are summaries of recommendations 1 and 3.

Professional understanding

The first recommendation is vital to all who seek to use and encourage the successful use of metacognition. Recommendation 1 explains the three-part metacognitive regulation cycle, which it argues is key to successful understanding of one's own learning. The report then breaks down the complexities of *thinking about thinking* into an understandable example.

In essence, combining learners' explicit understanding of their prior knowledge of the task, subject or strategies (metacognition) with the regulation cycle culminates in the following sequence (which will be experienced not just the once but multiple times during a single task):

- Planning how to approach a task: likely to be based on previously used strategies and knowledge.
- Monitoring the strategies used whilst completing the task: to consider whether they are working successfully or not.
- Evaluating the overall success of the approach given: the concept that self-regulated learners will be motivated to find successful approaches and return to the beginning of the cycle if an attempt is not successful.

This recommendation is simply an introduction to metacognition. The example in the report helps to make some of these ideas more understandable and concrete. It is not a strategy in itself but the report states that 'unless teachers have a strong understanding of the metacognitive demands of the topics they are teaching, they may miss opportunities to develop pupils' knowledge and skills'. This suggests to me that subject- and task-specific knowledge (regardless of the phase you are teaching) is key because the demands of each topic or task differ greatly. Without in-depth knowledge of the specific requirements and skills needed for that task, it is impossible to know when a student has mistakenly used a different skill or approach that may not be the most appropriate. It reminds me of the perils of covering a lesson where the task set is so subject-specific that although I (as the cover teacher) may understand the expected outcome or have access to the right answers, I cannot support students who are struggling in getting there as I don't have the subject-specific knowledge to know the steps they should be taking and therefore cannot intervene at the correct points to clarify their understanding or improve their knowledge.

The same can be said of our understanding of metacognition – unless we have an understanding of how we learn (you may wish to read more on cognitive load theory – see further reading after this section), then how can we hope to teach successfully?

Teacher modelling

Each of the recommendations deserve their own explanation and review; however, recommendation 3 stands out as a key idea for all teachers to understand regardless of your learners' age or ability. Once again, the report states that most teachers model and use such metacognitive techniques 'naturally'. However, it is important for both new teachers and novice learners that modelling is explicit.

Teacher modelling is described and presented as demonstrating and explicitly showing students the thinking behind the successful completion of a specific task. Whether that be a physical task or completing a particular type of exam question, teachers often outline their thinking (their metacognitive regulation cycle) verbally to their students. Teachers often do this without even realising it and it is simply about making ourselves aware of our own processes, which in turn can make us more effective. It is also important to make new teachers aware of the most effective processes and not allow them to attempt only to imitate modelling but to do so effectively.

In recommendation 3, there are a few ideas that help to improve teacher modelling and that I feel, if we are fully aware of, can help us in the modelling process:

- In order for teacher modelling to be successful, students require some prior knowledge and understanding. Therefore, it makes sense for students to see a successful outcome before modelling commences.
- Students need to be engaged in the process, and providing an opportunity to practise immediately after the modelling can be effective.
- Scaffolding should be in place but not too specific: a level of difficulty is desirable to encourage monitoring and evaluation.
- Scaffolding should be removed over time to encourage internal independent metacognitive processes.
- Metacognition is not more valuable than cognition and knowledge: knowledge of a subject will allow you to access the appropriate strategies and evaluate how well they have been used. Without the relevant knowledge or thinking, metacognition will not successfully move students forward.

These suggestions can be used to ensure teacher modelling is completed in the most effective way, and although there may not always be a need to plan every example of modelling to students, we should consider how we use it and what comes before and after and be aware when we choose to use modelling as a learning technique in the classroom.

Overall considerations

This guidance report is all about making the implicit explicit and this is something that I believe we should aim to do more often and in a more honest way. Often, our response to new strategies and techniques is thinking they are not relevant to us because it is something we already do. I think the metacognition report from the EEF is a great example of where we can continue to learn about our craft without having to start from scratch. It is the type of guidance that can help teachers at all stages regardless of their experience.

If you read the overview of the EEF Toolkit in Chapter 4, then you will know that one of the aims of the organisation is to level the playing field for disadvantaged students. Interestingly, in recommendation 2, the report mentions that students from disadvantaged backgrounds are less likely to use the metacognitive skills and therefore require further support in understanding and using them effectively.

The most important consideration when reading this report is to understand that it is generalised on purpose and that, throughout, it repeats the requirement to put the strategies into context, to have a deep knowledge of the skills and subject you are teaching and to constantly consider how to make the strategies suggested part of your everyday teaching rather than an additional strategy you might only use temporarily and therefore unsuccessfully.

Further reading

- A summary of the recommendations poster can be found on the EEF website and is a great way to remind yourself of the key features once you have read the whole report: https://educationendowmentfoundation.org.uk/public/files/Presentations/Publications/Metacognition/Summary_of_recommendations_poster.pdf.
- An introduction to cognitive load theory by Greg Ashman (2015b), which links well to the additional thinking we are asking students to do when we encourage metacognition: www.theconversation.com/why-students-make-silly-mistakes-in-class-and-what-can-be-done-48826.
- The EEF's (2018e) Early Years Toolkit has further recommendations for younger children and self-regulation: www.educationendowmentfoundation.org.uk/evidence-summaries/early-years-toolkit/self-regulation-strategies/.

4. What makes great teaching? (Coe et al., 2014)

Overview

Published in 2014, this paper reviews key research about a number of areas in education. From classroom practice to teacher characteristics and the best ways to evaluate teaching, this paper has it all in one place and the recommendations are based on research and reviews that would be worth reading in themselves. In fact, the previously mentioned Barak Rosenshine's 'Principles of instruction' are listed fully in the examples of effective practice, along with a number of other suggestions of effective practice.

It is the breadth of this report that makes it worthwhile engaging with. It does not claim to have all the right strategies or answers and it is honest about how the research it reviews might be open to misinterpretation or misuse if taken purely on face value.

To begin with, you should be aware that the report focuses on three main questions:

- What is good pedagogy?
- What kinds of frameworks or tools could help us to capture this good pedagogy?
- How could this promote better learning?

You may find it insightful to read the original research questions as detailed in the appendix on page 56 of the document, as these give further insight into the process behind creating the report. The authors make it clear that their measure of effective practice and good pedagogy is student progress.

The paper reviews evidence from contemporary studies in order to suggest not just what might work best but also what *doesn't* work.

Key ideas to take away

The paper is split into sections, of which the first discusses what good pedagogy might look like and summarises key theories of effective practice. The list includes:

- Danielson's (2007) framework for teaching
- the classroom assessment scoring system
- Rosenshine's 'principles of instruction'
- Creemers and Kyriakides' (2011) 'dynamic model'.

All are summarised and in the final sections of the paper it is concluded that Creemers and Kyriakides' dynamic model has the most credibility and is the most effective of all the suggestions.

Of course, looking into these theories and frameworks for effective practice would be highly beneficial – Rosenshine's in particular is easy to access compared to some of the others. The paper does state that all recommendations are 'open to interpretation' and that this interpretation may not be as the authors intended.

The paper summarises that two particular elements are key to improving outcomes for students and they are, unsurprisingly:

1. quality of teachers' subject knowledge
2. quality of instruction, which includes questioning, scaffolding, modelling, etc.

A further four elements are noted in the introduction as having less but still reasonable amounts of evidence to suggest they are important to effective teaching. Many of these areas are complex, such as classroom climate and classroom management, so it is unsurprising that they do not necessarily have concrete evidence or strategies to inform our practice. It is evident that the authors of this paper are aware that classrooms are multi-faceted and that learning is complex. There are two areas in particular that I think make this paper stand out. They are the overview of teacher characteristics and beliefs and the list of ineffective practices.

Teacher characteristics

Unlike other reviews, this paper reviews evidence of how a range of teacher characteristics are linked to student achievement. The term 'characteristics' can be used broadly. Some research has focused on observable characteristics and other research looks at characteristics that are less obvious to begin with, such as subject knowledge. The paper looks at research that compared teachers' subject knowledge to their students' gains and found that there is evidence to show a positive relationship between teachers' subject knowledge and students' understanding. However, it does explain that more research is required in this area. Interestingly, one study (Sadler et al., 2013) identified that teachers were not able to identify their students' misconceptions particularly effectively – and the report suggests that perhaps this is an area we could focus on in professional development sessions to ensure that we are accurately predicting and addressing students' misconceptions.

Examples of ineffective practice

This might seem a strange area of the paper to highlight as a 'takeaway' but using research-informed practice is as much about knowing what doesn't work as knowing what could work. In this paper, you will find a list of strategies that at some point have been recommended in teacher training programmes or simply passed down to new teachers throughout the years – often unquestioned.

A few of the key practices the authors now deem to be ineffective are:

- using praise too often
- grouping students by ability
- attempting to address low aspirations prior to teaching content
- using learning styles.

In this section, the authors reference evidence to the contrary of these ideas, referencing studies that have found that these ideas do not have strong enough evidence to support their use in the classroom. Probably the most controversial of them all is the belief that students should be taught in a preferred learning style – or Visual-Auditory-Kinetic (VAK) as it is better known. The strength of feeling behind debunking learning styles is rather strong and the evidence likewise. The authors of this paper reference studies from 2008 to 2014 that argue against the theory and there are more recent blogs, articles and studies that continue to argue against this widely shared learning technique.

Overall considerations

The paper is an overview of previous research studies and therefore to gain further knowledge and understanding you would need to investigate individual studies cited in the bibliography of the paper. It is a great starting point for those looking for an accessible route into research-informed thinking and practice. The conclusion summarises the importance of sharing literature on effective practice with others. It suggests that one of the main issues in becoming research informed is the lack of information available. It asks readers to 'spread awareness' of the evidence available, emphasising that awareness is vital to improving our own practice.

I would also consider how this paper can be used not only to affect your classroom practice but also to instigate discussions about how judgements of teaching and learning strategies take place in your school. A large amount of the paper is given over to studies that have debated the best ways to measure the quality of teaching. There are important references to papers that advise to use lesson observations with great caution, along with commentary on other judgement-based evaluation techniques such as headteacher judgements, inferring performance based on classroom work (students' books, teachers' planners, etc.) and value-added measures. The paper concludes that supportive formative assessment of teaching might be better as there is little evidence to prove that summative value judgements are accurate or credible, and neither do they help improve students' outcomes.

Further reading

- Daisy Christodoulou's 2014 book *Seven Myths About Education*; read Chapter 2: 'Teacher-led instruction is passive' in particular.
- Chapter 8: 'Learning myths' in *What Does This Look Like in the Classroom?* by Carl Hendrick and Robin Macpherson (2017) – read this chapter to understand how many ideas and strategies in education are conceived and then continue to hang around even when unwanted.
- The article 'The influence of teachers' knowledge on student learning in middle school physical science classrooms' (Sadler et al., 2013).
- For more on myth-busting learning styles, read the blog post 'Question: What's your preferred learning style?': http://blogs.northampton.ac.uk/learntech/2016/06/16/question-whats-your-preferred-learning-style/.

5. A marked improvement? A review of the evidence on written marking (Elliott et al., 2016)

Overview

Regardless of the subject or age group we teach, marking and the impact it has or doesn't have is an issue for us all. Moreover, the time it takes and the impact it has on our wellbeing and work–life balance are issues that continue to dominate discourse about teaching as a career. Marking, as with all elements of pedagogy, has undergone scrutiny, and new strategies are continually explored before being discarded. For example, strategies such as triple marking were once lauded as the best way to ensure students improve. Marking has also often been confused with feedback. This review was the first of its kind to survey teachers in England about their marking practices, strategies and requirements. It is worth reading if you have concerns about whether or not you or your staff use your time effectively.

Key ideas to take away

There isn't much evidence... yet

The review is clear from the outset that, perhaps surprisingly, there is little evidence to support many of the marking policies commonly implemented in UK schools. The review found that studies that had taken place were too short-term, and many hadn't tracked the impact of the marking strategy over longer periods of time and therefore their findings were not robust. The report states that 'the findings from this review are necessarily more tentative than in other areas where more studies have been done' – due to the lack of trials and evidence to review. The report calls for further research to take place in order to make more robust recommendations.

It is interesting that, although the evidence does not exist to refute specific marking strategies, the lack of evidence sometimes points in a particular direction and suggests that strategies previously jumped upon should perhaps be considered more carefully. The review helpfully breaks down the key areas of marking and looks at the issues that surround each element, including evidence reviewed, a case study and the impact on workload. These elements are:

1. grading
2. corrections
3. thoroughness
4. pupil responses
5. creating a dialogue
6. targets
7. frequency and speed.

In Section 3, it is suggested that the impact of thoroughness of marking is further explored to provide more definitive advice but, in contrast to thorough marking, the report suggests that there is no evidence to support marking work simply for the sake of it; in other words the use of ticking or stickers to acknowledge work is there is seemingly ineffective. This links back to the common misconception that takes place in processes such as the dreaded 'work scrutiny' or 'book look', where quantity rather than quality of written work equates to learning. We know that just because students have completed a task or written down a definition, it does not mean learning has taken place, and the statements from the EEF about the lack of evidence to support acknowledgement marking might therefore have greater implications and make us consider more deeply what it is we ask students to write down, why and when. In doing so, we can be more selective not only with our marking but also with what we ask our students to do before and in response to any marking. Overall, Section 3 suggests that 'It is also clear that offering information on how pupils should improve their work is substantially more effective than simply marking an answer as right or wrong.'

Section 5 looks further into the impact of creating a dialogue between student and teacher through marking – or, more specifically, a dialogue after the initial marking leading to dialogic or triple-impact marking. The survey showed that in primary schools 14 per cent of those who responded to the survey said most work marked was then responded to by the student and again by the teacher in written format, and a similar 15 per cent in secondary schools. Considering the amount of marking that takes place, a huge amount of time and effort is being put into recording responses and answers in exercise books. The key finding from this section is that no research has looked further into the difference between this dialogue taking place in written format and verbally. The workload section recognises the huge amount of time such strategies take and the fact that at the moment there is not enough evidence to prove this worthwhile, although the report does make clear that the approach of answering teacher questions and responses to these did, in one study, show promise and help to stretch students.

All sections state that the evidence in each area is lacking and that further research is needed in the most appropriate contexts (evidence exists but a lot of it is from higher educational institutions or very short-term), yet this does not stop us from taking lessons away and, where necessary, encourages us to question why we use strategies that are time-consuming and laborious based on little or no evidence.

Mark smarter

The opening of the EEF report states that written marking is only a part of overall feedback strategies – others include verbal feedback, feedback on presentations or answers in class, peer-assessment and self-assessment. However, it also states that written feedback is often the source of teacher-to-student specific and helpful guidance, which has previously been found to be most effective over and above vague comments giving praise or comments about effort.

In Section 6, 'Targets', the specificity of targets is discussed, along with the idea that formative marking should include short-term targets rather than long-term targets. It was found that many in both secondary and primary schools currently use a target-setting system such as 'What Went Well' (WWW) and 'Even Better If' (EBI). In the workload section of this report, the EEF suggest that target writing is time-consuming and therefore one strategy that has been used to reduce the time taken up by marking is to use codes. Interestingly they state that 'research suggests that there is no difference between the effectiveness of coded or uncoded feedback, providing that pupils understand what the codes mean'.

This is one method in which the review suggests marking smarter. In Section 7, the review states that the speed of marking (in other words the turnaround time) can have a positive impact on student progress but it is not clear how large this positive impact is. This might seem contradictory to other studies that state that it is the feedback that is important but the timeframe in which it is given is not as important as receiving the feedback itself (this was summarised when focusing on feedback of practice-testing in Dunlosky et al.'s paper; see page 75). Merging together the little evidence they have, the report suggests it is a balancing act between marking in adequate time for the feedback to be helpful but avoiding marking for the sake of it and therefore not giving detailed and thorough feedback, which is deemed to be more helpful than simply quickly marking work.

Overall considerations

Marking is often seen as something that happens after the learning but the overall impression this report suggests is to reconsider fully where marking and feedback sit within the process of learning. Throughout the report, questions are posed that should be considered by teachers at all levels and even more so by those with responsibility for creating marking and feedback policies.

A key consideration when reading this document is to recognise it as a review of a variety of types of evidence – qualitative and quantitative – of which both have strengths and limitations. The review therefore creates more questions than it answers but this does not mean we should ignore it. Part of being research informed and engaged is the confidence and desire to ask the difficult questions, and moreover, this review provides you with valuable suggestions regarding decreasing workload or at least not adding to it with impractical and unqualified strategies. If nothing else, it is worth skim-reading and highlighting the questions you need to ask most of your particular context, but as with any review of your current practice it is important to work out what you are currently doing before you plan to change it.

Further reading

- *Marking and Feedback* by Sarah Findlater (2016) in the Bloomsbury CPD Library series follows the same structure as this book and includes a very clear and helpful 'train yourself' section, which is crammed full of time-saving strategies.
- Peer critique is a form of written feedback that encourages students to give kind, specific and helpful comments to their peers, thereby encouraging specific improvements. Read Ron Berger's (2003) book *An Ethic of Excellence: Building a culture of craftsmanship with students* to find out more about how and why this strategy works.

Want more?

Whether you are completely new to the idea of research-informed practice or whether by reading through the evidence above you've realised you knew more than you originally thought, there is always more to find out. I have only picked a few papers and reviews for starters. There is plenty more open-access research that can be accessed if you have the desire to do so and an interest in a certain topic.

In particular, I would recommend reading the following easy-to-access papers and summaries:

Cognitive load theory

'Cognitive load theory: research that teachers really need to understand' by Centre for Education Statistics and Evaluation (2017), available at: www.cese.nsw.gov.au//images/stories/PDF/cognitive-load-theory-VR_AA3.pdf.

A great summary of the PDF document can be read via the Chartered College of Teaching's website (Shibli and West, 2018): https://impact.chartered.college/article/shibli-cognitive-load-theory-classroom/.

The science of learning

'The science of learning', written in 2015 by Deans for Impact, a non-profit organisation, aims through this document 'to summarize the existing research from cognitive science related to how students learn' (p. 1). It is therefore excellent reading for those interested in the ways in which cognitive science can be used for impact in the classroom. It is available at: www.deansforimpact.org/wp-content/uploads/2016/12/The_Science_of_Learning.pdf.

I also suggest watching these videos by David Didau and the production company Mosaic. Based on David's work with BBC Bitesize, these videos animate and explore how we learn. On his blog, David links to the research behind all the claims in his post with these videos: https://learningspy.co.uk/featured/three-animated-films-about-learning.

Guided instruction

'Why minimal guidance during instruction does not work: an analysis of the failure of constructivist, discovery, problem-based, experiential, and inquiry-based teaching' by Kirschner et al.

Written in 2006, this paper discusses the trend for minimal guidance, discovery and problem-based learning, and in its conclusion states that 'there is no body of research supporting the technique' (p. 83) and suggests that evidence 'almost uniformly supports direct, strong instructional guidance rather than constructivist-based minimal guidance during the instruction of novice to intermediate learners' (p. 83). It is worth a read if you are considering taking on board some of the more explicit teaching strategies mentioned in the research summaries above – specifically the use of modelling or metacognition. The paper is available at: www.cogtech.usc.edu/publications/kirschner_Sweller_Clark.pdf.

It is definitely worth reading Greg Ashman's (2015a) review of this paper and the rebuttals to it: https://gregashman.wordpress.com/2015/03/16/minimal-guidance.

Further reading sources

For even more papers see Tom Sherrington's blog post 'Teaching and learning research summaries: A collection for easy access' at www.teacherhead.com/2017/06/03/teaching-and-learning-research-summaries-a-collection-for-easy-access.

What next?

I would suggest working your way through some of the key reading summarised in this chapter... slowly.

You will be able to decide which papers, articles or reviews are the most relevant to you by reading the summaries. If so far you have only read the overviews, then do ensure you then move on to read the original documents and decide for yourself what the key takeaways are for your context. It is important that you make your own judgements. The same applies to any CPD you take part in – one person's key takeaways will not necessarily be the same as your own.

In a short blog post on the issue of teachers implementing research-informed strategies, Nick Rose (2018) suggests that 'Good ideas – even when they are well-rooted in evidence-based research – can be implemented in ways which render them no longer effective, or even counter-productive; becoming examples of what Dylan Wiliam (2011) and others have dubbed "lethal mutations".' Rose continues to look at some of the possible issues with implementing spaced practice and cognitive load theory into your teaching without considering your context, the students' current learning or aims of teaching. It is worth reading the post as a cautionary reminder not to jump in head first and change all of your teaching or strategies at once.

In the next chapter, I will share ways in which teachers from various sectors have used some of these evidence-informed takeaways in their day-to-day practice, thereby providing practical research-informed strategies you can then consider reviewing for your own context.

Having read through the chapters on acquiring research sources and beginning to read key research, you should start to consider the following questions as your journey develops. These questions should aid you in deciding your next steps and help you to decide whether you need to spend a little more time discussing, reviewing, accessing and questioning the research before moving on to implementing ideas fully:

- What do you require (time, money, support, CPD) in order to better engage with educational research or evidence reviews?
- How has your school previously discussed, shared or provided research for teachers? Could or should this change?
- What are the obstacles you foresee in developing your understanding and use of research in your current environment?

Chapter 5 takeaway

Teaching tip

Don't be a magpie

Avoid reading an overview and changing your own practice without full consideration. It might be that you do need to make a change and adapt your methods but an overview can only give you so much, and you should consider how you can carefully introduce new strategies or ideas for the long term rather than just in one lesson. Students are quick at picking up on changes and even if they are evidence based, they will not appreciate your penchant for trying new teaching techniques every lesson. This will quickly make the most research-informed and effective techniques ineffective. How and why you implement your practice is just as important as what you choose to do.

Pass it on

This point in your research-informed journey is a great opportunity to review research yourself and share it with others. Now that you have a number of sources to refer to and have read some of the key papers, you could offer to write a blog post or article for an internal or external publication. Perhaps you have a newsletter for teachers at school or could offer to share your takeaways from a particular paper with your department at your next meeting. Bear in mind that you are summarising what you have found and may not have had the opportunity to put the strategies into practice yourself yet, so use the forum to begin a discussion rather than using the paper you have read to provide answers.

You could consider setting the paper as pre-reading and, much like a book club, encourage others to come along with their key takeaways identified and any questions or concerns they might have. Be fully prepared to discuss and engage with those who might disagree with you. They will likely have identified something you skipped over and your disagreements could prove fruitful in how to move forward.

CPD book club recommendation

What Does This Look Like in the Classroom? by Carl Hendrick and Robin Macpherson (2017).

This book does exactly what it says on the tin in the most engaging of ways: through a series of interviews with a vast range of people you just know could choose their given chapter title as their specialist subject if ever on *Mastermind* – and win.

Bloggers' corner

Read Nick Rose's cautionary blog post here: www.ambition.org.uk/blog/ avoiding-lethal-mutations.

TO DO LIST:

❑ Review your area of focus and decide on the research reviews you wish to read.

❑ Read the overviews and key takeaways carefully.

❑ Pick one or two reviews to read in full using the links.

❑ Make notes on your own key takeaways from the research – why have these stood out to you?

❑ Read Nick Rose's cautionary blog post here: www.ambition.org.uk/ blog/avoiding-lethal-mutations.

❑ Discuss how you can share your reading and views with others – talk to your manager and see what opportunities there are for you to share this informally with others.

6 Putting research into practice

It is now time to start considering how becoming research informed can have an impact on what you do in the classroom. It is all well and good attempting to use your PPA time or time during the holidays reading research summaries and reviews, but it is how this will affect, and in some cases transform, your everyday practice and how it informs your professional judgement that really matters.

Putting your reading into practice means considering how to use your knowledge of research to guide your choice of teaching strategies and techniques; it does *not* mean trying to emulate a study in the classroom. Your knowledge of research and its findings and theories should guide your thinking but not lead it – consider your professional judgement alongside using any new technique. As Rob Coe is quoted as saying in the Teach First report 'Putting evidence to work: how can we help new teachers use research evidence to inform their teaching?', 'Even when [strategies are] evidence informed, whatever that means, they are probably unhelpful because most things you can do well or you can do badly.' (Rose and Eriksson-Lee, 2017, p. 11) It is our responsibility to ensure that we take a thoughtful approach to implementation and, later on, evaluation.

It is important that you take your time when putting in place new ideas of any kind and it might be that you simply think more consciously about a particular element of your teaching having read through the research sources and papers, or you may wish to make a bigger change by trialling a particular strategy through action research. To aid you in moving forward, this chapter demonstrates how research can positively influence your teaching as you become more conscious, considered and deliberate in your choices. This chapter uses cases studies from both my own experiences and those of colleagues to demonstrate how some research-informed teachers are adapting their practice to provide a solution to previous issues and concerns. This book makes no claim that these case studies represent anything other than what worked in one particular context – the case studies and suggestions are to inspire debate and discussion rather than a magic wand for your specific issue. As reiterated throughout the book, you must consider the research you read in your own way and apply it as necessary to your setting and your context. These case studies are not research studies themselves but an insight into how research can be used to ask the right questions and find solutions.

Research-informed teaching strategies

In this rest of this chapter, I will refer to some of the suggestions of research-informed good practice mentioned in previous chapters and demonstrate how these ideas can be used practically in the classroom.

The strategies discussed draw on research about teaching and learning. In general, they are teaching strategies but some have a basis in the science of learning (cognitive science and psychology in particular), and others look more specifically at the impact of teachers' choices – for example the impact of marking on student outcomes. Most refer to evidence that has been mentioned in Chapter 5 but some new sources are referred to at the top of each strategy. I have used some case studies from my own classroom and others' experiences to clearly illustrate how the strategies work in practice.

Each strategy described:

- mentions the problem or issue that led to its use
- refers to the research that informed the practice
- includes an overview of the strategy in practice
- highlights the outcomes in that particular classroom (which of course might be different in yours!).

When reading this chapter, you have a few choices to make. It might be that you simply want to see what is being done in response to research or you may wish to use the ideas to develop your area of focus that you began thinking about in Chapter 3, page 46. It is possible that you might wish to implement one of the strategies. However, before planning tomorrow's lessons and immediately implementing one of these ideas, you should consider the steps below:

1) **Identify a problem by considering further your area of focus.**
   Start by picking a class or group of students to focus on. Consider what the issue is currently and clarify your reasoning for this. Spend some time doing this rather than jumping to an immediate decision – discuss with others what you would like to improve and why as they might have other, perhaps better, suggestions. For example, your homework tasks do not seem to support learning in the classroom. They are set randomly and completed poorly.

2) **Decide upon what you hope to achieve – the intended outcome.**
   Is your goal clear or do you see yourself as simply needing to improve in this area? Break the issue down into small, manageable chunks. Rather than saying a whole class needs to improve, consider when they find learning difficult, or when you struggle to impart knowledge to them. Then consider what would look different in a set amount of time (a term, a year, two years) if an intervention worked. For example, you would like homework tasks to be explicit in their relevance and for students to see the benefit in them.

3) **Decide on a set period of time to keep things as they are and observe your own practice deliberately.**
   There is no requirement to implement a change straight away. Give yourself a half term or longer to review what you currently do. For example, check

whether it is only your opinion that homework tasks are not functioning to support learning. Carry out a student and parent survey. Collate records of how well and how often the work is completed. Make a record of the types of tasks you set and the frequency.

4) **Consider the issues in changing something at this time.**
Change is never easy. The bigger the change, the harder it is to implement. As this is a change in your own classroom, then the main stakeholders are your students so keep everything else as stable as you can – make sure you have routines in place and don't disrupt these if possible. For example, ensure that your routines for the classroom are clear – give yourself time to embed these at the beginning of the year.

5) **Decide on your change and implement it carefully – focus on why and how something might work in your classroom rather than what you are doing.**
When you implement a change in your classroom, monitor and evaluate it as you go along but don't give up on it when success or change isn't immediate. Set aside a relevant timeframe to trial the change. This should be a fairly long period of time – at least two terms of one academic year. Allow time to adapt and refine the approach but don't seek to overturn and change it completely without good reason.

Overview of strategies

	Strategy and how it links to the research	Research source	Year	Links to key takeaway	Author(s)
A	Distributed practice homework tasks	Improving students' learning with effective learning techniques: promising directions from cognitive and educational psychology	2013	Distributed practice	John Dunlosky, Katherine A. Rawson, Elizabeth J. Marsh, Mitchell J Nathan and Daniel T. Willingham
B	Hinge questions and mini whiteboards	Principles of instruction	2012	Ask a large number of questions and monitor independent practice	Barak Rosenshine
C	Daily review tasks: know it all and image recall	Principles of instruction	2012	Begin each lesson with a short review	Barak Rosenshine

	Strategy and how it links to the research	Research source	Year	Links to key takeaway	Author(s)
D	WAGOLL (what a good one looks like)	Metacognition and self-regulated learning	2018	Teacher modelling	Alex Quigley, Daniel Muijs and Eleanor Stringer (EEF-commissioned review)
E	Metacognitive talk to improve exam technique	Metacognition and self-regulated learning	2018	Teacher modelling	Alex Quigley, Daniel Muijs and Eleanor Stringer (EEF-commissioned review)
F	'Do now' quizzes and knowledge organisers	What makes great teaching?	2014	Identifying student misconceptions – teacher characteristics	Rob Coe, Cesare Aloisi, Steve Higgins and Lee Elliot Major
G	Whole-class feedback sheets	A marked improvement? A review of the evidence on written marking	2016	Marking better and smarter	Victoria Elliott, Jo-Anne Baird, Therese N. Hopfenbeck, Jenni Ingram, Ian Thompson, Natalie Usher, Mae Zantout, James Richardson and Robbie Coleman (EEF-commissioned review)

Research-informed strategies in practice: case studies

Strategy A: Distributed practice homework tasks

Problem: Homework or home learning was a waste of time (for all involved!) and students kept forgetting what they had been previously taught.

Research and evidence to refer to:

- As summarised in Chapter 5, page 75, the monograph 'Improving students' learning with effective learning techniques: promising directions from cognitive and educational psychology' by Dunlosky et al. (2013a).

- 'Why do we forget stuff? Familiarity vs recall' by David Didau, available at: www.learningspy.co.uk/psychology/forget-stuff-familiarity-vs-recalls.
- 'Homework (secondary)' resource on EEF, available at: www. educationendowmentfoundation.org.uk/evidence-summaries/teaching-learning-toolkit/homework-secondary.
- 'Homework (primary)' resource on EEF, available at: www. educationendowmentfoundation.org.uk/evidence-summaries/teaching-learning-toolkit/homework-primary.
- 'Homework. What does the evidence say?' from Huntington Research School, available at: https://huntington.researchschool. org.uk/2017/11/10/homework-what-does-the-evidence-say.
- Watch Dylan Wiliam's talk at ResearchEd, which briefly mentions homework (between 3:30 and 5 minutes), available at: www. youtube.com/watch?v=6ajXJ6PbDcg.

Why this strategy?

'Homework', 'home learning' or 'extension work' (whatever you wish to label it) is a contentious issue. Most schools still have policies that require it. There is evidence (see the EEF secondary and primary reports) that homework, when planned poorly, has very little impact; therefore there are reports that suggest homework is a pointless waste of time for the majority of children. In particular, homework is not deemed effective for primary students and reportedly only creates a further advantage for already advantaged students, widening the gap between disadvantaged students and their peers.

So why discuss a strategy about homework when homework, according to the evidence, isn't effective at improving outcomes? The reason is that homework still exists in many schools and therefore it might cause a problem. The evidence states that the type of task set for homework is key to it having a positive impact. Therefore, rather than scrapping homework completely (as this may not be our prerogative), we could consider the type of homework, how it is set and why it is set, and take on board relevant research from cognitive science and evidence about learning and apply them to our learning context.

This connects to a number of takeaways identified in the previous chapter as we looked at how distributed practice can be used to improve student outcomes. Applying this knowledge to an area such as homework as well as in the classroom might be a valuable use of the knowledge acquired through research.

Case study: English GCSE class

The homework strategy used in my classroom and department over the past three years with our GCSE students uses pre-planned interleaved *and* distributed practice tasks based on prior learning and skills that require practice and revision.

- Each week, students are given three tasks to complete at home independently. The first task should take a maximum of ten minutes, the second 20 minutes and the final task 30 minutes.
- Students are encouraged to complete tasks in one or two sessions to encourage distributed practice. This style of homework is only set once students have a level of understanding and knowledge that will allow them to access the tasks; therefore I would not use this strategy without considering carefully what has already been taught and whether students have enough knowledge to complete the tasks set.
- The three tasks cover three different topics students have previously studied – one of which they may be studying at that time. It has been found that interleaving is most effective when there are subtle differences between the topics (Carvalho and Goldstone, 2015) rather than putting completely unrelated topics next to one another. This is fairly easy to do in some skills-based subjects or in particular phases such as Key Stage 4 where skills have been clearly identified.
- The quality of this task will depend on the quality of the overall curriculum planning – a clear curriculum plan allows for clarity in designing the homework schedule.
- Each week, two of the homework tasks cover the English literature content and one covers English language – teachers and students of both subjects will know that there are clear links between the skills required at GCSE.
- To ensure that misconceptions are picked up on by the teacher and that homework tasks are checked, each task will be tested or reviewed in class. Typically, this will use practice-testing in a low-stakes quiz or through self- or peer-critique.

The following table is an example template of three interleaved and spaced homework tasks per week for Year 11 (who have covered all the content previously).

Basic example template of three interleaved and spaced homework tasks per week for Year 11

Week	Task 1 (10 mins)	Task 2 (20 mins)	Task 3 (30 mins)
1	Shakespeare play character quotations – to be quizzed in class	Shakespeare extract analysis	Creative writing based on the play's theme
2	Transactional writing planning – writing to be completed in class	Poetry quotations revision – to be quizzed in class	Exam question on modern play
3	Novel character quotations – to be quizzed in class	Unseen 19th-century text comprehension	Unseen poetry analysis annotations
4	Creative writing plan	Shakespeare play character profile	Shakespeare extract analysis
5	Transactional writing plan	Modern play act summary	Poetry quotations revision – to be quizzed in class
6	Unseen poetry analysis annotations	Unseen 19th-century text comprehension	Novel character quotations – to be quizzed in class

The research suggests that spacing and interleaving combined is positive in the long term but not always beneficial in the short term; therefore this strategy was used well in advance of formal testing. It benefits the students immediately. According to The Learning Scientists (Weinstein and Sumeracki, 2018; see page 62), the spacing effect of distributing topics across the pre-planned weeks and returning to a topic at a later date boosts memory retention. The evidence from Cepeda et al. (2008) suggests that how far apart you choose to space the topics depends on how long you want the student to retain the information for. The authors suggest that if you intend for students to retain information for longer, then the time between revision of a topic should be longer. David Didau (2015a) created a table based on Cepeda et al.'s findings, suggesting that if we wish students to be tested on a topic in six months' time, then the optimal time between study periods is three weeks, and if they are to be tested in one year, the optimal time is four weeks. With this in mind, we choose to space overarching topics every three to four weeks after first being introduced before reducing the spacing as mock or real exams approached.

Benefits of this strategy are that expectations are clear to all students in terms of timings, quantity and quality. Unlike the basic example above, the students' version would have clear instructions for each task and links to relevant resources and advice. Students complete their tasks in a separate homework booklet and we use peer-critique, quizzing or self-assessment to check the work is complete. Again, these checks can be adapted as necessary. Tasks can also be adapted by teachers to suit their class and of course could be adapted to suit an individual school's timings, expectations and age group.

When surveyed about the homework tasks, students commented on the clarity of instruction, the fact that they enjoyed knowing what was coming next and that they could see a clear link to their outcomes even if it wasn't initially relevant to what they had studied that day or week.

Strategy B: Hinge questions and mini whiteboards

Problem: Determining whether or not the class have grasped a concept can be very time-consuming, create more misconceptions and have a varied success rate.

Research and evidence to refer to:

- Read Chapter 5's summary of 'Principles of instruction: Research-based strategies that all teachers should know' by Barak Rosenshine (2012).
- Watch Dylan Wiliam's 'The characteristics of hinge-point questions', available at: www.futurelearn.com/courses/assessment-for-learning-stem/0/steps/7332.
- Read *Inside the Black Box: Raising standards through classroom assessment* by Paul Black and Dylan Wiliam (1998), available at: www.rdc.udel.edu/wp-content/uploads/2015/04/InsideBlackBox.pdf
- Harry Fletcher-Wood describes the best approach in 'Do they understand this well enough to move on? Introducing hinge questions' (2013) and in his book *Ticked Off* (2016). Blog post available at: www.improvingteaching.co.uk/2013/08/17/do-they-understand-this-well-enough-to-move-on-introducing-hinge-questions.
- This is a useful website, particularly for maths, computing and science teachers (even though it doesn't include that much research evidence): www.diagnosticquestions.com.

Why this strategy?

The research reviewed by Rosenshine (2012) suggests that intervening early to avoid misconceptions increases positive student outcomes. As discussed in Chapter 5, page 83, it specifically suggests that we ask more questions of more students and check all the answers in order to find out where they are. We all know that questioning helps teachers to identify issues and problems and there are multiple strategies to do so – many of which were strategies created in response to *Inside the Black Box* by Paul Black and Dylan Wiliam, where formative assessment practices were reviewed and approaches to improve students' results through formative assessment were suggested.

Hinge questions are one way by which you can be sure you are not only checking *all* students' current understanding of a task, but that you are also considering where they are and whether or not you should move on. There are key features to be aware of when using and designing hinge questions. In particular, hinge questions require speed of response so it is useful to have something like mini whiteboards for students to use to write their response on, or they could create A, B, C, D cards to hold up. Questions should be multiple choice, with only one correct answer, and vitally, students should only be able to choose the right answer if they have done the right thinking. In other words, it should not be possible for students to get the answer correct for the wrong reasons, for example by guessing. Hinge questions therefore need to be designed carefully but, as with any useful strategy, you will find that after all the thinking and time you put into the preparation you will be left with a myriad of resources you can reuse again and again. For example, I have created a set of hinge questions for the key grammatical terms we teach and these can be used with different year groups whilst teaching different texts at different times.

When designing the questions, it is vital to spend time considering the wrong answers you give as options. Considering the common misconceptions and mistakes students make, create incorrect answers that will really make students consider them as correct ones before having to think to identify the right one. This process will mean you are able to give instant feedback to those who get the answer wrong. You should be giving verbal feedback such as: 'The answer is B, but if you put A that will be because you forgot to...', or 'The answer is B, but if you put C it will be because you confused X with Y so remember that X is... and Y is...'.

In other words, your wrong answers shouldn't be completely random with no justification of why a student might have got it wrong. At this point, you can then decide who requires further intervention, whether or not you need to reteach an element and how or whether the class are ready to move on.

Case study: Mark Enser – geography

Questioning plays an important role in almost every classroom. We ask questions to check that pupils are following our explanation and are clear on what they have been asked to do, to ensure they are still awake and to help deepen their understanding through discourse about the subject at hand. Hinge questions add another string to our bow; they allow us to make quick and easy assessment of what pupils have understood and how well they have understood it.

Hinge questions tend to be a question with a range of multiple-choice answers for the pupils to select from and are often designed to help flush out misconceptions and check that pupils have a deeper understanding of the topic. They are called 'hinge' questions because what happens next in the lesson hinges on how they answer the question. They are a great example of responsive teaching.

One example of how I have used hinge questions recently was to ask the class: Why did Boscastle flood? Select the best answer:

A: There was heavy rain.
B: There are steep slopes leading down from the hills.
C: Recent urban growth in the drainage basin.
D: River straightening.

Pupils wrote down the letter on a mini whiteboard and revealed the answer at the same time. The idea was to check that they were able to discuss the specific causes of the Boscastle flood rather than the causes of flooding in general (all of these increase the risk of flood – both A and B are correct for Boscastle but I would suggest B is a better answer as almost all floods start with heavy rain).

I was able to quickly ascertain who had followed my explanation and who needed me to go over the key points again. If most of the class had got the question wrong I would also know that I needed to change the way I taught this lesson in the future.

Over the years I have changed the way I use hinge questions somewhat. When the idea was first introduced to me, about ten years ago, it was suggested that pupils should run to a corner of the room to indicate their answer; this would apparently be a good thing as it got them moving. The problem with this is firstly it takes far too long and breaks the flow of the lesson, and secondly, you don't know how many people are just following the crowd. I am now much more careful about ensuring each pupil answers the question themselves and reveals it at the same time.

A second way I have changed how I use hinge questions is to give all of the responses much more thought. I want to include things that are common misconceptions or answers that *could* be right but are less good than other possible answers. This can be far more revealing than a simple right/wrong response. For example, for the question 'Which of these landforms are created by the low energy of the Nile Delta region?', I have the following possible answers:

A: Sand dunes (a feature of the region but also need wind energy to form).
B: Underwater bars (a feature of tideless seas and low energy systems).
C: Stacks (not a feature of the low energy at all and rare in this area).
D: The Delta (a feature of low energy but also of plentiful sediment).

This question allows me to address a common misconception that just because the Nile Delta is a low energy system, all the landforms must be a feature solely of low energy.

Hinge questions, if well planned and well used, can be transformative in making teaching more responsive, as they allow you to make what has been learnt somewhat more visible. They are now a regular feature of my classroom as a diagnostic tool that allows me to close any gaps in students' knowledge and address misconceptions before they become embedded.

Mark Enser is Head of Geography and Research Lead at Heathfield Community College. He is a TES columnist and author of Teach Like Nobody's Watching *and* Making Every Geography Lesson Count.

Case study: Chloe Woodhouse – English

Hinge questions are a diagnostic tool to be used to check understanding and see which students need to move on and which students require more help. It is a question asked that students get right *but for the right reasons*, not a lucky guess or a fluke or by copying good old Sarah Smith sat next to them.

A hinge question is normally multiple choice and there can be more than one correct answer. They help to identify any misconceptions quickly in that moment in the classroom. The beauty of them is that they are designed to be answered by the whole class at the same time and should not take too long to ask nor take too long to answer. As a result of the answer(s) given, your lesson may go on different journeys. However, there has to be a health warning with the multiple-choice format: if there is only one right answer and you only give two options, then the odds of students getting it right for the wrong reasons are 50/50. Increase the number of options for students and throw in some misconceptions and then the odds of students getting it right for the wrong reasons decrease rapidly.

On the next page is an example of a hinge question used when teaching *Dr Jekyll and Mr Hyde*. This followed two lessons reading, discussing and analysing the relationship with Dr Jekyll and Mr Utterson and how Hyde was viewed by both characters.

Which words sum up how Dr Jekyll is presenting Hyde to Mr Utterson?

A: Dangerous
B: Gone away forever.
C: A risk to his reputation.
D: A person he no longer cares about.

Now a popular misconception here would be that Dr Jekyll would present Hyde as dangerous, as we know that he is dangerous, having (spoiler alert!) trampled a young girl and killed a man. However, Dr Jekyll would not present Mr Hyde to Utterson as that as he wants Utterson to stop worrying and drop the issue. Therefore, the correct answers would be B / C / D. For the students who selected A as an answer or part of their answer, we went back over the chapter and discussed what we had learnt about the characters so far and looked at key details. For the students who answered the hinge question correctly, they were given an extension task to find evidence from the text to support the answers of B, C and D, with the challenge of not selecting the most obvious reference.

Hinge questions can be asked at any point during the lesson; they can be asked at the beginning of the following lesson to test knowledge and understanding of what had been previously taught. They can be the final activity of a lesson to help inform your planning. It is all about being able to accurately assess students at the time of the learning, as opposed to six weeks later when you complete a summative assessment and then realise that students had been carrying misconceptions with them for all that time.

I have found hinge questions really useful and they have allowed me to have a clearer handle on what students have understood more quickly so time is not wasted. They do take a little longer to think of than a typical multiple-choice question but the benefits most definitely outweigh that.

Chloe Woodhouse is Learning Director, English and SLE at The Bemrose School, Derby. She is a PiXL associate, blogs at alwayslearning.blog and tweets at @AViewaskew.

Strategy C: Daily review tasks: know it all and image recall

Problem: Students are forgetting previous learning and struggling to make connections between prior and new knowledge. Starters are not effective in progressing the learning.

Research and evidence to refer to:

- Chapter 5's summary of 'Principles of instruction: research-based strategies that all teachers should know' by Barak Rosenshine (2012).
- Chapter 5's summary of the publication: 'Improving students' learning with effective learning techniques: promising directions from cognitive and educational psychology' by Dunlosky et al. (2013a).
- 'How to study using dual coding' from The Learning Scientists, available at: www.learningscientists.org/blog/2016/9/1-1.
- 'Lesson starters: An outdated idea or a meaningful teaching tool' (Stephens, 2014) is a very interesting read about the multiple purposes of a starter and concludes that a structured and formal approach is useful. The paper itself focuses on the link between starters, teachers' choices and expectations and students' behaviour, available at: https://journaleducationalresearchinformedpractice.files.wordpress.com/2014/08/3stephens2014june.pdf.

Why this strategy?

When thinking about the beginning of a lesson, there are many elements that we might consider vital – settling students, encouraging engagement with the topic of the lesson, establishing behaviour expectations and recapping knowledge. All of these can be achieved in different ways and some strategies do more of some than the others. As mentioned in the previous chapter, Rosenshine's (2012) first principle of instruction is to begin lessons by recapping previous knowledge in order to improve student outcomes.

One way of doing this effectively is to use quizzing of key information set for homework. Later in this chapter I discuss the ways in which knowledge organisers can support you in doing this. However, although extremely effective and engaging in terms of their accessibility and competitive element, you may wish to have more than just quizzes up your sleeve when it comes to recapping prior knowledge.

Two strategies I use to intersperse quizzes and knowledge organiser starter tasks are the 'know it all' recap and 'image recall'.

Case study: KS3 English

Know it all recap sheet

The 'know it all' sheet started life as a blank piece of paper that students had to fill in with everything they know about a particular topic. In an attempt to make it more sophisticated, useful and effective it has morphed into a tool for identifying misconceptions, and the task involves more than simply filling it in.

The sheet is given to students on entry to the classroom and typically focuses on the previous relevant lesson's learning. We have an interleaved curriculum meaning that the previous lesson on that topic might have been a few days or a week ago and therefore it is really important that students have a chance to recap the relevant knowledge for today. The good thing about having the sheet pre-populated rather than using a blank sheet is you can use it as a chance to give specific clues and hints or direct the process of retrieval in a particular direction. For example, the know it all sheet might have sections for particular chapters or characters in English, particular events or years in history or processes and theory in science.

Once students have the sheet, they fill it in as much as they can. I encourage students to do this in note format, including key dates, figures and words rather than using up valuable working memory trying to create perfect sentences too. At this point, you can move around the room to ascertain current retrieval, address misconceptions individually or as a whole class and consider how best to advance the lesson. It is of course not as specific as a hinge question but does give you an overview of the current knowledge your students have.

When five minutes are up, students typically put the sheet to the side of their exercise books and the lesson begins. The lesson might start by discussing an element from the know it all sheet. Students can add any missing information mentioned by a classmate on their sheet in a different-colour pen (I first saw this idea in practice at Michaela School and it seemed like an effective way of differentiating between a student's previous knowledge and new notes based on the teacher's or other students' feedback).

The other option is to place the sheet to the side and teach a lesson that builds on this knowledge, and towards the end of the lesson students can add to their sheet in a different colour. Completing this task every few weeks gives real confidence to those who believe they aren't taking anything in. Even those not keen to partake in lessons immediately have a desire to fill an empty sheet in some way.

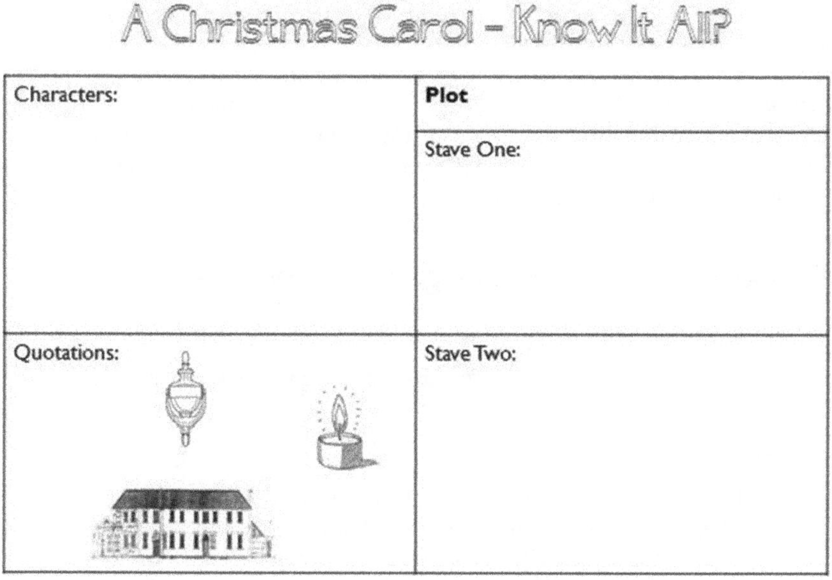

A Christmas Carol – Know It All?

Characters:	Plot
	Stave One:
Quotations:	Stave Two:

Fig. 5 Know it all recap sheet for *A Christmas Carol*

Image recall

In Chapter 9 of their book *Understanding How We Learn*, Yana Weinstein and Megan Sumeracki (2019) explore why and how dual coding is an effective revision technique. The use of images in teaching is not new, but it is the associations and links to these images that can make the use of dual coding and retrieval of prior knowledge effective. As a simple adaptation to the know it all sheet, you can include key images that students have previously been exposed to in order to encourage recall of specific key words, quotations, equations and so on. The theory suggests that as long as students have been repeatedly made aware of the images alongside the knowledge you have taught them then they will be able to retrieve the information that is now stored in their long-term memory when they see the image. This works well if done in stages. First of all, introduce the full information alongside the image and slowly take away key words or sections before finally leaving the image itself. This can take place over a few weeks, a half term or a year, with the intention of revisiting to avoid forgetting.

The use of images for recall does not have to work alongside the know it all sheet. Students can receive the image and have to identify key elements by talking to their partner or they might be given an image and you can encourage a choral response of a particular quotation.

There are, of course, numerous ways of recapping prior information, but with the prevalence of quizzing for retrieval we can easily forget that students are experiencing quizzes in numerous lessons each day and there is a requirement sometimes to mix it up just a little.

Strategy D: WAGOLL (what a good one looks like)

Problem: Students do not produce work matching your high level of expectations.

Evidence to refer to:

- The EEF's report 'Metacognition and self-regulated learning' (Quigley et al., 2018) summarised in Chapter 5, page 86.
- This website called 'Literacy WAGOLL resources' includes example WAGOLL texts to use with your primary classes. Available at: www. literacywagoll.com/resources.html.
- Read Andy Tharby's blog post called 'Modelling for excellence', available at: www.classteaching.wordpress.com/2013/11/24/ modelling-for-excellence.

Why this strategy?

Modelling our expectations and thought processes to students is key to student progress according to a wide variety of educational research. Both Rosenshine's (2012) principles and Creemers and Kyriakides' (2011) dynamic model identify modelling in its various forms as effective practice. Very much linked to direct instruction, modelling serves to give both good and bad examples and thereby expectations guiding students towards the desired outcome and providing the frameworks they require to be successful. Of course, there will still be misconceptions and miscommunications along the way, but through modelling approaches students were more likely to be effective in communicating the skills required to reach successful learning outcomes. Modelling is also a valuable tool for successful metacognition, providing an example of appropriate planning, monitoring and evaluation of a task usually through metacognitive talk.

We may sometimes forget that we are constantly modelling simply by being in a classroom, from how to greet someone and how to resolve problems to expected quality of work. If we have issues with students completing work in a haphazard way, if work is not of the quality we would expect, if students are trying to solve problems in an ineffective manner or struggling to complete a task, then *explicitly* rather than implicitly modelling how we would successfully go about it ourselves is the best way forward.

One time-saving method to do this, which has been kindly shared by a lead practitioner in art, Samantha Whitfield, is to use a models book. A models book is a way in which Samantha collates her models during demonstrations of subject-specific techniques. This book can be used again as a reminder or as a resource for students who missed a lesson or to demonstrate progress of a particular skill over time. The models book can be adapted to any subject. It is both a brilliant resource and a time-saving opportunity. I find myself referring to my models book almost every lesson and add to it often. Sometimes, it is best to begin a model from scratch to demonstrate the metacognitive process taking place, and at other points in learning it is necessary to have a complete model to refer to. The book can be easily given to students to provide scaffolding and can be built on year on year.

Modelling using examples is a strategy that can be easily applied to any classroom and found in most – but how it is done matters hugely. Both the following case studies give some advice on how to use modelling effectively in the classroom.

Case study: Samantha Whitfield – art

In my classroom I use this strategy to model high expectations and promote higher standards of work. The majority of my lessons will start with a WAGOLL; it lends itself perfectly to the obvious visual nature of art. Sharing what a good one looks like in this subject can be done using a model created by the teacher or a piece of student work. I have found that using a teacher or expert model can be highly effective in raising standards at Key Stage 4. However, at Key Stage 3, student work, even that of students older than them, is the most effective as a model. I believe this is because it feels more attainable for younger students.

When using a WAGOLL with a class for the first time, I would do so with caution, especially with low-ability students or those students who lack in confidence, as they may be intimidated. Perhaps start with separate stages of a piece or a specific skill focus before sharing finished and refined pieces or a body of work. It is also important that the thinking is modelled and students know how a painting, for example, was made. It is important that they are not simply shown a finished outcome with no explanation.

In art we often share a piece of best work and ask students to deconstruct the painting, sketchbook, etc., picking apart specific elements such as the strengths, skills and originality; this helps students understand what makes a really good piece of work. A WAGOLL can also be used to set out success criteria; this works well as a group task, where students can work together to identify effective elements. Equally, a more independent approach can work well, allowing students to personalise criteria by looking at a WAGOLL and making connections to their own stage of learning or skill set.

At Key Stage 4 we also teach our students to analyse a WAGOLL in the format of a full project or portfolio against the GCSE mark scheme to deepen their understanding of what high-grade work looks like. Students confidently ask to see high-grade work, and are showing higher levels of expectations of themselves and what they can achieve.

Samantha Whitfield is Lead Practitioner in Art at The Mountbatten School. She works as part of the teaching and learning team and tweets at @SL_Whitfield.

Case study: Kelly Brooks – religious studies

In religious studies teaching, I use WAGOLLs as a form of modelling to increase student progress and boost confidence in their interpretation and, latterly, application of the mark scheme in their extended writing. I often find that the language used by the exam board is too difficult for many students to access. Therefore, they need to see it in simple terms to be able to repeat the process and apply the knowledge for themselves.

My strategy tends to be to use a WAGOLL mid-way through a unit – not too early. Students need to feel confident in their knowledge and understanding before they can write a good evaluative piece. I always start with a WABOLL (what a bad one looks like!) as this gets students used to using the mark scheme and gives me an opportunity, with the visualiser, to draw out key points.

With a WABOLL, students can easily see what is missing and what has perhaps been poorly written (on purpose). I always talk aloud to model my thinking and approach, the aim being that they know what I and the exam board are seeking before they begin their own attempt.

The highest-attaining students find this especially useful, as they must write in a non-formulaic way. Their essays must read as a discussion and some find this difficult – they want to default to a PEE paragraph that will undoubtedly limit their grades. Through the use of WAGOLL, I find their confidence increases as they know what to aim for. It also highlights that it is not about writing more but about the quality of their writing! Overall, the qualitative feedback has been incredibly positive as students show more awareness and understanding of the mark scheme when they are used, and when I don't do this, students ask me when they will be getting a WAGOLL to support them! It is a form of scaffolding but not restrictive. In terms of impact, students' marks and speed of answering have increased.

My advice to someone writing a WAGOLL is to have the mark scheme on the left-hand side of an A4 page and your WAGOLL on the right. I highlight or arrow where I am meeting the criteria. This is deliberate so that students can interpret and therefore hopefully mimic the expectations. I always finish by setting a different question to the one we have looked at in class. I then ask that the A4 sheet provided (that includes the mark scheme and WAGOLL) is used to support students in answering the new question that might be set for independent work at home, where students now feel supported through the use of a great example that has been explained and explored fully.

Kelly Brooks is Lead Practitioner in Religious Studies at The Mountbatten School. She works as part of the teaching and learning team and tweets at @Kbrooks_mb.

Strategy E: Metacognitive talk to improve exam technique

Problem: Students struggle to remember how to combine knowledge and skills in an exam response.

Evidence to refer to:
- The EEF's report 'Metacognition and self-regulated learning' (Quigley et al., 2018) summarised in Chapter 5, page 86.
- John Tomsett wrote about his findings in a post entitled 'This much I know about... The Sutton Trust/EEF toolkit and the golden thread from evidence to student outcomes, via deliberate intervention', available at: www.johntomsett.com/2015/02/13/this-much-i-know-about-the-golden-thread-from-evidence-to-student-outcomes.
- I wrote a post called 'Research and revision' based on my classroom some years ago, available at: www.littlemisslud.wordpress.com/2015/05/01/revision-and-research.

Why this strategy?

Recommendation 5 in the EEF's metacognition report suggests that promoting and developing metacognitive talk in the classroom helps to make the cognitive strategies required to complete a task explicit so that students are better placed to use them in their approach to solving problems. The recommendation cites Professor Robin Alexander's (2017) work on dialogic talk, which distinguishes a variety of talk, differentiating learning talk from teaching talk. The report quotes Alexander stating, 'Learning talk includes narrating, questioning, and discussing; teaching talk includes instruction, exposition, and dialogue.'

The report suggests all types of talk are important but that discussion and debate are required to encourage learning talk, which leads to metacognitive thoughts and evaluation. The metacognitive process described in recommendation 1 of the report is reviewed in Chapter 5 and it is this process of planning, monitoring and evaluating that takes place numerous times in an exam situation, which is often skirted over when teaching students in the run-up to an assessment. In particular, lessons leading up to a formal examination such as SATs or GCSEs traditionally involve practice questions and a reminder of key timings. These are two very important elements but, as a new teacher, it did not occur to me to voice the internal narrative that takes place during assessments until I read John Tomsett's blog on metacognition. The process of voicing your decision-making processes throughout what is normally a silent situation (an exam!) is an eye-opening one. If you have never done this with a class before then I suggest narrating your car journey as a great starting point! Narrating your drive as you drive along means more than just pointing out what you can see – instead you should explain aloud what you see and the actions you will take. For example, why you are about to indicate, what issues you might have to deal with at the next junction, how you might deal with these issues, why you are braking early and so on.

Using metacognitive talk when approaching a formal assessment provides students with a range of information that without such explicit discussion would remain implicit, and our students would not have the advantages they could in an exam. Teachers have long been criticised for teaching to the exam but I believe that being aware of this strategy can in fact avoid this by creating a balance between teaching the content required, enjoying learning and covering strategies that students will need to succeed in their assessments, whether they be formal or informal. Rather than asking students to complete yet another exam question in the run-up to exams, when there may be misconceptions or misunderstandings about how to approach a question, pausing to model our own metacognitive strategies would be a better use of time and, research suggests, it is an effective tool in improving student outcomes.

Case study: Siân Cumming – English

Metacognitive talk is embedded in our English classrooms as it has had a transformative effect on both our students' awareness of their own thinking and my self-awareness around my own thought processes.

In English, I take a metacognitive approach when going through an exam paper to help students with their planning. Students each have a blank exam booklet as do I. The teacher copy is underneath the visualiser. I share my thought processes and questions out loud with the class, annotating the paper. These thoughts and questions include:

- 'I am reading the questions a second time **because**…'
- 'Which English skills are being tested here?'
- 'Which part of the questions is the most important?'
- 'I am highlighting this section **because**…'
- 'This question is worth X marks so I will spend X amount of time **because**…'
- 'I am going to write the time down **to help me keep to the exam timings**.'
- 'I know I need to use short, specific quotations **because**…'
- 'I am highlighting this key word **because it is the key thing I am looking for in the extract provided**' (and then I will draw a magnifying glass or a pair of eyes to remind them and me).
- 'The first thing I am going to do is plan my initial ideas **because**…'
- 'Now I am going to highlight the ideas I want to use; **I decide this by**…'

As I am modelling my thoughts out loud to the class, I annotate the paper. Students must annotate alongside me – copying everything I do. At no point do I include any English-specific answers; the annotations are totally focused on how I think about the questions and how I will approach the given task.

It is important to explain each decision and how I came to that decision, so the word 'because' is really powerful here. I also spend time pointing out common misconceptions whilst modelling my thought processes, e.g. 'I know that some students forget to put quotation marks around their quotations so I must remember to use them.' Students will then have to go through the process for themselves using a different exam paper or question.

Metacognition is also used in English as a form of monitoring to help students learn to self-regulate. During 'live' modelled work (either under the visualiser or on the board) I will model a written response and the thought processes I am going through. I will write the first couple of paragraphs and then, in a different-colour pen, go back through and consider how I am getting on. I will ask questions such as:

- 'Am I answering the question being asked?' – I would then re-read my answer and circle where I am explicitly linking back to a key word or idea in the question.
- 'Have I embedded short, specific quotations?' – I would then highlight them and ask, 'Is this short?', 'Does this quotation support my point?', 'Have I remembered quotation marks?'

Asking these questions to myself, out loud, whilst annotating my work models to students how to self-assess progress. It relies on a good understanding of the task's success criteria. When proofreading an answer at the end of a task, I go through a similar set of questions to help me evaluate, edit and improve my work.

These are embedded processes, not one-offs. Every time we have a question, I will annotate it and use metacognitive talk, always encouraging my students to do the same thing. Eventually, students will be able to do this independently. They will spend time annotating their questions, consciously planning and considering their approach. I now see students making notes in the margins of their mock exams as they self-regulate during a task.

Siân Cumming is Director of Learning at a secondary school in Hampshire and tweets at @TLMountbatten and @Siancumming1.

Strategy F: 'Do now' quizzes and knowledge organisers

Problem: Starter tasks were varied and ineffective.

Research and evidence to refer to:
- Overview of 'What makes great teaching? Review of the underpinning research' by Coe et al. (2014) in Chapter 5, page 90.
- Chapter 6: 'Memory and recall' in *What Does This Look Like In The Classroom?* by Carl Hendrick and Robin Macpherson (2017).
- Do now tasks are explained in Doug Lemov's book *Teach Like a Champion* (2015) and briefly on his website. Available at: www.teachlikeachampion.com/blog/now-primer.
- Joe Kirby writes about knowledge organisers and their use in practice-testing here: https://pragmaticreform.wordpress.com/2015/03/28/knowledge-organisers.

Knowledge organisers

Knowledge organisers are now commonly used in schools in a number of ways. Primarily, knowledge organisers are sheets detailing the essential and vital knowledge required by a student to best understand and explore a specific topic, for example Weimer Germany in GCSE history, UK geography in Year 4 or *Macbeth* in Year 9 English. Joe Kirby (2015), who introduced them to his school in 2015 whilst he was deputy head, states on his blog that 'Knowledge organisers clarify for everyone, from the headteacher to brand new teachers, exactly what is being taught.' There are a wide number of ways in which they can be used to aid retrieval and improve memory. They can also be used as reference sheets in the classroom, as cover work and as homework through self-quizzing and revision. Trying to distil all the key information onto one sheet can be a challenge but they are very beneficial once made. The process of making them only serves as a reminder that remembering and understanding knowledge, as we expect students to do, is not a lower-level skill, as Bloom's taxonomy pyramid is often misinterpreted as suggesting, but instead a large and vital level that cannot be ignored in favour of those skills often labelled as higher-level. (Read Doug Lemov's (2017) critique of Bloom's taxonomy: 'Bloom's taxonomy: that pyramid is a problem' and note that the pyramid was not created by Benjamin Bloom and doesn't appear in the original theory.)

Knowledge organisers work for every subject and phase. They can be used for long- or short-term subjects and once created can be reused year on year. In most subjects, the knowledge we require students to know does not vary hugely unless there is a change in specification for an examination, and therefore the energy put into making them isn't wasted. Hundreds of ready-made knowledge organisers can be found online but should be adapted for your students' requirements.

Case study: Hayley Cummings – science

We use knowledge organisers in science as a standard pre-learning homework task for all year groups across the science department. We have a large number of topics in our scheme of work (36 in Key Stage 3 and 49 in Key Stage 4) that all require pre-learning at home to enable maximum use of lesson time. Each topic has its own knowledge organiser, which is handed out and stuck in books at the beginning of that topic, to be learnt for homework. We recommend the use of look-cover-write-check to learn the content. On the date homework is due, the knowledge organiser is displayed to the class, but this time with ten sections missing. To prove that they have completed their homework, the students must complete the ten blank sections in complete silence, with 80 per cent being the accepted 'pass'.

This recall of definitions, equations and essential facts means that far more lesson time can be devoted to addressing misconceptions, the further application of knowledge and completing exam questions. The knowledge organisers can also be used as a great differentiation tool during lessons or as a catch-up aid for individuals who have missed lessons.

When introducing knowledge organisers to a new class, I would recommend briefly explaining to the students what they are, the research behind using them and why they are being used as homework. I found that the knowledge organiser homework was most effective when the students were clear about how it would impact their learning and ultimately their grades.

Hayley Cummings is Head of Key Stage 3 Science at a secondary school in Hampshire and tweets at @MissHCummings.

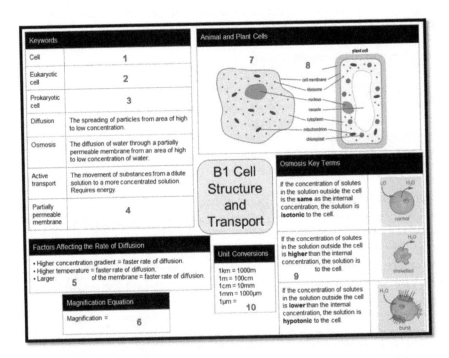

Fig. 6 A Key Stage 3 knowledge organiser ready for a recall quiz; ten key pieces of information have been removed

Do now

The second research-informed strategy you could try alongside Hayley's suggestions is Doug Lemov's 'do now' tasks. Doug Lemov's (2015) strategy-filled book *Teach Like a Champion* describes a do now activity as a short activity that students know to start immediately on entering a lesson. This form of starter activity should conform to a few directives in order for it to be effective according to the guidance.

- Firstly, it should be in the same place each lesson so students know where to find it.
- It should last around three to five minutes.
- Students should be able to complete it independently.
- It should either recap previous learning or preview the next lesson.

Ideas for using do nows and knowledge organisers together as starter activities are as follows:

- At the beginning of a unit, give students time to self-quiz using look-cover-write-check, focusing on a particular section of the knowledge organiser.
- Encourage retrieval practice using fill-the-gap exercises where sections of the knowledge organiser are blanked out.
- Hand out a blank knowledge organiser or project an empty section on the board and ask students to complete it.
- Remove all the information from the knowledge organisers but leave the diagrams and ask students to label them.
- Ask students to quiz a partner by giving a definition aloud.
- Provide quiz questions based on previous topic content: two questions on a topic this week, two from last week and two questions on the previous topic.

Strategy G: Whole-class feedback sheets

Problem: Marking takes hours and developmental feedback is ignored by students.

Evidence to refer to:

- The EEF's report 'A marked improvement? A review of the evidence on written marking' (Elliott et al., 2016) as summarised in Chapter 5, page 94.

- Jo Facer's overview of whole-class feedback: 'Giving feedback the Michaela way', available at: www.readingallthebooks. com/2016/03/19/giving-feedback-the-michaela-way.
- Greg Thornton's post 'Marking crib sheet and whole class feedback', available at www.mrthorntonteach.com/2016/04/08/ marking-crib-sheet.
- Examples of feedback sheets collated by teacher Victoria Hewett: 'Mrs Humanities shares... 5 whole class feedback examples'. Available at: www.mrshumanities.com/2017/10/15/ mrs-humanities-shares-5-whole-class-feedback-examples.

Why this strategy?

Marking and feedback are two separate entities that have on many occasions been unhelpfully merged into one. The EEF's written marking review (Elliott et al., 2016) does give some findings and implications from their review of the evidence, one of which is that 'some forms of marking, including acknowledgement marking, are unlikely to enhance pupil progress. A mantra might be that schools should mark less in terms of the number of pieces of work marked, but mark better.'

With ever-increasing demands on teachers' time, one strategy that saves time is the use of whole-class feedback. Whole-class feedback is shorthand for the practice of reading, acknowledging and giving targets to a specific piece of work completed by a large number of students but without the onerous task of writing comments and feedback on every piece of work. It also acts as a strategy to encourage students to focus on the feedback and targets and is often combined with strategies to encourage engagement with feedback such as directed improvement and reflection time (D.I.R.T).

An example of our English department's whole-class feedback sheet is provided on page 129. It is based on examples from many other teachers and has been adapted over the years to suit our context. Individual class teachers may also use it in different ways but the process remains similar:

1) Inform students that the work they are completing will be read and reviewed for a specific set of criteria.
2) Take in students' books (from either the whole class or a range of abilities depending on the task and how often you wish to give feedback).
3) Put the kettle on.

4) Read through the specific piece of work with a pen and paper or the whole-class feedback sheet open on a computer.

5) Make your hot beverage.

6) Note down common errors, misunderstandings, literacy issues and (very importantly) great examples from the work.

7) Complete the class feedback sheet and whilst doing so consider your next steps: how to correct misconceptions, what trends there are between the work and who needs extra support or development.

8) Finish your hot beverage and consider what to do with all your free time (only joking – what is free time?).

This practice can take some getting used to. Not writing comments on students' work (not even ticks in some cases) can be a difficult routine to get into. This is not to say that you cannot correct mistakes on students' work, which can be a helpful approach if it is a mistake that only one or two have made. However, this feedback approach avoids students concentrating purely on a grade or level and encourages teachers to concentrate on what matters – the feedback and teaching that will truly improve outcomes rather than how to phrase a particular target or which colour pen to use.

Feedback on Curley's wife/Crooks paragraphs		10th November	
Write out these key Spelling errors x3: Curley's wife – apostrophe!! Insecure Symbolises Implies Encourages **Sp** Please copy out your spelling corrections three times Microcosm	**Best bits:** 'She has adapted her mannerisms to 'make do' with what she has'.– Amy 'This is a clever way of telling, or rather making us think about what Curley's wife is really like' – Stephen 'Curley's wife is seen as incongruous' – Mary 'The writer demonstrates the negative conditions black people faced through this quotation…' – Joe		**Class Improvements/Discussion:** Why is it important to say that Steinbeck did something and Curley's wife is and not the other way around? In your analysis, could you use more than one short quotation from different areas to prove your point? What part of the success criteria would this hit?
Style improvements: - Your quotation must link to your point. Do not analyse a quotation that you haven't mentioned as this can get quite confusing. - Don't always use the word 'also' for your next point. Could you use 'moreover' or 'additionally'? - Be careful how you write about context – make sure it is accurate and don't make assumptions or use words that might be deemed inappropriate.		**Immediate Individual Tasks:** 1) Change I think/I believe/We believe to – perhaps, interestingly or arguably 2) Begin your planning for Curley's wife – consider whether or not your draft piece could be used and what you would improve.	

Fig. 7 An example of a whole-class feedback sheet

When James Grocott shared how he had used whole-class feedback methods on Twitter, he was overwhelmed by the response for his resource and advice. Below, he generously explains how he uses whole-class feedback with his primary class.

Case study: James Grocott – primary classroom

Assessing children's understanding of taught concepts is obviously a key part, if not *the* key part, of teaching and learning. There are obviously different ways of doing this; however, the most time-consuming and in my opinion least impactful way is writing comments in books. Teachers can spend hours of their working week marking work and it is one of the biggest contributors to workload issues. It is the impact of this marking that I believe to be an issue. Are children reading the feedback? Are they responding to the feedback? How could I make sure without having to talk to every child?

A year or so ago I decided to venture into the world of EduTwitter and I noticed a few people were talking about whole-class feedback. I decided to trial my own version. I started to use whole-class feedback after each lesson and haven't looked back!

In practice, teachers plan and undertake lessons as usual. At the end of a lesson, my children have lots of opportunities to peer-mark and self-mark their work. After the lesson I go through books and make notes on a sheet with headings: 'What you all did well', 'Work to praise and share', 'Presentation', 'LO (learning objective) misconceptions', 'Non-negotiable errors' and 'FIT (feedback and improvement time) activities'. Each of these boxes contains the names of individual children. Using the boxes I then formulate the FIT activity section. If children have certain misconceptions then they will have a FIT activity that will help to address that misconception (quite often with the teacher or teaching assistant). If there are children who have achieved the learning objective, then they will have a FIT activity that moves their learning on – which can be done independently. At the start of each lesson, work is praised and shared, presentation is shown on the big screen and FIT activities are undertaken in their books (we have the heading FIT written in their books and any FIT work is done in green pen). This FIT time lasts for around ten minutes and then we move into the next session.

Children were being given constructive, impactful feedback and during our FIT sessions were able to be 'moved on' or supported in their learning of the previous concept. Children responded amazingly well to the 'work to praise and share' when showing fantastic examples on the screen. Children are now desperate to get their work on the big screen and to be included in the work to praise and share. Every child now knows how they have achieved in each lesson and the impact has been substantial compared to individual written feedback in books.

One of the things to be aware of is that FIT activities need to be very well thought out. If you are setting an extending activity, it needs to be that. It cannot be a tag-on activity for children to get on with whilst misconceptions are addressed. The activity needs to move the children on.

Another issue that led to me tweaking my sheet was that some non-negotiables were being overlooked due to the previous sheet and the boxes it contained. This was added to the new sheet and allows for teachers to set what they would consider to be non-negotiables for a particular lesson. These could be errors that weren't part of the initial learning objective but may have been picked up through detailed marking – for example, a child may have achieved the objective to write a newspaper report but may be writing the letter i in lower case when writing the word I. Although they have achieved the objective, it would be something to pick up on quickly during the FIT and on a one-to-one level.

James Grocott is Deputy Headteacher at a primary school in Suffolk. He writes 'The Hopefully Helpful Teacher' blog at https://deputygrocott.blogspot.com/ and tweets at @deputygrocott.

Practical advice

With each of these examples, the teachers involved have continually adapted their practice as they deem necessary. The practical suggestions demonstrate a starting point with which you too could apply the knowledge you gain from reading educational research summaries or findings in your school or classroom. There are, of course, numerous issues with this:

- You could apply strategies left, right and centre without taking into consideration contextual issues.
- You might rush into a process and expect an immediate positive outcome.
- You might not understand the evidence provided but use it regardless.
- The evidence may not be robust.

Although these are all issues we may stumble upon at different times, it is only by working through such problems that we can seek to solve them. Not rushing into using too many strategies takes foresight and patience whereas the other issues are more complex and may require you working in a team (we'll come to this in Part 2) to avoid misunderstanding or avoid applying evidence that isn't as robust as you first thought. Ensure that you use the steps outlined at the beginning of this chapter on page 104 to give yourself the best chance of using the research and strategies effectively.

You need to be aware that the evidence may suggest a certain outcome, but in your classroom, for whatever reason, the results simply may not materialise as you expect. However, this does not mean your application or findings are a failure. By engaging with the research in this practical sense, you are undoubtedly keen to know more and can now identify, using the self-assessment in Chapter 7, page 138, what else you need to read about or learn to become further research engaged.

Chapter 6 takeaway

Teaching tip
Open your door
In Chapter 4's teaching tip, I suggested paying close attention to your current practice and decision-making so that you are aware of what you are doing or what others are doing to make decisions. My next suggestion might be wildly out of your comfort zone but I suggest inviting someone you trust into your classroom to do the exact same thing. You may wish to give them an area to focus on, but what you are after is feedback on what you *really* do rather than what you think you do.

For example, if you often have trouble with students being confused when you think you have taught as well as you can, then you may wish to ask someone to come in and write down the way in which you explain key ideas (perhaps they could record you) or ask them to notice how you question (how many questions, who you ask, what type of questions you ask). You are not expecting nor do you want a judgement on your overall teaching, but a specific set of information related to your chosen focus. Creating an open-door policy where you can ask for constructive data on your own teaching will be hugely beneficial.

Pass it on
Find a friend
Perhaps the same person you invite into your classroom will also be keen to trial strategies with you. It is always useful to have someone to bounce ideas off. If you are planning on implementing a new strategy, perhaps

they could too? Is there anyone with similar problems or thoughts as you who might want to trial a strategy for a term or two? It is always important to work together on implementing the strategy and share your woes and findings along the way. Set a date to meet up and explore your findings – either anecdotal or data – but be sure to discuss the differences between your classes even if on the surface they seem similar.

CPD book club recommendation

Read David Didau's *What If Everything You Knew About Education Was Wrong?* (2015a) in order to consider how best to put ideas into practice from the outset and how to become aware of your own biases.

Bloggers' corner

Jon Bruskill's use of knowledge organisers in primary schools is worth a read if you are not sure how these might apply in the primary classroom.

Link: https://pedfed.wordpress.com/2016/12/30/using-knowledge-organisers-in-primary/#comment-398.

TO DO LIST:

❑ Check the table of research and linked techniques – do any of them stand out to you as of interest due to a particular student, class or area of focus?

❑ Pick one or two of these areas and strategies to consider implementing in your classroom based on your area of focus that you began thinking about in Chapter 3. If you teach more than one class, identify which class you will focus on. Don't attempt to change everything all at once.

❑ Complete any further reading in this area. Evaluate how these ideas could work in your own classroom by using the guidance steps at the start of this chapter.

❑ Enquire with others about whether or not they have used such techniques – tweet out a question using the #UKEdChat or #UKEdResChat hashtags.

7

Evaluating progress

Hopefully by this stage you will have begun to engage with some of the key resources to access discussions and findings about research-informed practice and have read some of the reviews and research presented in previous chapters. You may have considered your research area (identified in Chapter 3) and begun to make plans to trial one of the simple but effective strategies presented in Chapter 6 – perhaps you have already done so and found that the strategy either worked well or didn't suit your particular context. You can consider why and how a strategy impacted your teaching and students' learning further through Chapter 8, once you have considered your overall research understanding and current practice.

This chapter provides a questionnaire to help you to step back and reflect on where you are and what you've learnt so far. It is important to take time to complete this questionnaire in order to evaluate your progress. This will support you in planning the next steps for excelling at and embedding research-informed practice.

How to complete the questionnaire

Exactly like the questionnaire in Chapter 2, you have two options as to how you approach this questionnaire. Here is a reminder.

Quick response approach

If your preference for the self-assessment is to go with your gut only, then simply fill in the quick response section after each question with the first thing that comes into your mind when you ask yourself the question. Do not mull over the question too long; simply read carefully and answer quickly. This approach will give you an overview of your current understanding and practice of using educational research in your decision-making processes both in the classroom and beyond and will take relatively little time. Just make sure you are uninterrupted, in a quiet place and able to complete the questionnaire in one sitting with no distractions so that you get focused and honest answers.

Considered response approach

If you choose to take a more reflective and detailed approach, then you can leave the quick response section blank and go straight onto reading the further guidance section under each question. This guidance provides prompt questions and ideas to get you thinking in detail about the question being asked and is designed to open up a wider scope in your answer. It will also enable you to look at your experience and pull examples into your answer to back up your statements. You may want to complete it a few questions at a time and take breaks, or you may be prepared to simply sit and work through the questions all in one sitting to ensure you remain focused. This approach does take longer, but it can lead to a more in-depth understanding of your current practice, and you will gain much more from the process than the quick response alone.

Combined approach

A thorough approach, and one I recommend, would be to use both approaches together regardless of personal preference. There is clear value in both approaches being used together. This would involve you firstly answering the self-assessment quick response questions by briefly noting down your instinctual answers for all questions. The next step would be to return to the start of the self-assessment, read the further guidance and then answer the questions once more, slowly and in detail, forming more of a narrative around each question and pulling in examples from your own experience. Following this you would need to read over both responses and form a comprehensive and honest summary in your mind of your answers and a final view of where you feel you stand right now in your use of educational research to support decision-making regarding your teaching and learning.

- I have done this self-assessment before.
- I only want a surface-level overview of my current understanding and practice.
- I work better when I work at speed.
- I don't have much time.

Quick

- I have never done this self-assessment before.
- I want a deeper understanding of my current understanding and practice.
- I work better when I take my time and really think things over.
- I have some time to do this self-assessment.

Considered

- I have never done this self-assessment before.
- I have done this self-assessment before.
- I want a comprehensive and full understanding of my current understanding and practice and want to compare that to what I thought before taking the self-assessment.
- I have a decent amount of time to dedicate to completing this self-assessment.

Combined

Fig. 8 How should I approach the self-evaluation questionnaire?

This is the longest of the three approaches to this questionnaire but will give you a comprehensive and full understanding of your current practice, thoughts and feelings in relation to research-informed practice being used in schools. You will be surprised at the difference you see between the quick response and the considered response answers to the same questions. It can be very illuminating.

Rate yourself

The final part of the self-assessment is to rate yourself. This section will ask you to rate your confidence and happiness in each area that has been covered in the questionnaire, with a view to working on these areas for improvement throughout the course of the book. The table below shows how the scale works: the higher the number you allocate yourself, the better you feel you are performing in that area.

Rating	Definition
1	Not at all. I don't. None at all. Not happy. Not confident at all.
2	Rarely. Barely. Very little. Very unconfident.
3	Not often at all. Not much. Quite unconfident.
4	Not particularly. Not really. Not a lot. Mildly unconfident.
5	Neutral. Unsure. Don't know. Indifferent.
6	Sometimes. At times. Moderately. A little bit. Mildly confident.
7	Quite often. A fair bit. Some. A little confident.
8	Most of the time. More often than not. Quite a lot. Quite confident.
9	The majority of the time. A lot. Very confident.
10	Completely. Very much so. A huge amount. Extremely happy. Extremely confident.

Fig. 9 Rate yourself definitions

Research-informed practice reflection questionnaire

QUESTION 1: Which new resources (such as publications, apps or recommended sites) have you used that have helped you to engage with research-informed discussions?

Quick response:

_____

_____

_____

_____

_____

Questions for consideration

- Which resources did you decide to access first and why?
- How easy did you find it to access the resources?
- Do you feel you understand the purpose and drive behind the resources you've started to use?
- Were there any resources that you have recommended to others?

Considered response:

_____

_____

_____

_____

_____

Rate yourself

QUESTION 1: How confident are you about accessing resources to help you to engage with research-informed discussions?

1   2   3   4   5   6   7   8   9   10

QUESTION 2: How has your research-informed network developed?

Quick response:

_____

_____

_____

_____

_____

_____

Questions for consideration

- Who would you look to in order to discuss any educational reading or research?
- Have you broadened your network to include those outside of your own school or context?
- What do you consider to be the benefits of discussing pedagogy and practice with others?
- How do you feel sharing your thoughts and ideas with others?

Considered response:

_____

_____

_____

_____

_____

_____

Rate yourself

QUESTION 2: How confident do you feel that you've developed a useful research-informed network?

1   2   3   4   5   6   7   8   9   10

QUESTION 3: How would you describe your current knowledge and understanding of educational research and research-informed practice and how has it developed?

Quick response:

_____

_____

_____

_____

_____

Questions for consideration

- How has your perception of what constitutes 'research-informed' changed?
- Do you find you are trying more or fewer research-informed strategies than you used to?
- Do you find you are reading more or less than previously? How has the content of your reading changed?
- Do you feel you consider your practice and decision-making more or less than before?

Considered response:

_____

_____

_____

_____

_____

Rate yourself

QUESTION 3: How confident do you feel about the development of your knowledge and understanding of educational research and research-informed practice?

1   2   3   4   5   6   7   8   9   10

QUESTION 4: How has your general reading informed or influenced your practice in the classroom?

Quick response:

_____

_____

_____

_____

_____

Questions for consideration

- What led you to search for a change of strategy or approach in this area of your pedagogy?
- Which piece of educational research influenced your practice or led you to look at further research in more detail?
- Have you recommended this reading to others and if so who?
- Do you feel this has led you to critique your current practice effectively?

Considered response:

_____

_____

_____

_____

_____

Rate yourself

QUESTION 4: How much has your general reading informed or influenced your practice in the classroom?

1	2	3	4	5	6	7	8	9	10

QUESTION 5: Are there any specific pieces of research you've read that you think could be relevant to your learning context and useful to implement in your classroom?

Quick response:

_____

_____

_____

_____

_____

Questions for consideration

- What paper, article or review did you read that resonated with you the most?
- What about this piece of research stood out to you?
- Was all the information new to you or did it confirm some of your previous understanding?
- How did you initially plan to implement this research in the classroom?

Considered response:

_____

_____

_____

_____

_____

Rate yourself

QUESTION 5: How confident do you feel that you've found research that is relevant for your teaching context?

1   2   3   4   5   6   7   8   9   10

QUESTION 6: Do you feel confident that you know what the next steps are for implementing relevant research you have found in practice?

Quick response:

_____

_____

_____

_____

_____

Questions for consideration

- Have you read the steps for implementation of strategies in Chapter 6?
- Do you have an idea about when best to implement a new strategy?
- Which group of students or sub-group of students would you focus on? Why?
- What issues do you feel you might come across when trying to implement a new idea?
- Are you confident that the evidence you have read is robust in its findings to justify making a change in your practice?

Considered response:

_____

_____

_____

_____

_____

Rate yourself

QUESTION 6: How confident do you feel about implementing research in practice?

| 1 | 2 | 3 | 4 | 5 | 6 | 7 | 8 | 9 | 10 |

QUESTION 7: Do you feel more confident when it comes to assessing the reliability of research you are exposed to?

Quick response:

_____

_____

_____

_____

_____

Questions for consideration

- Have you asked questions of the research you have read recently?
- Have you found yourself questioning the research that is presented to you?
- Do you feel you know which sources to look at in order to find robust evidence?
- Do you take time before implementing new ideas based on research you have read?

Considered response:

_____

_____

_____

_____

_____

Rate yourself

QUESTION 7: How confident do you feel about assessing the reliability of research?

1   2   3   4   5   6   7   8   9   10

QUESTION 8: Where do you feel your strengths lie when it comes to research-informed practice?

Quick response:

_____

_____

_____

_____

_____

Questions for consideration

- Do your strengths lie in finding the time to engage with reading research?
- Do your strengths lie in discussing research with others both in your school and beyond?
- Do you feel that you have the ability to differentiate between what might work for others and what might work for you?
- Do you feel your strengths lie in translating the research into something suitable for your own context?

Considered response:

_____

_____

_____

_____

_____

Rate yourself

QUESTION 8: How confident do you feel about your research-informed practice?

1   2   3   4   5   6   7   8   9   10

QUESTION 9: Where do you feel your weaknesses lie when it comes to research-informed practice?

Quick response:

_____

_____

_____

_____

_____

Questions for consideration

- Are you certain that you have access to the relevant resources to support you on your journey?
- Would you like to know more about the key research in Chapter 5?
- Would you like to know more about how to translate evidence into classroom practice?
- Would you like to understand the research strategies and statistical analysis in more depth and detail?

Considered response:

_____

_____

_____

_____

_____

Rate yourself

QUESTION 9: Do you have a clear understanding of your weaknesses when it comes to research-informed practice and how you can best address them?

1   2   3   4   5   6   7   8   9   10

QUESTION 10: How has your decision-making process changed when it comes to implementing a new strategy in the classroom?

Quick response:

_____

_____

_____

_____

_____

Questions for consideration

- Previously, when implementing a change, how much thought did you put into the process of doing so?
- What are the first things you consider when deciding whether or not to implement a change?
- Realistically, how much time do you spend considering the possible effect of that change on stakeholders?
- What do you record before you implement a change?

Considered response:

_____

_____

_____

_____

_____

Rate yourself

QUESTION 10: How happy do you feel about your new decision-making process?

1   2   3   4   5   6   7   8   9   10

QUESTION 11: What have you shared or discussed with colleagues in your school regarding research-informed practice?

Quick response:

_____

_____

_____

_____

_____

Questions for consideration

- At what point did you feel confident and happy to share your ideas with others?
- Who did you decide to talk to first and in what capacity?
- Have you felt the discussions have been worthwhile? Why?
- What impact do you feel your discussions have had or might have in your school?

Considered response:

_____

_____

_____

_____

_____

Rate yourself

QUESTION 11: How confident do you feel about sharing your ideas with colleagues?

| 1 | 2 | 3 | 4 | 5 | 6 | 7 | 8 | 9 | 10 |

QUESTION 12: What do your colleagues think about your interest in educational research- and evidence-based practice? How do you know?

Quick response:

_____

_____

_____

_____

Questions for consideration

- How do you know what others think about your approaches and considerations when making classroom-based or management-based decisions?
- Do you ever purposefully discuss your thoughts and feelings towards how decisions are made in schools?
- Did you find a variety of reactions from different colleagues? Why do you think this is?
- Have you provided others with any findings or knowledge based on your reading? What was their reaction?
- If you are leading others, how do you justify your sources and findings to them? What has their reaction been?
- Do you find that your approaches match well with the school's ethos and methodology?
- Moving forward, how would you like to see others' opinions develop (not necessarily to be the same as yours!)?

Considered response:

_____

_____

_____

_____

Rate yourself

QUESTION 12: How do your colleagues rate your interest in educational research- and evidence-based practice?

1	2	3	4	5	6	7	8	9	10

QUESTION 13: Have you joined any research-informed practice discussions outside of your school, either in your local area or online?

Quick response:

_____

_____

_____

_____

_____

Questions for consideration

- Have you identified a local Research School and contacted it?
- Have you written a blog post about research-informed practice and your engagement with it?
- Have you attended or signed up to attend a research-led event such as a ResearchEd conference?
- Have you reached out to discuss research with teachers from other schools?
- Have you taken part in an online discussion with others about a particular paper or theory?

Considered response:

_____

_____

_____

_____

_____

Rate yourself

QUESTION 13: How confident do you feel about joining research-informed practice discussions outside your school?

1   2   3   4   5   6   7   8   9   10

QUESTION 14: Now that you have begun, is there anything in particular that is stopping you from developing your knowledge and skills in educational research- and evidence-based practice further?

Quick response:

_____

_____

_____

_____

_____

Questions for consideration

- What areas or skills do you now wish to develop and why?
- What training do you feel you require in order to make these next steps?
- Have you discussed your requirements for CPD in this area with anyone?
- Have you tried to find ways forward through your newly developed support network?

Considered response:

_____

_____

_____

_____

_____

Rate yourself

QUESTION 14: Do you have a clear understanding of anything that is holding you back from progressing and how you can address this?

1   2   3   4   5   6   7   8   9   10

QUESTION 15: What impact have the changes you've made to your practice so far had on your students? How do you know?

Quick response:

_____

_____

_____

_____

_____

Questions for consideration

- What did you record before implementing a change?
- Did you consider your own beliefs and bias before implementing the change?
- What do you consider to be an 'impact' – either positive or negative?
- How has the impact on students manifested itself in your classroom?

Considered response:

_____

_____

_____

_____

_____

Rate yourself

QUESTION 15: How happy are you with the impact the changes you've made have had on your students?

1   2   3   4   5   6   7   8   9   10

QUESTION 16: What do you consider to be your next steps when it comes to your own research literacy and improving that of those around you?

Quick response:

_____

_____

_____

_____

_____

Questions for consideration

- Have you considered an action plan for taking your understanding and participation in educational research further?
- Have you identified areas in your own research literacy that require further thought?
- Are you in communication with your own leaders about how and why you should proceed with your research journey?
- Do you feel supported to continue with your interest in educational research, considering the time it requires?

Considered response:

_____

_____

_____

_____

_____

Rate yourself

QUESTION 16: How confident are you about your next steps when it comes to your own research literacy and improving that of those around you?

1	2	3	4	5	6	7	8	9	10

The results

Take a look at how you rated your answers for each question in the questionnaire and compare your ratings with the chart below, which will guide you in taking the next steps towards becoming a research-informed practitioner.

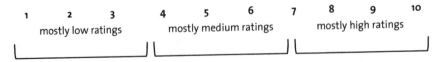

Fig. 10 How did you rate yourself?

Mostly low ratings

You still have some distance to go before you would consider yourself research informed. This is an understandable position to be in, considering educational research is such a large and time-consuming topic, but remember that being informed does not require you to be an expert in running research projects – far from it. We are still teachers and the experts in research will always be the researchers! However, if you do feel lost or confused, then go back and ensure you've completed the 'to do' sections at the end of each chapter and read the suggested posts in Bloggers' corner. It is important to bear in mind that becoming research informed won't happen overnight. The relevant reading takes time to read, consider and, if you so wish, apply. Make sure you give yourself an achievable timeframe within which to complete further reading, and find yourself a colleague or friend to discuss your reading with.

Mostly medium ratings

You are likely to have engaged with a number of articles, journals and blog posts regarding current educational research and topical issues and have started trialling practical strategies informally in your classroom. You might feel that you now know where to look and how to find what you require. Now, it is important to consider where you wish to go next. Use the areas in the questionnaire where you received a lower score to create a checklist of skills you wish to improve. Consider a reasonable timeframe in which to become a master in this field through diligent reading, continual conversation with others and building your network (outside of your own school and online) to ensure you are open to views that contradict your own. Use the contacts you have created to organise visits to Research Schools and national networking events.

Mostly high ratings

You are in a strong position regarding your knowledge and skills relating to educational research and are in the perfect position to begin sharing this knowledge with others. Remain aware that this is an evolving and continually controversial area, which requires you to stay on the ball and communicative. If you simply sit still then research findings and discussions will bypass you and perhaps even contradict your original understanding. It is vital that you remain open to change and new findings as well as considering new ways to incorporate findings so that student outcomes are improved. You can, however, be confident that you could lead others in beginning their journey by equipping them with the skills you have now developed. Use the training plans and ideas in Part 2 to begin developing your most vital network yet: a network that, if you work together, continue to learn together and keep an open mind, will likely lead to continual development for yourself and ensure progress for your team and students.

Moving forward

Once you've used the self-assessment process to identify where you currently are, it is imperative that you find time to stop and reflect in order to move forward. If there are areas that you need to review then make some time to do this. Go back to the relevant chapter to identify references and suggestions of further reading. It might be that you felt you knew a lot in the chapter already, but every article, paper and review has additional links through which you can build on your knowledge and instigate new discussions.

You may have already started trialling new strategies and read a lot of the research suggested in this book (both that summarised and through links) but now the next step is to implement the process for yourself, from defining the problem to investigating and reading relevant research, implementing it in the classroom and reviewing its impact. The final elements of this journey are summarised in Chapter 8.

As with any change, it is important that you trial it (despite setbacks) for a reasonable period of time and only make one change at a time.

The most important step moving forward is to feel secure in your convictions – to be sure that you feel confident when making a change but also be open to finding some things you don't inherently agree with. It is true that we will tend to find what we are looking for if we look hard enough; however, your job now is not to create a scientific experiment but to ask the right questions based on empirical evidence where possible and observe the effectiveness of your interventions.

Chapter 7 takeaway

Teaching tip

Don't give up your style!

It is tempting when reading about what others do and how they do it to change your style as well as your way of thinking. Most of us have an individual teaching style that has been created (purposefully or otherwise) over thousands of lessons and developed over a number of years. In order to apply a new strategy or idea, you do not need to give up your own style of teaching. If you have ever observed another teacher and thought, 'I might try talking/walking/moving/pointing/laughing like that', due to the success a particular personality trait seemed to have in the classroom, then no doubt you've found yourself in a muddle! Not only will it not fit you or your teaching style but students will be aware that you are not being yourself. So it is vital you maintain your teaching style when adapting your teaching strategies so that you focus purely on the pedagogy and less on performance.

Pass it on

Share your findings

Find an opportunity to share your ideas with staff in your school, preferably in a formal setting like a staff meeting or training session. This could take the format of sharing a piece of educational research you feel others should read – summarising it for them and presenting how you have used it in your own practice to improve outcomes. You could offer to present this to a department group or even the whole staff. If you don't feel happy standing up in front of others, then perhaps you have a department or school newsletter you could contribute to. Either way, it is important to begin sharing your findings and journey as this will inspire you to continue with yours and doubtless find you kindred spirits.

CPD book club recommendation

When Can You Trust the Experts? How to tell good science from bad in education by Daniel T. Willingham (2012)

This text is worth a read as you start to share your ideas and thoughts with others. There is a clear strategy for finding clarity in the sea of research, which can become overwhelming and can occur when discussions develop and more questions are asked than answered.

Bloggers' corner

Check out this TES article on in-house CPD by Nikki Carlin, called 'How our department is taking a DIY approach'.

Link: www.tes.com/news/cpd-how-our-department-taking-diy-approach

TO DO LIST:

- ☐ Complete the self-assessment questionnaire.
- ☐ Reflect on your current knowledge and skills and create a list of the reading you have already done.
- ☐ Reflect on your successes so far, especially the key texts you have read and considered, and tweet your thoughts.
- ☐ Offer to speak to colleagues about your recent reading and discuss the changes you might make to your practice. Be sure to emphasise the longevity of your changes and trialling and only discuss one area at a time.
- ☐ Read the blog post: 'How our department is taking a DIY approach'.
- ☐ Get your hands on a copy of *When Can You Trust The Experts? How to tell good science from bad in education* by Daniel T. Willingham and start reading it.

8

Embedding and developing research-informed practice

As with any change, it is vital to spend time embedding new knowledge and considering how to develop your research-informed practice, and this process can take a great deal of time. It cannot happen overnight and with the reading and research that you have started, you will be aware that research-informed practice is a time-consuming approach and that there will never be an end point where you are fully aware and read-up on all the relevant research at all times. Some may wish this to be the case but, in reality, I believe it is better for teachers to be research informed and make clear they are not trying to be the researchers with all the answers. However, with persistence, there will be a point where you feel confident about how to use research within your teaching, how to apply it to any decision-making and how to find out more if you need to.

The research community is ever evolving and developing so it is also a matter of keeping up to date with the latest arguments and theories. The EEF itself continues to look into how research is being used by teachers and what impact that has in classrooms. The important thing is to ensure that the impact it has on you, your students and your school is not to the detriment of your work–life balance. Whenever you consider making any change, especially one as big as changing your approach to pedagogy and practice as a whole, there are things we can do to make the transition easier for ourselves and others.

By this point, there are a few particulars I am sure you have experienced: you will have disagreed with some of the findings you've read; reread some strategies to check they really are that simple; questioned your and others' previous decisions; and started to wonder whether or not it is easier to live in ignorant bliss instead of embracing a research-informed path! If this is the case, then this is the perfect place to be. This is more likely to be the case if you have embraced the 'improve' section by dedicating some reading time and thinking time to implementing the strategies. If you haven't yet forced yourself (and let's be honest, there is always something else to do or something else that creeps to the top of the never-ending to-do list), then I implore you to do so. And now...

Stop.

No really, pause and give yourself a chance to consider what are the *nagging* issues you have with that one class, that one student, the NQT you mentor, that specific process or policy that constantly trips itself up (homework policies or feedback policies, for example).

By taking the time to consider why this particular focus might need an intervention you are giving yourself a chance of finding a solution. Not a one-size-fits-all, magic-wand-style solution, but a way of stepping back to truly and effectively question what it is you currently do, why you do it and whether or not a small change could make a big difference.

Remind yourself of your answers to the questions originally asked in Chapter 1 and repeated below. We want to ensure that as time goes on, the answers to these develop to include reference to the knowledge you have acquired and the research you will continue to engage with.

- What was the last big decision you made about your teaching practice?
- How quickly did you come to this decision?
- Who or what did you or would you turn to when making a decision about your practice?
- Did you feel confident in your decision-making process?

Embedding research in your classroom

In Chapters 3 and 4, you were encouraged to consider an area to focus on as you read through the research summaries and were provided with sources to engage with. It may be that you want to continue with this idea or that you want to change to a different one. In Chapters 4 to 6, you refined the tools needed for embedding research-informed changes. Now we're going to look at how you can implement the whole process yourself if you should wish to. The focus of this chapter is to give you advice on how to implement change successfully.

First take a look at Fig. 11 for a diagrammatic overview of the whole process of embedding research in your practice through informal action research.

You may already have an area of development in mind based on your reading throughout the book. For example: what strategy would help my students work more independently? What classroom-based intervention might improve my students' reading ages? How can I improve the rate and quality of students' homework?

To help decide upon your area of focus for this term or year, ask yourself:

- What areas of your teaching do you deem to be your strongest? Why?
- Have your areas for development changed since you started teaching?
- If so, in what way have they changed? If not, why do you think they have remained the same?
- What element of pedagogy would you like to develop the most?
- Why does this area stand out to you?
- Is this a reoccurring theme or a more recent issue?

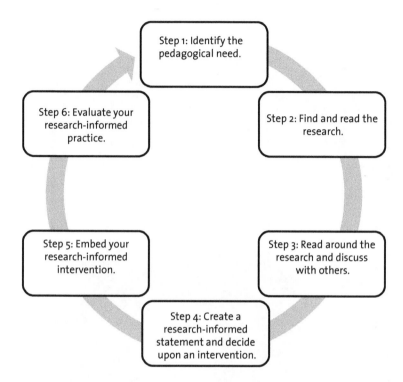

Fig. 11 The process of embedding research in your practice through informal action research

- What have you already done to tackle this area for development?
- Is this merely your opinion or have you learnt about this area through discussion with others (perhaps through lesson observation feedback)?
- Is the problem with the pedagogical approach or with a particular class or subgroup of students (for example, boys, Pupil Premium students or students with high prior attainment)?

To help you consider which area to focus on, you could look at the pedagogy focus infographic (Fig. 12), which was created by our teaching and learning team and my amazingly artistic Director of Teaching and Learning, Siân Cumming, to encourage our staff to consider every element of their teaching when deciding on their focus. We gave staff around 12 weeks to truly consider where they wanted to put their focus in the following term, so this is not a 'close your eyes and pick an area' exercise but something to consider carefully.

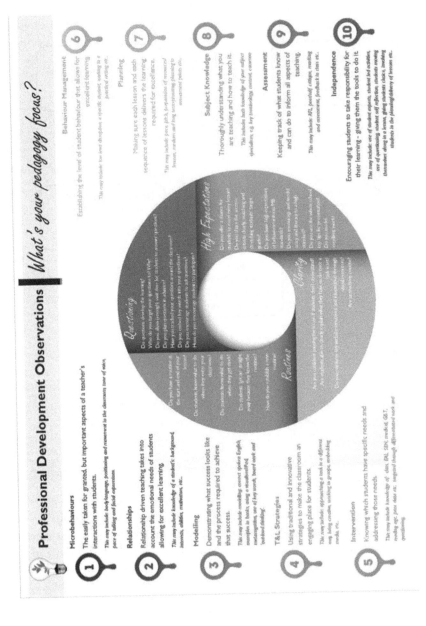

Fig. 12 Pedagogy focus infographic

Writing your PICO/PIO statement

In Chapter 3, I explained that a good way to begin a research project is by identifying a need (step 1) before spending time researching and discussing the problem in order to find a suitable intervention. Then, I would suggest turning your thoughts thus far into a PICO question or statement. Whether you create a statement or question does not truly matter – essentially they encourage the same thinking, although we found that writing your intention as a statement helped participants consider the process as an action and encouraged participation.

As a reminder, a PICO statement (or question) is defined as:

P – Problem with pedagogy: Specify which group of students you will focus on.
I – Intervention or strategy: What intervention are you going to trial after considerable thought and reading?
C – Comparison (not always needed to begin with): Which class or group will you compare your outcomes to?
O – Outcome: What would you like the outcome to look like if the intervention is successful?

To begin with, you might want to trial an intervention without a clear comparison or the comparison might be the same group without the intervention but earlier on in the school year. The PICO statement or question would then be a PIO statement or question. If possible, do try to have a comparison group, but as no one is suggesting this will be a fully scientific experiment, it is not detrimental to your engagement if you do not.

Examples of possible PICO statements:

I want to improve my modelling with my Year 4 class by using WAGOLL compared to a class not using WAGOLL in order to improve students' quality of extended written responses.

I want to improve the use of peer assessment with Year 9 by using Ron Berger's peer critique compared to a class using WWW and EBI in order to ensure students can successfully and accurately critique their own and each other's work.

I want to improve the recall and retention of my Year 13 class by using distributed practice compared to a class not using distributed practice in order to improve students' examination scores.

I want to improve my questioning with my Year 10 class by using hinge questions compared to a class not using hinge questions in order to identify students' common misconceptions and address them in a timely manner.

Examples of possible PICO questions:

For Year 5 students, how does the use of whole-class marking, compared to a class whose work I mark individually, ensure students receive relevant and effective feedback?

For low-attaining students in Year 7, how does implementing metacognitive techniques, compared to a class who are not explicitly taught using metacognitive techniques, ensure students can successfully approach mathematical questions?

For Year 10, how does deliberate use of image recall sheets as starters, compared to a class who have starters linked to that lesson, ensure students successfully remember subject content over time?

Use these examples to create a bespoke statement or question (whichever you prefer) through which you can engage with your identified research on a more practical level, whilst always bearing in mind that this is your method of engagement. As David Didau (2015a) writes, his reading of research 'was useful because it allowed me to test a theory that was underpinned by empirical evidence'. Remember, you are the teacher and the scientists and researchers are pointing us towards the right direction but not showing us exactly how to get there.

Evaluate your research-informed practice

At this point in time, there are some ways in which you can begin to evaluate the impact your research-informed practice is having on students and the impact on others.

The EEF 'DIY self-evaluation' website can be used to guide you through a deliberate evaluation process and requires you to consider your question or statement in advance. It provides you with hands-on support and summaries, although you will need a comparison and will need to decide on your measures before and after before completing it. Get started at: https://educationendowmentfoundation.org.uk/tools/diy-guide/getting-started.

More informally, you can collate evidence to consider the impact of your intervention through assessment data, marking and feedback given, student voice questionnaires, journals or logs of a series of lessons, photos and videos or observations of your teaching. All of these can give you an indication of how effective the intervention was. You need to be aware of your own bias and beliefs that will likely influence your perception of how successful your own project was. If all of the above are deemed evidence then you will be able to create evidence, however legitimately, that supports your intervention. This is the same as searching for research that supports a theory or strategy you hope to use. We have to be cautious and have to ask ourselves:

- What was the intervention? How rigorous was I in embedding it into my teaching?
- Why did I choose this intervention? Why did I not choose a different one? How does this demonstrate my beliefs in education and preferred methodology?
- How did I measure the starting point and final outcomes? How can I adapt the intervention to better suit my students' needs or my teaching style?

Often, in evaluation, we focus purely on the 'what': what we did and when we did it. As part of an ongoing process, try to focus on the why and how. It is impossible to be objective when completing your own action research project – which is why the time you spend considering and investigating the validity and credibility of the scientific research that influenced your choice of intervention is so important. By ensuring you pick credible evidence to point you in the right direction, you at least know that you are considering an intervention worthy of your time and that of your students.

Implementing change successfully

When it comes to embedding a new idea or strategy, there are some elements we must consider at all times. Without considering some of these factors, change cannot be sustained and you will quickly find yourself unconsciously falling back into old habits. In his book *Leading Change*, John Kotter (2012) presents his eight-step process to successful change. It is a model that can be applied to changes within education on a small or large scale. Below, I consider some of the steps, applying them to the specific issue of embedding your own practice with a view to forming effective habits when implementing new ideas.

Consider why

In order to successfully embed any new idea or framework you need to consider all the reasons for *why* you are making a change. It is vital that you consider your approach and feel confident about it before passing your ideas on to others. If you are considering discussing ideas with colleagues in a more formal setting and seeking to inform them about how they can become research informed, possibly in the form of the training plans that follow in Part 2, then you need to be convinced you are doing the right thing.

In order to achieve change successfully, Kotter (2012) suggests you require a sense of urgency. Aside from perhaps the middle week of the summer holidays, I struggle to think of a time during my career in teaching when everything didn't feel urgent or a change necessary! However, some situations prove more urgent than others when it comes to change being required.

Factors that have led to a sense of urgency for change in recent years include:

- the introduction of terminal examinations at GCSE
- new specifications for Key Stages 2 and 4
- the removal of levels at Key Stage 3
- funding cuts to the arts subjects
- increased student numbers
- the new GCSE grading system (9–1)
- the need for improved retention and retrieval
- the requirement of a better work–life balance for teachers.

Before deciding on the approach you are going to take to moving forward with your research-informed practice and the changes you'd like to implement in your team or department, make a list like the one above. Make sure it is specific to your key stage, school and subject and focus on concerns that you feel have recently created a sense of urgency for change in your own teaching, department or school. In doing so, you are considering whether or not change is required and whether or not you can justify it fully to yourself and others. I am not encouraging you to come up with problems or issues that don't exist, but I find it unlikely that even schools that have not had to conform to some of the above changes won't have ongoing challenges that may require a new and different approach.

Once you are aware that there is a sense of urgency surrounding the areas you want to focus on to change, and that developing your practice may help to find solutions to these issues, it is more likely you will be convinced in your purpose and therefore feel validated in your ongoing efforts.

Bumps in the road

When embedding and developing new practice, there will inevitably be bumps in the road. Being too keen could definitely be one of them! However, this shouldn't mean you should give up on your intention to change and improve. Instead, as mentioned above, you just need to stop, slow down and consider what comes next. Sometimes, there are too many ideas to consider at once and after all the reading and networking you have done it is difficult to know where to start. This is why deciding on a specific issue and action research project can be a good place to start.

With an area as large as trying to become research informed, and even larger if you are hoping to engage and train others to do so as well, you need to be realistic. No Research School became a Research School overnight. No teacher considered an expert in this area became so by writing one blog or reading one article on a Sunday evening. It takes time. Convincing yourself and others that reading and discussing research can save you time and effort in the long run is difficult. Most days, it seems improbable that you will catch up on what is going on in the world let alone complete your marking and planning as well, so asking colleagues to spend time seemingly just sitting and reading can seem like a waste. This is another bump you need to overcome and, considering you may need to read a lot to come to a decision or solution, it can seem unmanageable. This is why it is important to use the helpful hints and practical resources to engage with research detailed in Chapters 4 and 5 without wearing yourself thin before you can see the benefit.

Further bumps in embedding research-informed practice in your classroom include doing something that you feel goes against the grain. If you are considering changing your teaching strategies and you think the changes may contradict the school or department's policies, it is important to be honest with those around you on whom this might impact. For example, if your school insists on using learning styles to differentiate and due to your reading you are against this, then rather than become the maverick teacher, you should use this as an opportunity to trial something new, evaluate the findings and present them in a considered manner. All of this should be prefaced with a discussion and reasoning as to why. Doubtless, the strategies and ideas you may now disagree with were only put in place with good intentions for student outcomes and therefore it is important that this bump in the road doesn't lead to animosity or isolation from your colleagues. As a classroom teacher, leader or both, this will encourage others to see you as open and considerate when implementing changes, rather than dogmatic and shortsighted.

In my own experience of wishing to get things moving quickly and up and running, I now realise that bumps can be good things. They can send you in the right direction so don't give up when problems come along. Take a step back and remember that good things come to those who wait!

Creating your vision

Regardless of your position in school, creating a vision is important for moving forward with something new. Whether that's envisaging what an after-school club could achieve, what your role might look like in two years' time or how your department will approach curriculum planning over the next term, you need a goal and personal targets. The term 'vision' can seem cheesy. I used to draw badly sketched glasses on a notepad whenever I heard it at a conference but that was before I realised the importance of knowing where you want to go and why. So despite the overly used term, a vision is key and ensuring that your vision works alongside that of others and your school's is just as important as having one.

Considering whether or not research-informed practice can become your approach to teaching and learning at all matters. Then considering how you can demonstrate this in a day-to-day sense as well as a more philosophical way needs to be part of creating your vision. It is all well and good believing in an approach to teaching, but if the pressures on your current practice mean you will never be able to implement any of your beliefs or ideals then something does need to change. Moreover, for the benefit of your students it is important you are consistent with the school's approach to teaching and learning. You should create a vision that can adapt as needs be and ensure you reflect on your vision often. Preferably, this vision can become a shared vision where those involved volunteer their ideas and you adapt yours too.

I originally wrote a vision for my role as head of research and more recently as a head of department. The first draft was entirely selfish and written on my own, but in discussions with others it has evolved into something better than I could have hoped. My finalised vision is revisited each year and adapted based on my department's thoughts and feelings at the time.

When deciding upon a summary of your vision, brevity and avoiding too many modal verbs is key. If your vision includes too many 'could' or 'should' statements, you might find yourself drifting away from what seems impossible. I believe a vision should be possible, attainable and achievable if the right conditions are created. It is definitely worth writing down your ideas about how you wish to develop your research-informed practice, whether or not anyone is going to ask to see it. You can do this by asking some of the following questions:

- What do you hope to achieve in the short term through engaging with research-informed practice?
- What do you hope to achieve in the long term through engaging with research-informed practice?

- What values do you hold dear to your teaching practice? How can you ensure these remain in your vision?
- If you developed as you wish, describe how your teaching or leadership would look different in five years' time.
- What impact do you want your change in approach to have on your students and their outcomes?
- What efforts have you made so far to engage with sources, resources and networking so that you know what you do want to take forward and what works for you?
- Do you feel you have done enough to know what you like and dislike?

Developing alongside others

Developing yourself and your own vision is vital to beginning to work with others. There are many benefits of working with people who are more or less informed than you, as they bring to light new questions and ideas you may not have considered. In Part 2, you will find specific training plans for those at different stages of their careers and tips about how to work with others on creating a research-informed environment in your school. Before we get to that, below are some short pieces of advice about how to begin working with different groups of staff in order to engage them in research-informed practice and improve everyone's knowledge of research including your own.

Your department or key stage

- Use your shared knowledge and goals to explore new territory. For example, pick a particular subject-specific or age-specific area that you know requires work and suggest a research-informed solution.
- Provide the research evidence but don't make people feel threatened – use the evidence as a discussion point and ask for feedback.
- Don't insist that all changes are based on your ideas. Come up with, for example, two options that you wish to trial and split the group into two. This way people can choose which strategy they go with and how far they push it. They will feel engaged by the process but not forced into the decision.
- If you would like to implement a whole-school or whole-department change, drip-feed ideas through different mediums – planning sessions, short presentations, newsletters, etc. One meeting does not always lead to the perfect outcome.
- Listen to experience. There are likely to be colleagues in your department or key stage who are more experienced than you in some ways. Listen to them

and consider their points carefully – if this really has been tried and tested before, ask how and why it failed and what they would do differently.

Outside your department or key stage

- Listen to other areas of expertise. If you are being asked to work with colleagues with whom you do not share the same unique area of knowledge or specialism then ensure you respect this. The key is to ask questions so that you can learn as much from them as you can. Ask them, 'How might X work in your particular area?'
- Avoid making assumptions. As an English teacher, I dread to think how many times I have heard people tell me that English is easier as it's all about skills not knowledge, or how I should teach reading based on the way they learnt to read. Every subject or key stage has its stereotypes and I am sure that as teachers we fuel these in cross-curricular discussions. Try to avoid making assumptions and instead ask honestly how the evidence you have found could be applied in a range of subjects.
- Outside of your department, you may need to work harder to build strong relationships like those you've already built with your departmental colleagues. Trust is key to encouraging change and needs to be built quickly. Encourage an emotional engagement with your ideas and remove barriers early on – whether they be related to time, money or confidence.

Working informally with colleagues

- Encourage others close to you to give things a go – enlist what Kotter (2012) calls a 'volunteer army'.
- Ensure that you identify those who could contribute to moving things forward by spotting those who are keen, supportive and on board early on. Ask them for their support and advice so that they feel part of the change.
- Make it simple. If you are going to ask people to work on something additional and potentially time-consuming, then you need to keep it as simple as possible. Could you agree to meet once a fortnight at a local café or pub to discuss the latest findings? Ensure that you provide the information for them but also ask others to contribute so that it becomes more of an informal working group than a rebellion!
- Don't threaten the *status quo* on purpose. Consider a small change or an area of interest that you believe could only be seen as a positive and beneficial response to an issue. For example, a group of colleagues from various subjects might want to look at ways to make revision and retention of information across their subjects similar and more streamlined. This does not require much more than

cross-moderation and discussion before agreeing on the next steps and it can be done in an informal way without minutes, notes and to-do lists being created, so that all are engaged in a purposeful yet unthreatening mission.

If you're interested in learning more about developing change, I recommend you read *Leading Change* by John P. Kotter (2012) and watch Kevin Bartle's talk from the conference Teaching and Learning Takeover 2013 about teacher autonomy and being brave enough to make your own change: https://dailygenius.wordpress.com/2013/10/20/the-gruffalo-an-allegory-for-trojan-mice.

Final steps

Considering all of the issues and next steps listed in this chapter, it is now time to be the one who makes the change and continues with what they believe in and the vision they have created. Once you have considered why you want to continue and who you want to work with and when, you can spend time ensuring you're happy with your own understanding and practice and then perhaps embark upon sharing this more widely and formally with others, using the training plans in Part 2. Remember, this is a long journey but a worthwhile one.

Chapter 8 takeaway

Teaching tip
Action research
Spend some time looking at projects that have already been completed in your school or at others and talk through the issues with action research. Use the EEF guidance and self-evaluation to make sure you have clear steps ahead. Give yourself a clear timeframe in which to implement your action research but also evaluate it (I suggest at least two terms!).

Pass it on
Offer to lead an informal discussion on a particular area in your next department or whole-school meeting. Ensure there is time to lead and give others time to talk. This is not so much a presentation on what you know but a way of asking questions, perhaps about a particular area of change (see the sense of urgency list!) and how it has been dealt with. If you don't fancy doing this in your school, offer to lead a weekly chat on Twitter where you can ask a number of set questions and respond from

the comfort of your own home. Consider buddying up with a friend if you are not sure you want to go it alone. #UKEdChat and #UKResEdChat are worth getting in touch with.

CPD book club recommendation

Having considered your journey thus far and focused on embedding research, now find out about cognitive science and its application in the classroom in detail by reading: *Make It Stick: The science of successful learning* by Peter Brown, Henry L. Roediger III and Mark A. McDaniel (2014).

Bloggers' corner

Log into TES to read this article by Milly Nevill called 'Action research in the classroom: a quick guide'.

Link: www.tes.com/news/action-research-classroom-quick-guide

TO DO LIST:

❑ Create a list of issues and situations that may be seen as creating a sense of urgency in your own context and therefore could require or justify changes.

❑ Plan and design your own PICO statement or question.

❑ Share your PICO statement or question with others.

❑ Consider how you will implement the intervention and begin to collate evidence prior to embedding the intervention.

❑ Spend some time looking at the EEF self-evaluation website to guide the process.

❑ Identify your volunteer army – those who can help support you in your mission, as they are engaged, keen and supportive.

❑ Identify key elements of research you could share with others that would not be overwhelming.

❑ Offer to lead a discussion that will gather others' views about an issue and offer up some evidence as a starting point for new solutions.

Part 2

Train others

1 Preparing and planning your CPD

A smorgasbord of CPD

As in many professions, continuing professional development (CPD) is something that we are all made aware of when we enter teaching. In our formative teaching years, we are keen to take part but too often, once the form filling and panic of our training and NQT years have melted into a hazy memory, CPD sessions take on a new meaning and can incite a wide variety of responses depending on our previous experiences.

Our experiences of CPD sessions may range from never having taken part in a CPD session other than those we are expected to attend (INSET days) to having organised and arranged our own CPD outside of our own organisations and perhaps attending conferences or TeachMeets in our own time.

The wide variety of CPD opportunities currently available may lead you to believe that one style of CPD is better than another. You may have access to voluntary after-school sessions, have taken part in INSET days where you organise your own CPD, enjoyed academy CPD days, visited local universities and speakers, listened to podcasts, taken part in an educational book club, attended weekend conferences and spoken at TeachMeets *or* you may have done none of the above in the past five, ten or even 15 years. You may be required to complete a set amount of hours each term, you may thoroughly enjoy doing 'extra' training at the weekends or you may see CPD as something to 'get away with' by simply attending INSET days (in which you play bingo waiting for a straight line of buzz words recently coined by Ofsted – *'rapid and sustained', anyone?*). Whatever your current appetite for CPD or that of those you wish to train, it is essential to remember that everyone's previous experiences of CPD will determine how they approach your training and what they wish to get out of it.

Many of the CPD sessions suggested could be considered 'external' CPD – the highlight of which might be the free lukewarm coffee and subsidised sandwiches for lunch! External CPD typically refers to sessions that take place outside of your own school run by an organisation or individual not associated with your individual context but it could also refer to a visiting speaker. In the traditional sense, these sessions are those you may be sent on by your school to attend on a weekday requiring cover and travel costs. Such sessions have recently suffered a bad press with costs rising and the impact on student outcomes often unclear. Have you ever heard of someone going to a training session and then never hearing anything about what they heard, read or learnt on their 'day out'? I know that I have even been the person to attend courses elsewhere and struggle to find the relatability and information to bring back to my own department or school. The reason this might happen is that a course or session may have been well titled and well intentioned but it often may not be relevant to your setting at that particular time. I know that I have attended numerous meetings and events and thought, 'That would have been useful two years ago but not anymore' or the trusty favourite: 'That wouldn't work at my school because...' Therefore the only outcome of my CPD is a long to-do list made up of all the other things I could have done with my time. Some of the best CPD events I have attended (both externally and internally) have resulted in me making a different type of list: lists of discussions I wish to have with others, lists of questions, lists of changes and lists of things to stop doing. More often than not, these events have been the free DIY events or in-house sessions that I have dragged myself to after a long day or long week but never regretted going to once there.

In recent years, there has been considerable growth in weekend and after-school events being run by teachers for teachers. This DIY landscape seems to be on the rise as more and more schools struggle to afford the costs necessary to send staff to CPD sessions during the school day and as the growth of such events becomes better known. As an organiser of one such weekend CPD event, I am undoubtedly biased towards their purpose and place in the development of teaching practice, but for one particular reason I have found these DIY events more affecting and purposeful than others. Simply, I have found there to be a more informal and discussion-based format at these events, which often allows attendees to question and relate the key ideas to their own setting more easily. The feedback from our first Teaching and Learning Takeover event in 2013 was primarily about the positive and relaxed atmosphere delegates experienced, allowing them to share and discuss their thoughts and ideas freely – something that is perhaps not experienced during a more traditional, corporate-style CPD session on a rainy Thursday afternoon in a grey council building in Bristol city centre.

The most engaging and helpful CPD sessions I have been to (internally and externally) have been run by those who currently teach or only recently left the profession and are therefore aware of the current pressures and constraints of our educational world as it stands. Moreover, I have found that the most helpful sessions are ones where there is time to discuss, to question and therefore to relate what you have taken away to your own circumstances. Whether you are organising anything from a short in-house CPD session to a large national event, I would suggest including time in every session for discussion between delegates and speaker and, if possible, just simply between delegates who wish to share their knowledge and experiences with others.

Understandably, there are arguments against the rise of DIY CPD. These arguments focus particularly on the weekend CPD opportunities, suggesting that not all teachers have the opportunity to take part and that the rise in such events could lead schools to ignore their responsibility to develop their own staff. These arguments are all understandable but I believe the greatest lesson we can take away from the developments in how we partake in CPD is that despite cuts to CPD budgets there remains a strong desire to develop and improve, and I believe that the more informal style often found at these DIY events can be easily brought into any in-house CPD sessions, leading staff to engage more effectively and more genuinely with the process.

Why 'where' matters

The reason that 'where' matters is rather simple when it comes to sharing research-informed findings and ideas. There is no one-size-fits-all strategy to use or a fixed methodology in which to immerse yourself that will ensure you are research informed and that your school's practices are all research informed. It is an evolving process that requires thought, time and discussion, and this is not something you can get on a one-day course. The resources, tips and advice provided in Part 1 are a starting point and your research journey will undoubtedly evolve as educational research becomes more widely spread, as government policy develops and as debates about approaches to teaching and learning rage on. Therefore, although there are extremely valuable events at which people will talk about the research they have used in their own educational setting, nothing will beat talking about these findings in your own setting. This is not to say that you shouldn't seek out further opportunities to see what others have done with the same findings. Events such as ResearchEd conferences and many other smaller, more local events make this possible – you can listen to other teachers discuss their use of the educational research and the changes made to their practice, but having done this it is then key that you return to your setting and speak to your colleagues about how this could work for you.

Whatever your current beliefs about the purpose and effectiveness of the CPD you have taken part in, having taken an interest in and started your own research-informed journey it is time to share it with others and see how far you can take it. I would argue that in this day and age of limited CPD budgets and schools having to consider carefully the cost and impact of cover, it makes the most sense to consider in-house CPD from the very beginning – particularly when focusing on a specific piece of evidence or advice that does not need expensive or time-consuming resources in order to ensure it has an impact on outcomes. In-house CPD does not need to mean round tables of tired teachers completing diamond nine activities. CPD might look short, suitable and subtle. CPD sessions might look like a discussion or debate. CPD sessions might even be silent reading or a series of questions you discuss at length. CPD is never one size fits all, which is why there are a range of training plans to suit different experiences, positions and interests in the following chapter.

Regardless of how CPD sessions might look from the outside, they should be informed and considered by those leading them and primarily they should only take place to help improve student outcomes through improving teacher practice rather than take place for the sake of someone's teaching and learning responsibility (TLR) or as a directed-time activity. CPD is far too essential to school improvement to be decided upon the night or week before. CPD can, if done badly, be simply considered another way of using up teachers' precious time and you do not want your training sessions to be considered in this way. Therefore it is important that you consider what your CPD sessions might look like – make them inclusive, make them considered and make them matter if you want to get results from them.

In 2017, at the Wellington Festival of Education, I listened to Andy Tharby and Shaun Allison describe how their in-house CPD stemmed from always considering the wide variety of opinions on teaching from their staff and the 'wisdom of great teachers' they had worked with over the years. It struck me at this point that every school has the tools to make the developments they described – almost all schools have experienced teachers who have seen trends and fashions come and go working alongside teachers who astutely consider their practice regardless of their experience. It is a mix of these teachers that you need to engage in your CPD sessions on using research in the classroom. I am fully aware of the irony that I thought this whilst attending an external CPD opportunity – on page 180, I will discuss how some external opportunities could be considered for yourself in order to develop your own interests in research and leading others in this area, all whilst creating in-house CPD opportunities for others.

If you can, as Andy and Shaun explained, consider the views of others and combine them with research-informed discussion, then you are likely to have a winning formula on your hands compared to if you stroll in as the self-anointed expert in research-informed practice. When considering running in-house CPD sessions, it is vital to think about your audience carefully and not to restrict access to some sessions unnecessarily, so that staff who have lots to share – particularly those who are more experienced – don't feel excluded. Of course, there are times when you will want to focus your CPD session towards particular groups of staff, but do not consider yourself the expert in the room nor the only one who is truly interested; it is vital that you speak to those who know the strengths and weaknesses of your staff and that you consider the wisdom of others before and whilst delivering content. CPD sessions should create questions as well as answers and opportunities as well as outcomes. You can find Andy and Shaun's presentation on their blog: https://classteaching.wordpress.com/2017/06/25/growing-a-culture-of-great-teaching.

Think, pair, (now it's time to) share

The purpose of Part 1 was to develop your own ways of engaging with, reading and digesting external research. It may be that there is an argument that the best way to then further understand evidence and research in education is to go the source of the research to question and explore it further – in order to continually develop your professional understanding of it. However, it is unlikely that the majority of the evidence you engage with has a course or seminar related to it. Much of the research you might engage with could be decades old and those who conducted the experiments or wrote the analysis may not be in the field of sharing their thoughts and evidence further – if they are and it is an area of particular interest to you and you believe it could positively impact student outcomes then it may be worth investigating, but this does not have to entail an expensive CPD outing for one or two staff alone. Once you have individually explored the relevant research you believe could impact your teaching (and that of your colleagues) and students' learning, it is time to pair up with another person and consider their point of view. Many of the takeaway tips in Part 1 suggested you share your thoughts and practice with others. For example, in Chapter 5, page 100, I suggest sharing your thoughts on a particular paper or finding in a department meeting or newsletter, and in Chapter 6, page 132, you're encouraged to find a friend and invite them into your classroom to observe a particular strategy. Hopefully, having completed one or more of these tasks to pass your knowledge on, you are now in the position to share your findings and thoughts with others, and therefore completing a CPD session on research alone may not be the best way forward if your purpose is to envelop others in your passion for research-informed practice.

With your primary source being the research itself, CPD sessions involving research should focus on how the research could work in your context or indeed why it might not. In order to consider your own context, and how this research could inform your own practice to improve student performance and outcomes, it makes sense to consider reading and exploring the research alongside those you work with whilst sat in your own school. Rather than searching high and low for an expensive course with a guest speaker in a faraway city, it would be much more beneficial to use your number one resource (the staff) to their full potential and engage them in research and evidence without extra cost or hassle.

If at all possible, consider discussing your CPD preparations with others. Even if you have been charged with leading the CPD in this area, you should discuss and plan with others, gaining an insight into the possible tangents and questions that could come up – not in order to avoid them, but in order to embrace them. If you are part of a team leading on CPD or have been asked to discuss a particular area with staff, then it is important that you use the wisdom of those around you to support you and perhaps to lead parts of the session. It is important that CPD allows staff from all departments and levels of experience and confidence a platform to share what they do well. I have also seen how extraordinary it is to hear from a quiet and unassuming member of staff about their experiences and findings, and see them both grow in confidence and gain a new-found respect from their colleagues who were unaware of their expertise and diligence prior to them taking part in or leading an aspect of CPD. Sharing the task of leading CPD with others will ensure that you do not feel alone in your endeavours and will also ensure that you are working with others in creating a sense of purpose built upon your school's specific strengths and needs, which is extremely powerful and will help you in moving towards a research-informed culture.

Top tip

Depending on your role, you may feel that you require your own further professional development in the area of research in education before you can run CPD sessions for others. There are a number of courses you could look at further should you wish to develop yourself in this area. I do not believe that not having a particular accreditation should stop you from sharing your thoughts, findings and outcomes with others but there are some programmes out there that you could investigate. If the location and timings work for you then I would certainly recommend the Research Leader in Education Award, an award programme supported by Sheffield Hallam University (https://researchersinschools.org/current-participants/2015-cohort/rleaward). For shorter CPD opportunities and research lead training programmes, visit the websites of the current Research Schools through https://educationendowmentfoundation.org.uk/scaling-up-evidence/research-schools and click on 'training' and 'events' on each of the Research Schools' websites. I would recommend doing this if you are looking for training local to you.

Having a clear vision

The term 'vision' was first visited in Chapter 8, page 168, when we explored how to excel in and embed your own goals and wishes regarding your research-informed practice. Considering a vision that will involve others fully and that you wish to have regarding the purpose of your CPD is slightly different. Instead of considering simply what you want to occur in your own practice and what your classroom will look like in five years' time, you need to change and widen your perspective to consider what you want others to take away from the CPD you will endeavour to provide. It is important for all the reasons stated in Chapter 8 to have a clear vision and, this time, to consider fully the impact of your decisions on all stakeholders. From watching others develop and implement CPD plans, it is evident when someone simply wants you to do something exactly as they desire or when they are truly invested in making the development a two-way process. You need to consider how your vision might be expressed but not dictated through the CPD you would like others to take part in. You must also consider how any vision for a successful CPD programme to improve the use of research-informed practice sits alongside your school's ethos and core values. There will need to be a number of conversations with those who lead your school's vision and development plan (likely your headteacher) if you wish to push forward a research-informed CPD programme.

When building any vision, but particularly one that will involve influencing and changing the habits and patterns of others, it is important to consider where you have been and where you are now. I would advise asking staff to share their current understanding with you in some way – either formally or informally depending on your role, number of staff and purpose. The key information you need in order to successfully plan any CPD sessions or long-term strategy includes:

- staff's prior training and understanding of educational research
- how staff might have previously used educational research in the classroom
- how this information has been acquired and when
- staff perspective and beliefs about approaches to teaching and learning
- staff's queries and concerns
- how these responses vary depending on staff experience and position in school.

There are many ways in which school leaders and CPD leaders work together to build and share a vision with others. I cannot claim to be an expert in this area as I do not lead on CPD in my school nor am I a senior leader; however, I believe I have seen it done well and know that there are similarities between leading change and a vision at any level. Having created and implemented a plan to achieve an evidence-informed vision at a department level, I believe the following key questions could be applied before embarking on a CPD programme to ensure that the focus remains on what matters: student outcomes.

1. Why is there a desire to change?
2. Why do you wish for teaching to be research informed?

3. When the CPD programme is implemented and acted upon, how will things look different in terms of:

- the attitudes of staff?
- outcomes for students?
- discussions about teaching and learning?

Audience and purpose

As anyone who has taught any type of writing task knows, you need to know and understand your audience and purpose before you write. It is exactly the same rule for presentations and requires you to consider well in advance who you are talking to and why. In the following chapter of training plans, you will find a range of suggested CPD sessions that could be adapted for different groups of staff, but the following advice could then be used to tailor a particular session or approach for your school and context. It might be that you have particular responsibility for a group of teachers such as NQTs and you wish to tailor a number of sessions to them. In which case, take on board some of the advice below before implementing a session that is aimed towards leadership or all staff, as no doubt you will need to change a few things.

Before any session, in order to correctly decide upon your style and approach, there are some basic questions you should ask yourself and those you are running the session for and with – in the exact same way as you would plan a lesson, plan your CPD sessions to avoid misconceptions, the correct use of time and successful outcomes:

1. Who is the session aimed at and why?
2. What prior knowledge do they already have in this area?
3. How could you find this out before or during the session?
4. What do you want them to understand by the end of the session?
5. What three things would you like them to take away from the session?
6. What is the long-term plan?
7. How does this session fit into your long-term planning?
8. Who would be the best person to lead this session and why?

Advice for running CPD targeted at NQTs and recently qualified teachers

- Ensure that this group of teachers are aware well in advance of the sessions you want them to attend. NQTs in particular have a lot on, including paperwork, which can vary depending on their training provider. A schedule at the start of each year or term would help with this.

- Ensure the training is targeted. For both these groups of teachers, it might be worth beginning with the key principles of teaching, which they are still getting to grips with.
- Avoid overwhelming or overcomplicating the tasks.
- Ensure that any training that takes place is discussed with curriculum mentors and NQT mentors so that they are aware of what their mentees are doing and can continue discussions with them.
- Ensure there is an opportunity for questions to be asked at a later date. Teachers within this group may not immediately have questions but when they later go on to experience a situation, they should have the opportunity to question how it links to their CPD training. Keeping channels of communication open is important for everyone's development.

Advice for running CPD targeted at experienced teachers

- Be conscious of timings and tasks. Experienced teachers are likely to have other responsibilities in the school and therefore already have to-do lists as long as their arm. Consider the possible outcomes of your session – how can you ensure it is engaging and worthwhile?
- In order to do this, identify three to four teachers whom you would expect to take part in this training and ask them for their advice. Ask them what would make the sessions most relevant and timely. You don't want to feel as though you are wasting anyone's time after you have worked so hard preparing.
- Be honest – it is important to be honest at all times but when talking to colleagues who may have more experience than you, it is even more important that you don't present yourself as the expert at all costs. Doubtless, there will be people in your session who know more about areas of your presentation or have more experience to draw upon – use them by directing questions towards them or asking them to contribute in advance.

Advice for running CPD targeted at subject, stage or department leaders

- As with experienced teachers, middle leaders will be spinning a lot of plates. Ensure you acknowledge this and don't be tempted to set more complex tasks purely because of a person's position in the school.
- With a complex topic such as research, it is important that you allow the reading the time it deserves. Rather than sending out reading in advance to middle leaders, you may wish to provide reading time in the session. Everyone will respond kindly to some dedicated reading time – if you simply hand

reading out and ask them to do it later there is every chance it will end up at the bottom of a large pile of other, often more urgent tasks.

- As with any session, consider in your mind one or two people you hope to aim your thoughts and key ideas towards. Personalising your audience will help you to engage with them.
- Avoid lengthy debates that focus on department or key stage politics or issues – although this might come up, you don't want to engage with the idea that an area of research or evidence-based strategy would not work in a certain subject or key stage without further information. Instead, consider in advance how you use examples to make it relevant to all involved.

Advice for including SLT in CPD sessions

- Rather than running CPD sessions strictly for senior leadership, consider the importance of SLT (senior leadership team) presence at training sessions. For many staff, this validates the importance of a session, so when you have the training schedule and your responsibilities or contributions in place, ensure you share a schedule with your SLT and invite them along.
- You may wish to have certain members of SLT at certain sessions, depending on their responsibilities. A formal and polite invitation will likely be accepted as long as it is sent out in a timely fashion.
- Make clear to your SLT that you would like them there in order to encourage other staff but also to learn from their experience. Once again, it is important in these sessions that everyone shares regardless of their position.
- Ensure that SLT are in sessions that are focused on leading others so that they are able to guide and support the next generation of leaders too.

It is likely that you have experienced CPD being something that is done to you yet hopefully you have also experienced CPD in which your thoughts and ideas have been listened to and perhaps have been the driving force. In the following training plans, you will see that participants are often asked to complete tasks prior to the sessions themselves or sometimes during the sessions. This engagement seeks to encourage those involved to invest, consider and adapt the session to suit their own needs. As these sessions are based on the wide topic of research-informed practice, you are not putting yourself or anyone leading these sessions in the driving seat alone; in the training plans you will see lots of time for discussion, questions and reflection.

2 Training plans

The training plans in this chapter are based on a number of principles, which sometimes cross over or could be considered separately:

- introducing the idea of research to staff
- introducing specific research strategies and findings to staff
- an approach to action research and engaging staff in improving their own research-informed practice.

There are 19 training plans, amounting to over 20 hours of CPD. I have split them into six separate sections to help you find the sessions that will be of most use in your context:

Introducing research training plans (one hour each)

1. A brief guide to research
2. Getting to grips with sources of evidence
3. How to approach evidence

Twilight sessions: embedding research-informed strategies (one hour each)

1. Memory and recall
2. Metacognition in the classroom
3. Rosenshine's principles of instruction
4. Internal TeachMeet sharing practical ideas based on research
5. Evaluating your research-informed journey

Quick weekly training sessions: introducing research-based thinking to staff through strategies (15–30 minutes each)

1. A research-informed approach to homework
2. Knowledge organisers
3. Low-stakes quizzing
4. Whole-class feedback

Training for leaders (one hour each)

1. Leading a research-informed team: how to get involved
2. Leading a research-informed team: follow the leader
3. Leading a research-informed team: start spreading the news

Action research guide (one hour to one hour 30 minutes each)

1. Considering action research
2. Creating an action research question
3. Reflecting on your action research

INSET day (six hours)

Introducing research training plans (one hour each)

Overview of the sessions

In this first set of plans, the information from Chapters 1 to 4 has been transformed into three one-hour training plans. Preferably these would be run separately with enough time in between to allow thinking, application and embedding new ideas. These training plans are aimed at those with a real interest in becoming more research informed but this does not require staff to be in any particular leadership position. It is just as important, if not more important, that staff new to the profession consider research in their practice and seek to decide whether or not they wish to find out more about this particular route. Each training plan includes a planning document to help you cover the logistics of the session. The session layouts are designed to include plenty of time for discussion and participation from attendees.

Training plan 1: A brief guide to research

Planning document

Focus	Introduction to research: a step-by-step approach
Facilitators	Teaching and learning specialists (such as lead practitioners, research leads, SLT with responsibility for teaching and learning).
Topics covered	• An overview of educational research. • Basic resources to engage with when beginning a research journey.
Preparation tasks	• For those running the session, reading Chapters 1 and 3 is essential. They may also wish to audit staff using Chapter 2's self-assessment questionnaire in order to understand the current views and understanding of research in the school. • No preparation is required for those attending this session.
Resources required	• Download the relevant PowerPoint slides from the online resources or prepare a handout with the key information to give to attendees at the event. • IT resources – laptops, tablets or a computer room so that staff can access some of the research resources for themselves.

Session outline

Focus	Timing	Format	Content
Introduce	5 minutes	Spoken Explanation	• Introduce the session and make clear that this is the first of three sessions with the aim of encouraging people to become more research informed should they wish. • Explain that to begin with, it is important to reflect on the school's, department's and individual's current position regarding research.

Focus	Timing	Format	Content
Reflect	10 minutes	Small group discussions	• Using some of the questions on the PowerPoint slides or results from a staff survey, hand over the discussion to small groups. For the majority, the following questions could be used (I am presuming that if you are keen to hold such a session, this is not the first time the word research has been mentioned when talking to staff!): 1. What do we do well when using research? 2. What have we already done to use educational research in guiding teaching and learning? 3. What do we wish to further explore? Why? What do you think about the use of educational research? • Follow these discussions with some feedback from the group before introducing the next set of questions: 4. What have you already done to engage with research? 5. What do you still feel you need to improve? 6. What do you feel confident about in terms of using educational research?
Explain	10 minutes	Presentation	• Read aloud 'What does research-informed practice in education look like?' from Chapter 1, page 5, of this book. • It is time to pass on some practical information that might contextualise educational research. Use the slides to explore what research is and what it isn't and the current landscape.

Focus	Timing	Format	Content
Explore	20–30 minutes	Guided exploration of key sources	• Ask staff to log on to a laptop, computer or tablet. They will be spending some time exploring some of the online resources that are available to support research-informed thinking. Some they might be *au fait* with whereas others might be new to them. Encourage staff to look at the resources in the same order so that they can discuss their thoughts at the same time. You may wish to lead them through certain sites before giving them time to explore on their own. *The key sources to look at are:* ✓ The EEF Toolkit: https://educationendowmentfoundation.org.uk ✓ The IEE Best Evidence in Brief: https://the-iee.org.uk/what-we-do/best-evidence-in-brief ✓ The Learning Scientists: www.learningscientists.org ✓ The Chartered College of Teaching: https://chartered.college
Feedback and evaluation	5–10 minutes	Discussion	• End with a chance for questions and feedback about the information shared. Was it helpful or too basic? What do people think about the time required to engage with research and what could be done to support their needs? • Consider the next steps that you would like staff to take before the next session (see final PowerPoint slide).

Training plan 2: Getting to grips with sources of evidence

Planning document

Focus	How to get to grips with evidence sources
Facilitators	Teaching and learning specialists (such as lead practitioners, research leads, SLT with responsibility for teaching and learning).
Topics covered	• Where and how to look for evidence. • What to consider when using a variety of research sources.
Preparation tasks	• For those running the session, reading Chapters 1, 3 and 4 is essential. You may wish to focus on sources that you did not mention in the first training session or refer back to these as part of the recap. • It would be helpful to send reminder links to staff attending of the four evidence sources mentioned in the first training session.
Resources required	• Copies of 'Considering the evidence' from Chapter 3, page 49. • PowerPoint slides from the online resources. • Copies of the 'overview cards' from the online resources (print enough so each pair or triad has a copy of each card). These cards are made up of the information found in Chapter 4. They give a summary of each source in the research starter toolkit and where to find it. Print double-sided so the 'where to begin' and 'what else to consider' information is on the back of each card.

Session outline

Focus	Timing	Format	Content
Introduce	5 minutes	Spoken presentation	• Introduce the session and make clear that this session builds on the last. The aim is to give some more practical guidance and advice relating to using new resources to find and implement evidence in the classroom. • Explain why it is important to have a range of sources. • Explain why it is often difficult to find helpful resources and how this links closely to good time management.

Focus	Timing	Format	Content
Reflect	10 minutes	Discussion	• Check prior knowledge: where have staff been looking to find evidence and research since the last session? • Ask staff to read 'Considering the evidence' from Chapter 3, page 49. • Discuss the differences between information that has been provided in other CPD sessions (perhaps external CPD might be best to discuss) and more recent CPD sessions. • After reading the extract 'Considering the evidence', ask staff to consider what they do or think when given new strategies and ideas. What would their questions be of a new source or finding?
Explain	10 minutes	Guided questions and discussion	• Guide the group to think about any research or theories they have previously engaged with. Use common examples from training providers to jog their memory or to provoke discussion. • Ask staff to list all the places they would look or go to in order to find out answers about teaching strategies and pedagogy.
Explore	20–30 minutes	Paired or small group work	• At this point, you should look to introduce the new ideas and resources that you feel will help staff learn more about research-informed practice. • Hand out the overview cards for each of the evidence sources you would like discussed. In pairs or triads, ask staff to consider their first impressions of the source, any prior knowledge they have of the source and whether or not they would consider using it on a regular basis. • Ask staff to turn over the cards to find more information about the sources. They should then discuss what they deem to be the possible benefits of or issues with using this source.
Feedback and evaluation	5–10 minutes	Feedback	• Feedback – small groups should feed back their thoughts to the rest of the group, focusing on whether or not the sources seem practical, helpful and manageable. • Consider the next steps that you would like staff to make before the next session – see final PowerPoint slide.

Training plan 3: How to approach evidence

Planning document

Focus	What to trust and why: is research credible?
Facilitators	Teaching and learning specialists (such as lead practitioners, research leads, SLT with responsibility for teaching and learning).
Topics covered	• What constitutes 'evidence'? • What questions to ask about the evidence you find. • What to consider when applying the evidence to your practice.
Preparation tasks	This session is a guide to approaching evidence, including a shorter version of the self-assessment questionnaire in Chapter 2, page 15, and information from Chapter 3. Those running the session should: • Read Chapters 1, 3 and 4. • Read Alex Quigley's post on the stages of finding new ideas and the benefit of evidence in doing so: www.theconfidentteacher.com/2016/03/escaping-the-tyranny-of-our-old-ideas
Resources required	• Mini whiteboards and board pens. • Copies of the 'evidence cards' from the online resources (print enough so each pair or small group has a copy of each card). • Sticky notes. • PowerPoint slides from the online resources.

Session outline

Focus	Timing	Format	Content
Introduce	10 minutes	Paired or small group work	• Introduce the concept of trust through one of the following engaging exercises (you know your audience best so consider which option might work and which might put people off taking part!): o Have attendees stand in a circle. Instruct everyone to lock right hands with someone on the other side of the circle. Then have them lock left hands with someone else on the other side of the circle. Try to see whether they can untangle without unlocking hands – they will need to trust others in their team to do this.

Focus	Timing	Format	Content
			o Grab some mini whiteboards and ask everyone to pick a partner. Have them sit back-to-back. One person has the pen and whiteboard, whilst the other is given a picture with an obscure shape on it. The person with the picture instructs the one with the whiteboard about what to draw. No doubt hilarity will ensue! • Talk about the idea of 'trust'. Explain that when making research-informed decisions about teaching and learning, we must consider how much and why we trust the evidence in front of us. Just like the games at the beginning, trust is important if you don't want to look and feel daft at the end of it!
Reflect	5 minutes	Paired discussion	• Ask staff to reflect on their current practice. They should answer: 1. When you are told about a teaching strategy or suggested practice, what do you often think? 2. What do you do to check the validity and reliability of any suggested strategies? 3. What barriers do you find that might stop you from adequately checking the source and validity of some strategies and theories that claim to work?
Explain	10 minutes	PowerPoint presentation	• Explain that like all research fields, there are inconsistencies and inaccuracies in education studies that are likely to trip us up. Explain that there are some key questions that we need to consider when approaching evidence and especially when certain evidence is presented to us as the magic fix to a problem we have. See the PowerPoint slides for the key questions and sub-questions that support how to approach evidence in a more informed and slightly critical way!

Focus	Timing	Format	Content
Explore	20–30 minutes	Paired or small group work	• Using the evidence cards, ask attendees to work through the different forms of evidence and studies. For each study that is presented, they should comment on the three areas below. They could use sticky notes to make a note of their thoughts and initial responses. 1. accessibility 2. clarity 3. purpose. • The pairs or groups should work through each of the studies, discussing the key features but also comparing them. It is important to consider which studies, in the role of a busy full-time teacher, would be deemed the most useful.
Feedback and evaluation	5–10 minutes	Discussion	• Feedback – small groups should feed back their thoughts to the rest of the group, focusing on whether or not the sources seem reliable and whether or not this correlates with their accessibility. • Consider the next steps that you would like staff to take before the next session – see final PowerPoint slide.

Twilight sessions: embedding research-informed strategies (one hour each)

Overview of the sessions

In the following set of training plans, the research papers and related strategies explored in Chapters 5 and 6 are turned into informative sessions. These sessions are similar to those in the first set of training plans as they refer to simple, effective and evidence-based techniques; however, they differ in that they allow time for the attendees to read the research for themselves, question its appropriateness to their context and debate any issues the research may present. The quick weekly training sessions (see page 208) are a good teaser to these sessions. In fact, they could be used to advertise the following sessions and encourage attendance and participation.

As with the previous plans, each training plan includes a planning document to help you cover the logistics of the session. The session layout is a suggestion only and you may wish to allocate more or less time to different sections depending on the experience and expertise of your attendees.

For these sessions, the facilitators can be whomever you wish them to be but focus on picking those who have read and embedded the research into their practice. If you are a leader, this is a good time to consider and ask about who has an interest in a particular area or who has been trialling certain strategies. For each of these sessions, you may want more than one facilitator and the sessions could be led by a particular department or stage team willing to share their thoughts and practices together.

In terms of the location and set-up of these sessions, they do not have to be your typical 'presenter at the front and attendees sat watching a PowerPoint' configuration. Instead, consider finding a classroom, library or breakout-style space where you can all sit together, preferably facing one another, to allow for a more casual and relaxed discussion. At my school, we call such sessions 'Journal Club' and it attracts teachers from a variety of departments. These sessions are non-threatening and rely on participation and collaboration – something that is key if you hope to incite and encourage change. Cake is also usually necessary at such events.

Twilight session 1: Memory and recall

Planning document

Focus	Research session on strategies for improving memory and recall
Topics covered	• Overview of the Dunlosky et al. (2013a) paper. • Strategies linked to evidence within the paper. • Discussion of how to apply this to your own context.
Preparation tasks	• Facilitators should be familiar with the Dunlosky et al. (2013a) paper, including its history and methodology. They should also read this blog post: https://teachingtoptens.wordpress.com/2018/09/28/ten-testing-strategies-a-range-of-activities-for-varying-retrieval-practice (Lolder, 2018). • Ask attendees to read the summary of this study found at: www.aft.org/sites/default/files/periodicals/dunlosky.pdf (Dunlosky et al., 2013b).
Resources required	• Copies of the above summary to hand out. • Action plan cards from the online resources for participants to fill in. Print enough for one each.

Session outline

Focus	Timing	Format	Content
Introduce	5–10 minutes	Presentation	• Introduce the key topic for today and summarise the history, methodology and structure of the Dunlosky et al. (2013a) article.
Reflect	10 minutes	Discussion	• Describe your own experience with engaging with this theory and how you believe it has started to change your approach. • Open this question to the group and allow others to explain where they are at the moment and what impact evidence has had on their teaching so far.
Explain	10 minutes	Reading and discussion	• Ensure you have copies of the summarised article to hand out. Give participants the necessary time to glance back over the article (this could be five minutes). • Explain the ten learning techniques that were believed to be most effective when the article was written. • Explain that the two techniques the session will focus on are practice-testing and distributed practice.

Focus	Timing	Format	Content

Explore	20 minutes	Guided group discussion	• Use guided questions related to the strategies of practice-testing and distributed practice.
			• Begin with a summary of one of the findings before opening up the questions and discussion. Consider the following questions:
			  1. Is the approach clear?
			  2. How do you use practice-testing/distributed practice in your classroom?
			  3. How is this different from previous approaches?
			  4. What problems do you envisage with using this strategy?
			  5. How do you see this strategy working practically and logistically? What does it require you to create or know in advance?
			  6. What might the benefits be considering the format of assessment (formative or summative) for students in your classroom?
			• Share some examples of different styles of quizzing based on this blog post (it could be read in the session or you could pick out key parts to share in the session and then circulate it afterwards): https://teachingtoptens.wordpress.com/2018/09/28/ten-testing-strategies-a-range-of-activities-for-varying-retrieval-practice.
			• Ask staff attending to share their own strategies.

Feedback and evaluation	10 minutes	Guided discussion and pass it on	• Bring the discussion to a close by helping attendees to create individual action plans to take forward. Ask:
			  1. How will you apply this to your everyday teaching?
			  2. What do you need to adapt in light of the research findings (for example, the research on the timing of feedback)?
			  3. What longer-term implications does this have for your curriculum and schemes of work? Ask staff to fill in an action plan card that they can keep with them in a planner or put on their desk to remind them of the research they have read and their next steps.

Twilight session 2: Metacognition in the classroom

Planning document

Focus	Research session on understanding and using metacognition in the classroom
Topics covered	• A summary of the EEF's metacognition and self-regulated learning report (Quigley et al., 2018). • Practical strategies relating to the guidance from the report. • Next steps in your own context.
Preparation tasks	• Facilitators read the full EEF guidance report: https:// educationendowmentfoundation.org.uk/tools/guidance-reports/ metacognition-and-self-regulated-learning/#recommendation-1 • Download the free supportive materials related to the report.
Resources required	• Copies of the summary of recommendations poster from the report website. • Ensure you have sent copies of the full report to attendees so they can refer to it. • PowerPoint slides from the online resources. • Action plan cards from the online resources for participants to fill in. Print enough for one each.

Session outline

Focus	Timing	Format	Content
Introduce	10 minutes	Short presentation and reading	• Introduce the topic of metacognition and the Quigley et al. (2018) report. Explain that this is a guidance report from the Education Endowment Foundation. • Ask attendees to read through the summary from Chapter 4, page 57, of the EEF Toolkit resource. • Provide all attendees with the 'summary of recommendations' poster and briefly read through it together.
Reflect	10 minutes	Guided discussion	• Use the questions on the PowerPoint to guide the discussion. Discuss how the term 'metacognition' is used in your school at the moment and how staff feel about the strategies they currently use. • This could also be a time to informally use the EEF's school audit tool relating to metacognition: https:// educationendowmentfoundation.org.uk/ public/files/Publications/Metacognition/7-SchoolAuditTool.pdf.

Focus	Timing	Format	Content
Explain	15 minutes	Presentation	• Give attendees the necessary time to glance back over the article (five minutes). • Decide in advance which steps you believe will best benefit your audience and explain these sections of the report in more detail.
Explore	20 minutes	Small group discussions	• Ask staff to discuss with others from different subjects or key stages in groups of three or four. • Use the four levels of metacognitive behaviour grid to encourage staff to discuss their knowledge of learning in their own classroom. • Ask staff to share their findings with their smaller group. • Open up the discussions to the whole group to consider the issues and areas that require further development.
Feedback and evaluation	5 minutes	Guided discussion and pass it on	• Bring the discussion to a close by helping attendees to create individual action plans to take forward. Ask: 1. How could you apply this guidance to your everyday teaching? 2. What do you need to adapt in light of the research findings (for example, do you need to consider how you model your expectations to students)? 3. What longer-term implications does this have for your department, pedagogy and curriculum? • Ask staff to fill in an action plan card that they can keep with them in a planner or put on their desk to remind them of the research they have read and their next steps.

Twilight session 3: Rosenshine's principles of instruction

Planning document

Focus	Rosenshine's principles of instruction
Topics covered	• The purpose and methodology of the original paper. • How the evidence from the paper can be used in practical everyday strategies. • How this applies to our context.
Preparation tasks	• Facilitators to read Rosenshine's 'Principles of instruction' (2012) at https://files.eric.ed.gov/fulltext/EJ971753.pdf. • Facilitators to read the summary of the paper in Chapter 5, page 80. • Facilitators to choose two or three of the principles to focus on based on their specific context.
Resources required	• Copies of the nine-page summary linked above to be sent out beforehand. • Copies of the How2 poster available here: https://teachinghow2s.com/blog/principles-of-instruction. Print one copy for each attendee. • Sticky notes. • PowerPoint slides from the online resources. • Action plan cards from the online resources for participants to fill in. Print enough for one each.

Session outline

Focus	Timing	Format	Content
Introduce	10 minutes	Short presentation and reading	• Introduce Rosenshine's (2012) original paper and explain why it is a seminal piece of work. Explore the methodology and the fact that the paper still encourages a wide range of activities but based on quality basic teaching. • Provide all attendees with a copy of the How2 poster.
Reflect	10 minutes	Guided discussion	• Use the questions on the PowerPoint slides to guide the discussion as a whole group. • Give out sticky notes and ask attendees to decide whether or not Rosenshine's ten principles are something they do regularly or irregularly, purposefully or through habit alone.

Focus	Timing	Format	Content
Explain	10 minutes	Presentation	• Give attendees the necessary time to glance back over the article (five minutes). • Explain that you will not be going through all ten principles today but have chosen two or three specific principles based on your context to discuss further. Explain why you have chosen these.
Explore	20–25 minutes	Small group discussions: facilitators to record the key points of the discussions by circulating between the groups	• Pick one principle to focus on at a time. For each principle, ask the groups to discuss it using the questions below. Rotate the principle you are focusing on every five to ten minutes. 1) Why do you think this has been included in the top ten principles? 2) What experience do you have of this strategy? 3) How has your experience of this changed over your teaching experience? Why? 4) Do you use this principle on a day-to-day basis? How? 5) How much do you consider the impact of your choice to do this on students' learning? 6) What practical approaches can you share about including this principle in your teaching?
Feedback and evaluation	5 minutes	Guided discussion and pass it on	• Bring the discussion to a close by creating a wall of information relating to each principle based on what you have heard being discussed. The wall could be simply notes on a whiteboard or sticky notes. Ask staff to write down two new ways they could apply each principle to their teaching. • Ask staff to fill in an action plan card that they can keep with them in a planner or put on their desk to remind them of the research they have read and their next steps.

Twilight session 4: Internal TeachMeet sharing practical ideas based on research

I cannot imagine there are many people left in the world of education who have not heard of a TeachMeet as a form of CPD. A TeachMeet is typically a collection of short presentations focusing on one particular theme. The brilliance of a TeachMeet is the opportunity to hear from a wide range of speakers in a slightly more informal context than your traditional CPD. I have placed this under the twilight session for training as I feel that in the first instance it makes sense to have an internal TeachMeet as a celebration of the expertise in your own school. Should you wish, you could also run this as an external event or as a networking event working with linked schools or schools simply in your area. In other words, you can make this as large or as small as you wish. One thing I have always loved about attending and speaking at TeachMeets in the past is the fact that people feel happy and open to sharing their experiences rather than their purpose being to persuade you to invest in a product, which might be the case at larger, corporate-style conferences.

An internal TeachMeet should focus on allowing staff who do not always have the opportunity to share their practice and findings with others a platform to do so. Planning this as a twilight session takes away the pressures of time and, with a variety of speakers from different stages and subjects, allows conversations to begin that might not occur in a more formal CPD session.

Planning document

Focus	TeachMeet sharing practical ideas based on research
Topics covered	• The research that led to the strategies. • Practical application of the strategies used. • Problems encountered and advice.
Preparation tasks	• Invite attendees along but carefully consider the timing of your event. I would avoid putting this in the middle of a busy summer term and perhaps place it towards the end of a term instead. As odd as it might seem, such an event can be a good 'pick-me-up' in November or December or can be put in along with a staff BBQ at the end of the summer term as a celebration of the staff's hard work. • Ask your presenters to come up with titles for their sessions that will interest and intrigue the audience. • Send your presenters the 'top tips for a TeachMeet presentation' in advance to help them prepare. These are available on page 205 and in the online resources for you to copy and paste.
Resources required	• You will need enough space to host the event properly: a room with a stage, projector and computer for speakers. • Provide a variety of refreshments – try to make it something different by going all out! • You may wish to set up a working wall or Twitter feed to record key elements of the twilight session.

Session outline

Focus	Timing	Format	Content
Introduce	5 minutes	Presentation	• Welcome staff to the event. Make sure that they have all had time to grab some refreshments. • Have a rolling list of titles that will be covered on the screen – not necessarily in order but to encourage intrigue and interest. • Explain the format of this session. Encourage audience members to take notes but explain that the format is likely to be quick-fire presentations.
Presentations	20 minutes	3 x individual presentations	• Invite presenters up one at a time to give their presentations. • Either decide in advance on the order, or use a random name generator to add an air of excitement (although I imagine this might make some presenters a little anxious!). • Remind people to ask questions via Twitter or your working wall.

Focus	Timing	Format	Content
Break	5 minutes	N/A	• Ensure you book in a very short break to allow people to refuel, have a quick chat and sort out any technology issues. I once went to a TeachMeet that went on for three hours without a break – needless to say, I didn't take away a lot from the last few sessions!
Presentations	20 minutes	3 x individual presentations	• Continue with the rest of the presentations.
Closing	5 minutes	Presentation	• Ensure that you thank all those who have helped with the set-up – site management, IT, presenters and attendees. • Share where further information can be found and encourage staff to talk to those who presented if they wish to find out more. • Encourage staff to post more ideas, questions and comments to Twitter or on your working wall. Those in charge of CPD can look and formulate future plans based on these suggestions. Perhaps one presentation in particular proved popular and could be expanded upon. Perhaps one confused the majority and needs more clarification.

Top tips for a TeachMeet presentation

1. Avoid overusing PowerPoint – in five to ten minutes, there isn't much time to get through all the swirling, snazzy clipart!
2. Avoid including an introduction about yourself and your ambitions. Instead, you should focus on the research, strategies and findings.
3. Ensure that you have double checked your presentation in advance for spelling, grammar and punctuation errors, as well as repetitive information.
4. Ensure that further information can be found elsewhere after your presentation has finished. Send this to your organiser in advance.

Twilight session 5: Evaluating your research-informed journey

This final twilight session should take place either towards the end of a year or at the beginning of a year, following the four previous twilight sessions. Although it sits nicely after the internal TeachMeet, it is important to consider the time necessary to allow ideas to bed in. Do try to encourage those who have voluntarily come along to the sessions to attend this final one – this is where they can start to become the next leaders and your volunteer army, helping you to invoke change and increase research-informed practice in your school.

The session is focused mainly on an individual's reflection on their current practice, considering where they started at the beginning of the year. This session will certainly include lots of discussion but also a lot of time for reflection. Ensure you give enough time over to the questions on the PowerPoint to help guide the discussion, but also leave time for people to simply 'chip in' with their own thoughts.

Use the feedback time constructively to work out how you wish to move forward as a school. Are you happy where you are now or do you want to push the boundaries even further by connecting with other networks and schools and taking part in research projects as a school?

Planning document

Focus	Evaluating your research journey
Facilitators	Teaching and learning specialists (such as lead practitioners, research leads, SLT with responsibility for teaching and learning).
Topics covered	• Where have you come from – as a school and as an individual? • What are the key things you have learnt about research-informed practice? • What are the next steps?
Preparation tasks	• Send out the short questionnaire in the online resources and ask all attendees to complete it in advance of the session. These can be adapted to suit your sessions and requirements. • Create a map of your sessions so far to demonstrate the topics you have covered and information that has been passed on.
Resources required	• The evaluation questionnaire in the online resources based on Chapter 7. • PowerPoint slides from the online resources.

Session outline

Focus	Timing	Format	Content
Introduce	5 minutes	Spoken presentation	• Introduce the final twilight session as an opportunity to fully reflect and discuss next steps.
Reflect	5 minutes	Comparison grid	• Ask attendees to consider three words that describe their practice at the start of the process compared to now. • Briefly discuss how they feel things might have changed.
Explain	10 minutes	Presentation	• Share the map of the topics you have covered and the knowledge you have gained over the course of the twilight sessions. Not all staff may have attended all sessions so it is useful to see the journey as a whole. • Explain that the purpose of today's session is to reflect on their journey with research-informed practice as individuals – remind them that everyone would have started in a different place and with a different level of understanding.
Explore	30 minutes	Whole group discussion moving into smaller group work	• Hand out the evaluation questionnaires based on the twilight sessions. These can be adapted to suit your sessions and requirements. • Discuss the outcomes of these questionnaires as a group. Who feels they have made progress in this area and who thinks they require further support to develop their interest? • Divide your attendees up into smaller groups – preferably by stage or subject area so that they can work together to consider how their knowledge and findings might work in the long term and on a larger scale. Use the questions on the PowerPoint slides to guide the group discussions. They should be working towards creating a plan of how to embed research-informed practice into their departments.
Feedback and evaluation	10 minutes	Q&A	• Having considered their individual journeys and made steps for the next stages as a team, give staff the opportunity to ask questions about the next part of the journey. You will likely have a wide range of questions, spanning from questions about particular papers and strategies to how the school sees its current position regarding research-informed practice. Be prepared to answer questions at every level by ensuring that someone responsible for teaching and learning is available to field some of these questions.

Quick training plans: Introducing research-based thinking to staff through strategies (15–30 minutes each)

Overview of the sessions

These short and precise training sessions are a great way to engage staff of all levels of experience in quick and practical strategies that are linked to evidence-based thinking. They can be adapted to complete in different contexts such as whole-staff morning briefings or departmental meetings or combined with other sessions on an INSET day or twilight session. They also allow for flexibility in terms of subjects and facilitators but it would always be preferable that the facilitator had trialled and evaluated the strategy before delivering it to others – this provides credibility and ensures others will be keen to listen and become invested in the strategy and keen to trial it themselves.

On the following pages, you will find four training sessions that describe how to deliver specific sessions to a wide range of staff. This presumes that staff will be expected to attend such events and therefore there is less time for discussion or questions than normal as there may be time restraints. However, if you wish to adapt these sessions you could extend them by 15 minutes to include a question-and-answer-style session or link them together to ask for feedback at each new session on the success or issues with the previous strategy.

Quick training plan 1: A research-informed approach to homework

Planning document

Focus	Interleaved and distributed homework tasks
Facilitators	Research lead and/or staff who have trialled strategies in this area.
Topics covered	• What area for development led to trialling this strategy? • A brief overview of the research the strategy is based on. • An overview of the strategy. • An explanation of issues that teachers should be aware of before implementing the strategy in their own classroom. • Examples of the strategy in the facilitator's own classroom. • An evaluation of the strategy and next steps. • Suggestions of how to use the strategy in other subject areas or phases.
Preparation tasks	**Pre-reading** It is important that staff leading the session have not only read but trialled the use of distributed practice in their own classrooms and, in this case (although easily adapted), as homework tasks. To begin with, read the summary in Chapter 5, page 75, of the Dunlosky et al. (2013a) publication. Afterwards, you may wish to read the entire paper and identify any other areas of interest. It is worth delving further into other research and comment on memory and retrieval through the work of The Learning Scientists. Ensure you read the links and suggestions in Chapter 6, page 106, where this strategy is explained in further detail. **Review your current practice** Before exploring the issue of interleaved and distributed practice, you need to consider the norm in your current context. Similarly, perhaps there is already in place a robust and successful homework policy that doesn't require rewriting. In which case, consider how the research could be used to adapt other parts of learning – for example, how could the information affect how your teachers plan for the start of their lessons, for introducing new units or in the run-up to exams?
Resources required	This session lends itself well to a presentation with one or two talking about their findings and their advice. If it is being held as a whole-staff session then I would not suggest providing handouts but if you are presenting to a smaller number of staff you may wish to print off examples of your strategy in practice as well as the summary of Dunlosky et al.'s (2013a) findings. The summary can be found in the online resources.
Preparation time	25 minutes (35 minutes if you include time for questions).

Focus	Interleaved and distributed homework tasks
Potential problems and solutions	**Problem:** Staff have a range of experience and understanding.
	Solution: Ensure that in your presentation you make it clear that you understand this. Where possible, reference staff you know have already considered interleaving and distributed practice in their teaching.
	Problem: Staff teach a range of ages or subjects.
	Solution: Again, it is important that you make it clear you are understanding of the differences between classrooms. However, it is important to make clear that this evidence could be applied to a wide range of students and tasks.
Possible follow-up tasks	• After the session, ensure that you email out any resources and further reading so that those interested can take it further.
	• Encourage those who might be interested to seek you out at a later date to discuss how trialling the strategy is going.
Pass it on	You may wish (depending on how informed you feel your audience are) to send out the whole research paper and set a date where it can be further discussed. If you have the time, this could be at the beginning of your next training session; however, I would only consider doing this if you have time after school.

Session outline

Focus	Timing	Format	Content
Introduction – why are you talking?	5 minutes	Presentation	• Introductory discussion to contextualise why you are discussing interleaved and distributed practice. Consider: 1. current curriculum plans 2. current revision practice – for SATs, GCSEs or A level 3. current homework policies 4. any issues with the above.
Explanation – a brief overview of the research	5 minutes	Presentation	• Explain why you are referencing research in this presentation. The phrase 'research suggests' can seem vague and a justification, so explain exactly which paper you are referencing: 'Improving students' learning with effective learning techniques: promising directions from cognitive and educational psychology', by Dunlosky et al. (2013a). • Share the summary of the paper, available in the online resources.

Focus	Timing	Format	Content

Advice – any issues to consider	2 minutes	Presentation	• Focus on any specific issues you feel staff in your context may have and ensure that you have discussed these with SLT and leaders beforehand.
			• Some of the key issues are likely to be:
			  1. Time considerations – do not expect changes overnight.
			  2. Adapting current practice – you are not suggesting they implement changes immediately.
			  3. Resources – be honest about how long it took to create and adapt resources.

Example of strategy in use	7 minutes	Presentation (and possible handout)	• Show an up-to-date and legible copy of your current resource. In this case, it is likely to be a homework timetable that could be adapted to suit different stages or formats.

Evaluation	5 minutes	Presentation	• Evaluate the outcomes you have found based on your trial of the resource. This could include:
			  1. anecdotal evidence
			  2. student voice findings
			  3. data
			  4. parental feedback.

Questions	5–10 minutes	Group discussion or think, pair, share	• If you have time for questions, then it is worth asking the following to promote discussion before taking questions from the floor:
			  1. How might you use this in your own classroom?
			  2. What issues do you envisage when implementing this strategy?
			  3. What outcome would you like in six months' time?

Quick training plan 2: Knowledge organisers

Planning document

Focus	Knowledge organisers
Facilitators	Research lead and/or staff who have trialled strategies in this area.
Topics covered	• What area for development led to trialling this strategy? • A brief overview of the research the strategy is based on. • An overview of the strategy. • An explanation of issues that teachers should be aware of before implementing the strategy in their own classroom. • Examples of the strategy in the facilitator's own classroom. • An evaluation of the strategy and next steps. • Suggestions of how to use the strategy in other subject areas or phases.
Preparation tasks	**Pre-reading** • Read the summary in Chapter 5 of the publication 'What makes great teaching? Review of the underpinning research' by Coe et al. (2014). • Read Chapter 6 on 'memory and recall' of *What Does This Look Like in the Classroom?* by Carl Hendrick and Robin Macpherson (2017). • Joe Kirby writes about knowledge organisers and their use in practice-testing here: https://pragmaticreform.wordpress.com/2015/03/28/knowledge-organisers. • Read the overview in Chapter 6, page 125, of how knowledge organisers have worked for secondary science teacher Hayley Cummings. **Create your own** • Ensure that you have created your own knowledge organiser to demonstrate to others and have examples of use from your students' books.
Resources required	This session lends itself well to a presentation with one or two talking about their findings and their advice. If it is being held as a whole-staff session then I would not suggest providing handouts but if you are presenting to a smaller number of staff you may wish to print off examples of your knowledge organiser in advance.
Preparation time	30 minutes for reading and preparing resources.
Potential problems and solutions	**Problem:** Staff do not believe their subject has enough 'knowledge' to make this worthwhile. **Solution:** Ask staff to write down everything their students need to know in their subject area or pick an area in a key stage and give a key topic. They will soon realise they have created a knowledge organiser and no subject is immune to knowledge – no matter how skills-based! **Problem:** The knowledge organiser is deemed to be suitable for older key stages but not for younger year groups. **Solution:** Take it back to basics and explore how a knowledge organiser could be made visually appealing and useful to younger students.

Focus	Knowledge organisers
Possible follow-up tasks	After the session, ensure that you email out any resources and further reading so that those interested can take it further. Encourage those who might be interested to seek you out at a later date to discuss how trialling the strategy is going and ask them to present on it at a later session.
Pass it on	You may wish (depending on how informed you feel your audience are) to send out the whole Coe et al. (2014) article and set a date where it can be further discussed. If you have the time, this could be at the beginning of your next training session; however, I would only consider doing this if you have time after school.

Session outline

Focus	Timing	Format	Content
Introduction – why are you talking?	5 minutes	Presentation	• Introductory discussion to contextualise why you are discussing the use of knowledge organisers. Consider: 1. how students currently acquire and record knowledge 2. what assessments they are required to know this for – internal or external 3. how the process could begin.
Explanation – a brief overview of the research	5 minutes	Presentation	• Explain why you are referencing research in this presentation. The phrase 'research suggests' can seem vague and a justification so explain exactly which article you are referencing. • You may wish to use a video or podcast to explain the strategy here, for example: https://soundcloud.com/user-907153766/kirb-your-enthusiasm-for-knowledge-organisers-1.
Advice – any issues to consider	2 minutes	Presentation	• Focus on any specific issues you feel staff in your context may have and ensure that you have discussed these with SLT and leaders beforehand. Some of the key issues are likely to be: 1. Collective or personal responsibility – how will you ensure consistency across a department? 2. Resources – be honest about how long it took to create and adapt resources. 3. How to use knowledge organisers effectively.

Focus	Timing	Format	Content
Example of strategy in use	7 minutes	Presentation (and possible handout)	• Show a range of knowledge organisers in different subjects. • Identify the ways in which they can be used in class and at home. • Show students' work based on their use of knowledge organisers.
Evaluation	5 minutes	Presentation	• Evaluate the outcomes you have found based on your trial of the resource. This could include: 1. anecdotal evidence 2. student voice findings 3. data from assessments 4. parental feedback.
Questions	5–10 minutes	Group discussion or think, pair, share	• If you have time for questions, then it is worth asking the following to promote discussion before taking questions from the floor: 1. How might you use this in your own classroom? 2. What issues do you envisage when implementing this strategy? 3. What outcome would you like in six months' time?

Quick training plan 3: Low-stakes quizzing

Planning document

Focus	Low-stakes quizzes
Facilitators	Research lead and/or staff who have trialled strategies in this area.
Topics covered	• What area for development led to trialling this strategy? • A brief overview of the research the strategy is based on. • An overview of the strategy. • An explanation of issues that teachers should be aware of before implementing the strategy in their own classroom. • Examples of the strategy in the facilitator's own classroom. • An evaluation of the strategy and next steps. • Suggestions of how to use the strategy in other subject areas or phases.
Preparation tasks	**Pre-reading** • Read the summary in Chapter 5, page 90, of the publication: 'What makes great teaching? Review of the underpinning research' (Coe et al., 2014). • Read the summary in Chapter 5, page 75, of the publication: 'Improving students' learning with effective learning techniques: promising directions from cognitive and educational psychology', by Dunlosky et al. (2013a), with a focus on practice-testing and low-stakes testing. • This paper (Stephens, 2014) makes for a very interesting read about the multiple purposes of a starter and concludes that a structured and formal approach is useful; the paper itself focuses on the link between starters, teachers' choices and expectations, and students' behaviour: https://journaleducationalresearchinformedpractice.files.wordpress.com/2014/08/3stephens2014june.pdf. • Read an overview of retrieval practice here: www.learningscientists.org/blog/2018/11/6-1 (Coane and Minear, 2018). • In order to engage staff in the presentation, you could create a short low-stakes quiz that they have to take part in immediately. This could link to previous sessions, your school's theme or a less-than-serious quiz on the school itself!
Resources required	• PowerPoint slides from the online resources. • Quick low-stakes quiz. • You may wish to hand out the summary of Coe et al. (2014), available in the online resources.
Preparation time	One hour of reading and 20 minutes of preparing a presentation, including the quiz.

Focus	Low-stakes quizzes
Potential problems and solutions	**Problem:** Staff may see low-stakes quizzes as a waste of time when they have content to get through or skills to practise. **Solution:** Demonstrate the evidence through use of the research provided. Use real-life examples related to your context to encourage people to understand that if an idea isn't picked up on or thought about in a certain period of time it will be forgotten. You could reference a particular meeting, assembly or policy in the past and quiz them on it versus a quiz on something they commonly refer to. **Problem:** Staff are unsure how to make an effective low-stakes quiz. **Solution:** Explore the best approaches to questions – multiple-choice questions in particular – or how to use low-stakes quizzes to support interleaving topics. Ensure that the quiz is truly low stakes for your students and not just for you. Read this blog post to look for advice on how to ensure the quiz doesn't cause unnecessary anxiety: https://classteaching.wordpress.com/2017/03/23/is-it-really-a-low-stakes-quiz (Simmonds, 2017).
Possible follow-up tasks	• After the session, ensure that you email out any resources and further reading so that those interested can take it further. • Encourage those who might be interested to seek you out at a later date to discuss how trialling the strategy is going and ask them to present on it at a later session.
Pass it on	Ask teachers attending the session to follow up on this in a faculty or department meeting, and collaborate on creating low-stakes quizzes that could be shared to save time and ensure a range of questions.

Session outline

Focus	Timing	Format	Content
Introduction – engage your audience	5 minutes	Low-stakes quiz	• Create a short, quick and perhaps funny (if you can do funny!) low-stakes quiz for all staff to take part in. Staff might appreciate you laughing at yourself or referencing events at your school that everyone will know the answer to, for example, *'What is the school motto?'* or *'What was the last school production?'* Focus on questions that the majority will know easily.

Focus	Timing	Format	Content
Explanation – a brief overview of the research	5 minutes	Presentation	• Explain why you are referencing research in this presentation. The phrase 'research suggests' can seem vague and a justification so explain exactly which article you are referencing: 'Improving students' learning with effective learning techniques: promising directions from cognitive and educational psychology' by Dunlosky et al. (2013a). • Share a brief and succinct explanation about low-stakes testing: *Low-stakes quizzing is a strategy to use in order to encourage retrieval practice, often at the beginning of lessons, which will allow you to understand quickly and effectively what students remember. They are often short and sharp with little significance in terms of scores attached to them – in other words, they do not form part of a formative or summative assessment.*
Example of strategy in use	5 minutes	Presentation	• Using a range of subjects, show several examples of low-stakes quizzes but identify for staff the type of information being quizzed. For example, make it clear that these are knowledge-based quizzes and that students will have been taught this content explicitly. It is also a good idea to demonstrate some of the answers you would expect, to show their complexity.
Video focusing on issues	5 minutes	Tod Brennan video	• Show all staff this video about possible issues with low-stakes quizzes becoming high stakes if not well planned: https://classteaching.wordpress.com/2017/03/23/is-it-really-a-low-stakes-quiz/. Watch it and lead into a short discussion.
Summary	2 minutes	Presentation	• Summarise the key points of low-stakes quizzes using the PowerPoint slides.
Questions	5–10 minutes	Group discussion or think, pair, share	• If you have time for questions then it is worth asking the following to promote discussion before taking questions from the floor: 1. How do you currently use quiz questions in class? 2. Are you always conscious of the high-/low-stakes balance? 3. How do students receive quizzes? 4. Do you think it is beneficial for all or only some? Why? 5. How might you adapt your use of quizzing from now on?

Quick training plan 4: Whole-class feedback

Planning document

Focus	Whole-class feedback
Facilitators	Research lead and/or staff who have trialled strategies in this area.
Topics covered	• What area for development led to trialling this strategy? • A brief overview of the research the strategy is based on. • An overview of the strategy. • An explanation of issues that teachers should be aware of before implementing the strategy in their own classroom. • Examples of the strategy in the facilitator's own classroom. • An evaluation of the strategy and next steps. • Suggestions of how to use the strategy in other subject areas or phases.
Preparation tasks	**Pre-reading:** • Read the summary of the EEF's review of marking (Elliott et al., 2016) in Chapter 5, page 94. • Read Jo Facer's (2016) overview of whole-class feedback: https://readingallthebooks.com/2016/03/19/giving-feedback-the-michaela-way. • Look at examples of feedback sheets collated by teacher Victoria Hewett (@MrsHumanities): https://mrshumanities.com/2017/10/15/mrs-humanities-shares-5-whole-class-feedback-examples.
Resources required	• Examples of whole-class feedback sheets. • Examples of exercise books with the use of whole-class feedback sheets. • PowerPoint slides from the online resources.
Preparation time	One hour for reading and creating and using resources in class – trial them over a term or half term before presenting.

Focus	Whole-class feedback
Potential problems and solutions	**Problem:** Your school's marking policy. **Solution:** It is important that you discuss this issue with those in charge of the marking policy before you share with all staff your plan to change and adapt it! If you are in a position to do so then consider the following questions regarding your policy: • When was the policy created and what were the intentions at the time? • How often do you ask teachers to mark written work? Why? • Are the expectations the same for all or do they change depending on phase or subject? • How do you know whether or not marking has an impact in your department or school? • How do staff view your marking policy? If you consider these questions carefully, then you may wish to include a section in your presentation referring to your current policy, staff voice findings, student voice findings and possible adaptations – of which whole-class feedback could be one. **Problem:** Varying subject or year group requirements. **Solution:** Marking might be different for each of your teachers in the school. Depending on the students they teach, the subject they are teaching and their age group, it might mean different things to different people. Of course, a strategy such as whole-class feedback might be most beneficial to subjects based heavily in writing or examination year groups; however, it is not simply beneficial to reduce the amount of time looking at exam scripts and can be used in a number of ways to reduce workload, ensure record keeping of feedback and improve student outcomes.
Possible follow-up tasks	A staff and student survey both before and after implementing new techniques would be helpful. Staff and students are key stakeholders in any developments and research-informed changes that you make. It is important to include them fully along the way to give you a true reflection of what is happening in your school. Questions to ask yourself are in the 'problems' section above but it might be useful to use some of the following with staff and students. Staff survey questions: • How often do you mark one class set of books? • What is your 'go to' marking system? • How long would it take you to mark one set of books? • How do you provide students with feedback?

Focus	Whole-class feedback
	• What are the most effective ways in which you feel you feed back to students? • What factors affect your marking and feedback? • Why do you think your approach to marking works? • What would you like to change and why? • When are your 'pinch-points' in the year? Student survey questions: • How do you know how to improve your work? • What do you do when a teacher has marked your written work? • What do you feel when a teacher has marked your work? • What type of feedback do you find most helpful? • What do you do to act on your feedback?
Pass it on	Completing a staff survey before and after you have implemented new strategies will help you to pass on your knowledge. As with all these smaller strategies, encourage people in a range of roles and departments to trial it before you present. This will help get all staff on board, and presenting your staff survey findings will also ensure people know they have been listened to – as long as you do really listen and are not simply paying lip service to their responses!

Session outline

Focus	Timing	Format	Content
Introduction – why are you talking?	5 minutes	PowerPoint presentation	• Recap your current practice and policies if possible. • Look at staff and student survey results and explain why these might lead to a new strategy being trialled.
Explanation – a brief overview of the research	5 minutes	PowerPoint presentation	• Reference the EEF marking report (Elliott et al., 2016), which found more research was required but suggested that the time invested in marking may not have the impact many previously thought and that new strategies may be required to make marking manageable and more effective. (See Chapter 5, page 94.)

Focus	Timing	Format	Content
Advice – any issues to consider	3 minutes	Top tips on PowerPoint	• At this point, reference the different types of marking and feedback that exist. Make reference to different subjects and pressures. • Advise staff to use the following strategy after setting a particular piece of work or task rather than using it in hindsight.
Example of strategy in use	5 minutes	Example from exercise books	• Explore an example used in a student exercise book or from a teaching presentation. Explore how it might be adapted for different subjects – how might the box headings change?

Evaluation	5 minutes	Presentation	• Ask for staff voice from those who have used the strategy already.
			• Encourage staff to share the time it took to complete the strategy (honesty is the best policy!) and the pitfalls they came across. Likely pitfalls include:
			  1. finding it difficult not to 'traditionally' mark work
			  2. choosing the most appropriate areas to develop
			  3. identifying the next-steps tasks
			  4. differentiating the feedback for students.

Questions	5–10 minutes	Group discussion or think, pair, share	• Ask staff to consider on their own, then in pairs, the following questions:
			  1. How often do you mark students' work?
			  2. What is your 'go to' marking system?
			  3. How do you provide students with feedback?
			  4. How could you see this strategy working in your area?
			  5. What issues might you face when implementing this strategy?

Training for leaders (one hour each)

The following training plans are aimed at middle leadership in particular. Middle leaders are the most important group to target if you are hoping to implement change. They are at the core of the system by both knowing what is going on in the classroom (they are likely to still be in the classroom for a vast amount of time) along with having the unique ability to discuss and influence change with those at the top. They are likely to have strong relationships with all members of staff who report into them, along with those whom they report into, and therefore have a unique position in the school to push forward developments.

Of course, these sessions could be used for senior leaders too; however, it is likely that their use of research will be different to that of a classroom teacher. Senior leaders are more likely to spend their time using the research to influence whole-school decisions and policy. Moreover, their decisions will be focused on the use of research to make effective procurement and long-term decisions. The research they choose to access might include the papers and strategies discussed in this book but will also cover a range of other topics. Gary Jones's (2018) *Evidence-Based School Leadership and Management: A practical guide* is a good place for senior leaders intending to become more research informed and to use this in their leadership and management decisions.

The following sessions should be used either after more introductory sessions we have already covered in this section or after the INSET day on page 238. The sessions do reference the research that has already been mentioned but also focus on how best to evoke change in a team and what you require to keep you onside. These ideas reference research and theory on change rather than on practical teaching strategies or learning theory but may have a powerful effect when combined.

The planning document remains similar for all three sessions. You will present over time to the same audience and your purpose and facilitators should remain consistent throughout this set of training plans. The preparation tasks and resources will vary slightly and will involve reading outside of the previous reading mentioned in the book.

Training for leaders 1: Leading a research-informed team – how to get involved

Planning document

Focus	Introduction to research: a step-by-step approach
Facilitators	Senior leaders and/or research leads.
Topics covered	• An overview of educational research sources. • How and why you should get 'more involved' quickly. • Joining a network and building a network.
Preparation tasks	• Reread Chapter 4, page 53, and Chapter 5, page 72, of this book. • Ask staff to bring a device such as a phone or tablet along to the session.
Resources required	• Download and adapt the relevant PowerPoint slides from the online resources.

Session outline

Focus	Timing	Format	Content
Introduce	5–10 minutes	Spoken introduction	• Introduce the aims of the session and explain why this audience have been invited to take part.
Reflect	15 minutes	Discussion and feedback	• Divide the attendees into triads in which they can discuss their current leadership roles in relation to educational research using the questions on the PowerPoint slide. • Draw out small elements of feedback from the groups. Bring together strands that are reflected in every group, for example concerns about the diversity of experience or knowledge within their teams. Capacity and time are also likely to be concerns that come up. • Ask attendees to summarise what they hope to gain and change in their teams.

Focus	Timing	Format	Content
Explain	15 minutes	Presentation	• Explain that to begin with you may cover areas that some leaders are already aware of and that this is an ever-changing set of sources. • Briefly go through each of the various sources (based on Chapter 4) from engaging with research from magazines to apps and conferences. • Ascertain which sources are currently in regular use and which are unheard of.
Explore	15 minutes	Triad discussions – problem solving	• Mix the triads up so that leaders have a chance to talk to others with different responsibilities. • Give each group a set of problems relating to engaging their teams in a change such as introducing research-informed practice. Ask staff to discuss the possible solutions in their triads. • Present to staff some possible solutions and ways of both becoming part of external networks and creating their own internal informal networks to support the process.
Feedback and evaluation	10 minutes	Pass it on	• Bring the discussions to an end by asking leaders to choose one step they will take to embed their new knowledge and pass it on to begin building their network. There are a list of options that could be added to in the PowerPoint slides.

Training for leaders 2: Leading a research-informed team – follow the leader

Planning document

Focus	Leading a research-informed team – follow the leader
Facilitators	Senior leaders and/or research leads.
Topics covered	• What matters when and to whom. • How to trial research-informed ideas in your department. • How to decide when to expand.

Preparation tasks	The facilitator should:
	• Read in this book:
	   o Chapter 1, page 2
	   o Chapter 3, page 35
	   o Chapter 6, page 102
	   o Chapter 8, page 158.
	• Adapt a list of possible strategies and areas of focus depending on their school.

Resources required	• PowerPoint slides from the online resources. • A printed copy of the leadership change document (available in the online resources) for each participant to fill in.

Session outline

Focus	Timing	Format	Content
Introduce	5–10 minutes	Spoken introduction	• Welcome participants and introduce the aims of the second session, which are to encourage leaders to take the first leap and be the example to their team.
Reflect	10 minutes	Discussion	• Ask the attendees to reflect on the previous session's action points. 1. How have they used the sources covered in the last session? 2. What difficulties did they find? 3. How have they tried to 'pass it on'? 4. How has the idea of research-informed practice becoming more explicit been received by their teams? 5. Has anyone in their team shown a particular interest or strong opinion regarding their vision?

Focus	Timing	Format	Content
Explain	15 minutes	Presentation	• Explain some of the elements required to incite effective change: time, trust, volunteer army, etc. • Consider what issues will matter to their team at different points in their career – and why. • Ask staff to think about, based on the research presented in previous sessions, which research they would consider using to adapt their own practice in the classroom first.
Explore	25 minutes	PowerPoint and discussion	• Ask staff to think about themselves rather than the team for this next section. • Encourage them to identify an area that they would like to improve and consider some of the strategies previously explored in other sessions. If staff have not been in other sessions, you may wish to consider asking them to do some pre-reading of particular papers before the session – or you can add additional time to this session to ensure they know all the options. • Explain in brief how and why staff should begin implementing this strategy in their own classrooms before asking others to do so. The next set of training plans go into action research in more detail. You could run these sessions after the leadership sessions. • Ask attendees to consider who would be in their volunteer army to begin trialling strategies alongside them. Provide a model for evaluation.
Feedback and evaluation	10 minutes	Discussion	• Ask attendees to consider the positives and negatives of trialling ideas themselves first before implementing policies and practices in a team. • Discuss possible solutions as a team. • Encourage staff to begin trials soon and to discuss further with each other as a support network.

Training for leaders 3: Leading a research-informed team – start spreading the news

Planning document

Focus	Leading a research-informed team – start spreading the news
Facilitators	Senior leaders and/or research leads.
Topics covered	• Creating your vision. • Sharing your vision with others. • Methods of spreading the research-informed love!
Preparation tasks	Facilitators should: • Read Chapter 8, page 158, of this book. • Adapt the PowerPoint slides in the online resources to include an example vision relevant to your context. • Set up a school, department or team Twitter account. • Ask attendees to bring along any documents relating to their team's vision – you could provide a sample vision or questions to respond to that will help create one.
Resources required	• PowerPoint slides from the online resources. • Sticky notes.

Session outline

Focus	Timing	Format	Content
Introduce	5–10 minutes	Spoken introduction	• Welcome the participants and introduce the aim of the third and final session, which is to encourage leaders to think creatively to encourage change.
Reflect	10 minutes	Discussion	• Participants share with each other in triads the visions for their individual teams.
Explain	15 minutes	Presentation	• Explain that a vision should have certain elements. • Explain how a variety of visions might benefit from engaging with research.

Focus	Timing	Format	Content

Explore	25 minutes	Carousel activity	• On tables in the room, display a variety of ways in which leaders might want to drip-feed research to their staff to encourage a research culture.
			
			• For each way of sharing research with staff, ask leaders to consider the benefits of and issues with each. Ask them to add sticky notes of how they might use, adapt or improve the strategies for their own team. Strategies for spreading the news include:
			
			  o a weekly newsletter with a blog
			  o a half-termly reading or journal club
			  o reading briefings per half term
			  o research postcards
			  o a research focus for each term
			  o research posters
			  o action research triads.

Feedback and evaluation	10 minutes	Planning activity Q&A	• Ask leaders to create a timeline of strategies they would consider implementing with justification as to the timeframe. • Lead a final Q&A based on all three sessions.

Action research (one hour to one hour 30 minutes each)

These training plans can be aimed at any group of teachers. In my school, we have used action research in a multitude of ways – from asking everyone to develop their own action research (with varying degrees of success) to encouraging more research-informed projects developed by our second-year teachers, which are then presented to all staff at the end of the year. Action research projects often have a bad name in schools – their success depends on so many factors, not least the time and advice given to those undertaking them. It is important to understand that action research projects are small scale and based purely on the teaching in your context and your classroom. Although findings and results should be shared with others, it might be difficult to apply the findings and changes necessary to a whole school based on a very variable and sometimes messy process. That said, it should not be avoided. How are we to encourage research-informed practice if all we do is read the research and apply it without thinking about our own context and application? We must take the leap and encourage teachers to make the research their own, make the trials their own and make the changes necessary to improve students' outcomes based on evidence over assumptions.

These training plans are designed to be spread over a year, although I do suggest shorter catch-up sessions take place in between to encourage staff to discuss and share their current progress. I would suggest completing the first two sessions before the second term but waiting until after a break (preferably Christmas) to begin the actual process of the action research. This will help to iron out all other issues that might need sorting in a classroom and also to ensure a well-informed choice of action research project. Asking teachers what they want to focus on when they haven't yet met or got to know their class is like asking a doctor what to fix before having met the patient. It is too rushed and likely to be based purely on the most basic of details. Encourage the staff you have involved to attend some of the other sessions you run during the first term to engage them in research but wait until the second term before they begin their own unique action research project.

These sessions are likely to take between one hour and one hour 30 minutes to complete as they involve a lot of discussion and a lot of new ideas being explored. Consider carefully where you place them in the year so that staff always have the time to fully consider the session and their projects. I therefore suggest the following timings:

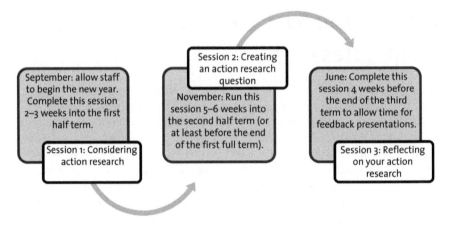

Fig. 13: Suggested schedule for running the action research training plans.

Once staff have taken part in these sessions, it is useful to share the action research project with others. Depending on the scale of the working group taking part, this could mean presenting projects in quick training sessions such as those detailed on pages 208–221. These are 10–20 minute presentations that could take place in front of all staff in the morning. If your working group is over around ten teachers, then this may not be possible. In this case, I would consider combining the action research project with the TeachMeet-style session (page 203), where the TeachMeet takes place two to three weeks after the reflection session and involves staff sharing their findings with others through short five-minute presentations instead.

Action research session 1: Considering action research

Planning document

Focus	What action research is and how to approach it
Facilitators	Senior leaders, research leads or teachers.
Topics covered	• What is action research? • How should you approach a new project?
Preparation tasks	Facilitators should: • Read the overview of action research in Chapter 8, page 158. • Consider example situations in advance that are relevant to your school context.
Resources required	• PowerPoint slides from the online resources. • Scenario cards printed and cut out. Prepare enough for one pack of cards per pair or small group. The cards are available in the online resources.

Session outline

Focus	Timing	Format	Content
Introduce	10 minutes	Spoken presentation	• Welcome the group to the session and explore the aims and outcomes of the session, ensuring you cover the fact that being there means everyone is willing to take a risk and explore a new way to improve their teaching. This means that an atmosphere of mutual respect and a supportive environment are key.
Reflect	10 minutes	Scenario sort	• Look at the scenario cards. Ask the participants to work in pairs or small groups to sort them into those events that are 'action research' and those that aren't. • Make sure you consider the possible experiences of action research your teachers may have had before.

Focus	Timing	Format	Content
Explain	15 minutes	Spoken presentation and PowerPoint slides	• Explore what action research is and how it links to reading evidence. • Refer to previous sessions that staff may have been to if possible. If not, do a quick overview of what it means to read research and how action research differs from simply implementing something new in the classroom.
Explore	15 minutes 15 minutes	Question-led discussion in pairs or triads PowerPoint presentation	• Use the questions on the PowerPoint slide to develop a discussion in pairs or triads about current areas of interest for the school, a department or an individual. This will feed into the next planning session. • Look at the model of action research provided in the slides. You may need to adapt this for your school. It follows the same principle that runs throughout the book – that you need a question and are looking for answers to inform your teaching and students' learning.

Feedback and evaluation	10 minutes	Presentation and reflection	• Provide a set of tasks to complete over the next term.
			• Make clear when you will next be in touch with participants as coordinator of these projects.
			• List the information you will require in just over half a term's time. This should include:
			  1) the class the teacher has focused on
			  2) some current observations of this class
			  3) an area that they wish to improve
			  4) current ways of working.

Action research session 2: Creating an action research question

Planning document

Focus	Writing an action research statement and embedding an evidence-based strategy
Facilitators	Consider asking a range of different teachers to present this session – where possible pick those who have completed some action research already.
Topics covered	• How to decide on a project focus. • Sharing action research projects. • Predicting issues and creating solutions.
Preparation tasks	• Consider how you have created and used the book to write your own question. • Edit the PowerPoint slides to include example questions that best suit your context. • Contact all teachers attending a few weeks before the day to discuss their possible areas of interest. • Collate the evidence you wish to share (include a range of books, papers and blogs). • Collate a list of possible strategies to share with others.
Resources required	• Access to evidence – either in books or online via tablets or computers. • PowerPoint slides from the online resources.

Session outline

Focus	Timing	Format	Content
Introduce	5 minutes	Spoken presentation	• Use this as an opportunity to thank everyone for their time and their preparations so far, which have included considering their possible action research project and chosen class or group of students. • Repeat the expectations of the action research project, ensuring you make clear the element of respect and notice the risk taken by all staff taking part.

Focus	Timing	Format	Content
Reflect	10 minutes	Spoken presentation	• Reflect on what teachers have done so far (in the first half term) and explain that it is important they spent the time teaching in this way and observing their normal practice. • Reflect on how previously at this time of year cracks might start to show and you might begin to use a plethora of strategies to solve these problems – explain how the action research project aims to focus any changes you make in a more considered and valuable way.
Explain	10 minutes	PowerPoint presentation	• Present the areas that you know attendees are currently interested in researching based on your discussions and email communications with them prior to the session. • Try to find links between the attendees' current interests and link them to your school improvement plans and areas for development. Keep these areas anonymous – it should be up to staff whether or not they share these areas with others.
Explore	20 minutes	Writing a research question	• Introduce the PICO statement or question format. • Give examples of the types of questions staff might wish to write. • Ask staff to begin writing their own question (mini whiteboards would be helpful here as people can keep editing and adapting the question as their discussions progress). • Ask staff to look at the suggested strategies lists in the PowerPoint slides to consider a possible strategy. • In discussion with senior leaders, others in the group, research leads and facilitators, encourage staff to create their more precise research question.
Explore (further!)	20 minutes	Group activity	• Pause the discussions so that you can move the groups on to look further at the strategies and resources you have provided for them to learn more about their new strategy. • Where possible, encourage staff to use the same strategy as at least one other teacher so that they can support each other, share ideas and reflect on the differences in outcomes.

Focus	Timing	Format	Content
Evaluation	10 minutes	Presentation and Q&A	• Explain the next steps in the project and timings. • Offer teachers a number of opportunities to catch up between now and the final official session. • Share your expectations of how teachers proceed. • Give teachers a chance to ask questions about their projects and how they move forward.

Action research session 3: Reflecting on your action research

Planning document

Focus	Reflecting on your action research
Facilitators	Plan to use a wide range of teachers who have taken part in the action research to present this session – perhaps pick those who have not previously presented at other sessions or are from under-represented areas of the school.
Topics covered	• Reflections on the project. • Findings and changes teachers are likely to make. • Planning for presentations to all staff. • Question and answer session. • CPD evaluation.
Preparation tasks	• Speak to all participants a number of times between Session 2 (November/December) and Session 3 (June). This will give you a better idea of how to coordinate this session but also lend support. • Consider how you wish the group to present their findings to each other – there are a few ways of adapting the suggestions below if you have a larger group or wish to make it less formal.
Resources required	• PowerPoint slides from the online resources. • A printed copy of the takeaway sheet for each participant (available in the online resources). • CPD evaluation sheet (to be sent out via email after the session; available in the online resources).

Session outline

Focus	Timing	Format	Content
Introduce	10 minutes	Spoken presentation	• Welcome teachers to this reflection session, which is created to help those taking part share their research with others and prepare for their final presentations, which will take place in a few weeks' time. • Explain the format of the session: a quick reflection followed by individuals presenting their ideas to three or four others in an informal setting. This will then be followed by a whole-group discussion where everyone will be asked to share what they will take away and consider further.

Focus	Timing	Format	Content
Reflect	10 minutes	Self-evaluation	• Share some information about the pros and cons of self-improvement in teaching and ask teachers to discuss how they feel about these in relation to their projects. • Use the questions in the PowerPoint slides to help guide the discussion.
Explain	5 minutes	Spoken presentation	• Explain how the session will now work. • Groups created in advance (based on topics and successes) will share their findings with each other. Findings can come in a variety of forms: data, feedback, student voice, logs, photos, videos or questionnaires. • Ask groups to sit at tables. These are informal seated presentations. • Hand out the takeaway sheets and ask for them to be filled in as each teacher talks through their project and findings.
Explore	40 minutes	Carousel sharing activity	• Each teacher is to have 5–8 minutes to share their project, outcomes and thoughts about their action research. • Those listening to each 'presentation' can write down how they think this might apply to their teaching and what they will take away to consider. This can be shared in the feedback session.
Feedback and evaluation	15 minutes	Discussion	• Ask those who have taken part in the three sessions to provide you with feedback on how to improve it next time. • Ensure that those who will later be presenting their ideas to staff are clear on the expectations and aims of their more formal presentations.
Handout	Circulate one week later via email; it should take 10 minutes to complete	CPD evaluation sheet	• Ensure that the CPD evaluation sheet is handed out to staff to complete and hand back to you within the week. Use this to adapt further sessions.

Whole-day INSET (six hours)

All of the previous training sessions work individually but can also be revisited and adapted to create a whole-day INSET, as is done in this section. I still believe it beneficial and preferable to split the sessions into individual ones to allow the thinking to really sink in and allow time to embed, but if you are looking for a way to introduce and inform staff about research-informed practice formally then an INSET day can provide a great opportunity. Some of the day will touch slightly on the sessions in previous training plans but you can simply adapt the one-hour sessions to go into more depth and detail when you then have the time. The INSET provides a taster session of all the key areas and can fit in well at either the beginning or end of a term.

As with the previous sessions, the INSET day plan presumes that the school is happy and keen to work towards research-informed practice and that they have made it their purpose, linked clearly to their overall mission, to improve knowledge of and access to educational research for their teachers. Without this purpose and this mission being made explicit by the school's leadership, this INSET day will not have the impact required and will seem obsolete and time-consuming rather than the start of something important.

One of the issues with voluntary twilight or after-school sessions is that they often clash with other events in school or end up ill-timed, meaning that attendance can vary and the people you were hoping to get the message to don't hear it. On the whole, INSET days don't suffer with that problem, although they can suffer from the preconceptions of long days sat in one place listening to one speaker alone. Try to avoid all the INSET clichés and bingo terminology when planning your day.

The aim of a whole-day INSET on research-informed practice is to encourage teachers to consider their current practice, the possibilities of the research out there and how it might apply to their classrooms or leadership. I would suggest considering which options you take depending on the timing of your INSET day and any training you have done beforehand. You may also wish to run different sessions for different audiences on the day, depending on who has already engaged with your sessions or their experience in teaching.

With a whole-day INSET, it is definitely best to let people know in advance how they will be using their time. We have all sat through INSET days unsure how long presentations will be going on for and this can make people disengaged and less likely to want to take part in this journey with you. It is also very important that you carefully consider your presenters and format. Although every format is now tried and tested, it is important you mix it up and hand over elements to a variety of staff.

Another reason to contact staff about the plans well in advance is to ask for them to bring along certain examples of work, schemes of work and curriculum maps that will help them consider where the research might best impact their teaching both now and in the long term.

Planning document

Focus	Evaluating your research journey
Facilitators	Senior leaders, teaching and learning specialists or department leads.
Topics covered	• An overview of educational research. • The different forms of research that might appear. • Self-reflection and assessment. • An overview of research resources. • Key papers and knowledge. • Effective strategies based on research. • Review of current practice and next steps.
Preparation tasks	• Send out a timetable for the day to all teachers attending. • Ensure that there are enough locations for the different sessions. • Decide who will lead and who will attend each sessions in advance.
Resources required	• Teachers should bring along some of their current planning – in whatever form that takes. • Curriculum leaders should bring along curriculum maps or plans for the sessions later in the day. • PowerPoint slides from the online resources.

Session outline

Focus	Timing	Format	Content
Introduction	30 minutes	Keynote	All staff (led by SLT in charge of T&L): • Welcome all attendees. • Link the day's focus to the school's ethos and mission statement. Remind staff of the purpose of the day: to further inform, enquire and consider the impact of research-informed practice on classroom teaching. • Set out clear expectations of the day. • Remind staff of the timetable for the day and logistics.

Focus	Timing	Format	Content
Session 1	1 hour	Presentation and debate	**Should we rely on intuition or science?** • Staff in leadership positions lead a debate on the above question. Perhaps recruit some staff with opposing opinions to discuss their points of view. • Use the PowerPoint slides to open up a debate about the science of learning and educational research about teaching versus the power of intuition.
Break	30 minutes		
Session 2	1 hour	Carousel activity	**What is educational research? Where did it come from?** • This session should be led by a number of staff and, after a ten-minute introduction, lead to staff taking part in a carousel activity where T&L leaders present on different research sources to each group.
Session 3	1 hour	Shorter presentations led by staff; staff watching to be split into four groups and move between rooms	**Application in the classroom: research-based strategies for effective teaching** This session should be led by a variety of middle leaders who have attended previous training sessions and by teachers who have undertaken the action research projects. This session can be run in a number of ways. Again, you could stick to the carousel format but this time split the groups between rooms. Each presenter has either 15 or 30 minutes (depending on your format) to present their strategy and the research it is based on (much like the 15-minute quick training plans on pages 208–221). The individual rooms will allow those listening to ask questions and not feel as rushed as all taking part in one room. You may wish to suggest certain staff attend certain sessions or run all four sessions simultaneously so that everyone gets to each session.
Lunch	1 hour		
Session 4	2 hours	Department meeting	**Next steps: applying research to our curriculum** All staff should meet in their respective department. See PowerPoint slides for the questions they should focus on.

Focus	Timing	Format	Content
Closing speeches	30 minutes	Presentation	**Reflections** • The end of an INSET day is not a time to ask for new ideas or thoughts. Instead, allow each department to meet with another and share their initial thoughts about the application of research to their curriculum and teaching. Make the pairings carefully. For example, in primary you may wish to pair together year groups or subject specialists who work well together. In secondary, you could pair together faculties such as humanities and English or science and PE to see where their strategies overlap. • Thank you.

3   Evaluating your CPD

This final section of the book is about evaluating your progress, fully focusing on the CPD you have put in place. This is one of those topics that will keep adapting and changing as more research takes place, as the elements of education that we want investigated change and adapt and as that research comes (hopefully) to the forefront of teacher training. The evidence cited in this book and the strategies suggested are just that – suggestions. There is a plethora of evidence out there for you to find but the whole point of the book is to point you in the right direction. As busy teachers with lives to lead, it is clear that finding the evidence is often the hardest part and I hope that the resources and strategies mentioned have put you on the right path to finding your own way through the ever-expanding, complex world that is research-informed practice. If nothing else, it might have made you critical and intrigued. Sharing these questions and ideas with others through the CPD sessions should have brought to light the areas you and others wish to focus on in an attempt to continually become a better teacher, without burning yourself out through last-minute changes and exhausting strategies that only last a few weeks.

Why it is important to evaluate CPD

Evaluating the impact of the CPD you provide is part of an ongoing process. Creating a CPD programme requires a lot of time and effort. It is unlikely that you have implemented all training plans over the course of one academic year and therefore it should be a long-term plan that may need adapting as you go along. In doing so, you respond directly to the needs of staff at the time. As you well know, one set of results, change in funding or change in leadership can swiftly change the course of your actions. As an English teacher, the phrase 'best laid plans...' comes to mind! Therefore, it is important you evaluate as you go along, both individually when running the sessions and also as a team. Ensure that you ask for feedback often and be as open as possible to constructive criticism. Remember, no one is going to love every CPD session all of the time. They may not be in agreement with your or the school's aims and objectives – and that is OK. Ensure that the questions you ask are about the content of the sessions over and above the presentation style. Presentation skills matter – of course they do – but first and foremost it should be about clarity, the content and the conversations that take place in these sessions to support teachers in their ever-exhausting quest to improve students' outcomes.

Ensuring that the CPD you provide is relevant to your context and moves with your school is vital. The word 'continuing' in CPD means that this is not a one-year-fixes-all programme. To truly embed a research culture, you are looking at half a decade's worth of CPD and change. In order to maintain momentum, you will need to adapt and consider the new requirements and update the training year on year to suit your school's needs. In one evaluation of the impact of CPD, it was concluded that 'the most effective types of CPD are perceived to be those that directly meet individual needs' (Goodall et al., 2005). In order to meet the individual needs, you will need to evaluate current practice to refine it every time those needs change.

One other reason for evaluating your CPD is to avoid too much of your own bias. In a report for the Department for Education published in 2005, Goodall et al. found that, unsurprisingly, those running the CPD sessions were more positive about the enjoyment and impact than those attending. It is impossible for us to see without a wider range of resources than what are dubbed 'happiness questionnaires' in the report whether or not the CPD really is making a difference to both teachers and students. There is an entire section in the report of the views of CPD leaders versus the views of teachers. There are lots of commonalities but also some differences about what those leading and those attending considered 'good CPD'. It is important to address some of these issues by considering who leads the sessions, when they are put on (consider the busier times of the year and other pressures) and the format in which they are presented.

There are a few different ways in which you can assess the issues, impact and changes required, and these link back to the opening of the book in which we explored what makes up evidence (page 4). There are very traditional ways of doing so, which may not always be the most effective, but, when combined with a number of different evaluative formats, should prove more illuminating for those running the sessions.

Timing

Despite the fact that the evaluation section is at the end of this book, it is important to evaluate as your CPD sessions occur and not simply wait until the end of one set or section. Ongoing CPD is like formative marking: it will help to improve your feedback and adapt your approach as you go on, rather than not addressing an issue or problem that has arisen. When planning your sessions and who will run them, build in time for some conversations with attendees. These do not have to be formal, interview-style conversations (unless you want them to be) but you should make a note of their views and preferences.

Similarly, when a set of training plans are complete or when an academic term or year ends, you will want to complete some summative evaluation. However, consider carefully the timing of these questions and whether or not this is the only thing you do to evaluate. Asking participants at 5.00 pm on a Monday afternoon how successful they felt a session was is not likely to help you plan your next session on its own. It isn't worthless but you may end up with some blasé answers or (worst case scenario) none at all. Responses could range from a curt response from a teacher who felt they'd seen it all before to a detailed essay plan from a keen NQT detailing everything they learnt and how they're going to use it tomorrow. Of course, these are stereotypes and you will also end up with some useful thoughts but what you do with these responses really matters.

Therefore, below there are a few ways to ensure you do evaluate your CPD sessions but also ensure that this evaluation is:

- relevant
- timely
- varied.

The job of collating the evaluations and findings should be given to one person who has been involved in but has not necessarily led the CPD programme. Some distance is required to fully evaluate and de-personalise the responses, which is certainly required to ensure effective CPD provision for staff.

Strategies to evaluate CPD effectively

Firstly, it is definitely worth reading the full report: 'Evaluating the impact of continuing professional development' (Goodall et al., 2005). For anyone in charge of CPD, this will not be a surprising read but might lead to some changes and conclusions that you had not yet had time to consider or to prioritise and put in place. Below are a few simple ways in which you can make the evaluation of your CPD more rounded.

Staff surveys

Depending on when you give these surveys out you will get one of two things: an immediate reaction or an after-effect. Both are useful and both might be necessary to take your next steps. If you are considering using a staff survey immediately after a session, then make it simple and short. This is a very common form of evaluation but is not always deemed effective due to the lack of changes and adaptations that may occur based on it. Make sure that you use a range of question types but perhaps use a simple system of multiple choice, a score or 'out of 10' responses. At the end of a session, however enlightening, teachers will want to go and you want to gauge how things went without taking up more of their time.

Staff surveys could also be sent out a week, a month or a term after the event. A combination of these would likely work well. The survey itself could act as a reminder of the CPD and encourage staff to consider the knowledge they gained. This works well with busy teachers who may have had an issue to sort out straight after the session, pushing the change they were about to embark on to the bottom of their to-do list. See the two possible evaluation surveys in the online resources and adapt them for your context.

Student interviews

Student voice has become a bit of a buzz word and can mean a wide range of things; however, if you are aware that a certain group (for example second-year teachers) took part in a specific element of your training, you could direct your questions towards their students to look for the impact in the classroom. This needs to be completed carefully and could be unreliable as there are so many factors that might affect student responses.

Having carried out student voice questionnaires in person and via online surveys, it is clear that both have benefits. A bit like the staff surveys, talking with students allows them to expand their responses and you to clarify your questions, whereas an online survey can lead to more blunt responses. An online survey can be easily made using Google forms and shared with students using your online platform – make all the questions 'required' to ensure you don't end up with lots of blank answers!

You could make these surveys anonymous to encourage more honest responses if you wish. Such surveys should focus purely on an initiative and research-informed strategy that has been introduced and allow plenty of time for the strategy to have been embedded and trialled before the first survey – it could be one of a few.

CPD journals

As part of an ongoing process of evaluation, you can provide teachers taking part in a number of sessions with a CPD journal. This is not a place simply to log the number of hours in attendance but a place to record immediate thoughts straight after a session, followed by plans to include new knowledge and strategies in lessons. You will need to encourage teachers to use the journal but it could form part of the evidence required for end-of-year reviews, for example. It is a non-threatening form of collating an individual's engagement with CPD. You could ask to review the journals at a certain point or take a snapshot of how they are being used and the impact they may be having on staff's planning and strategies.

Journaling is an important part of reflecting. It is also key for setting intentions and goals and therefore could be used to encourage engagement with new ideas and change or to help people remain organised with their goals and intentions. Tying this to a more typical form of evaluation, you could follow looking at these journals with learning walks or observations.

Learning walks

Organised and well-planned learning walks in response to training sessions can allow leaders to see the effect of the sessions in the classroom. Rather than making these full observations, you could aim to see a number of lessons simultaneously, and a learning walk can often seem less threatening than an observation. Looking at a variety of lessons will allow those running CPD to see how teachers are adapting and implementing the knowledge and advice they received. It is important to look at the learners in the lesson, the way in which the strategy is being implemented and any previous work that may provide evidence of the effect of training on the teaching and learning taking place.

Feedback should still be given on your observations in the lesson, preferably via face-to-face discussion. A learning walk could involve popping in and out of a lesson or staying in for a set period of time. Inform staff that you will be coming round and your aims and intentions. Make it clear that you want to see the strategy in their context and, where possible, make this clear from the outset – be this weeks or months before the learning walk with this aim takes place. From these observations, you can assess the requirements for the next sessions but also for any future adaptations to the training plans.

Student outcomes

Throughout this book, I have referenced improving student outcomes as the aim of the research-informed changes put in place. This is therefore an important part of the evaluative process but it is difficult to attach student results to one particular strategy. This might be possible with a test designed specifically with a research-informed strategy in mind – for example, if a teacher has changed and developed their teaching based on research on memory and retention, and they design a test that specifically tests the impact on memory over time. However, if we are to use 'big data' such as SATs, GCSE or A level results, there are a multiplicity of factors that influence these results and it would be very difficult to link any correlation directly with a strategy employed. As we know, correlation does not equal causation.

Therefore, this can only form a part of the evaluation process. Alongside some of the other evaluative processes, the data should always be considered as a way to indicate areas of focus and interest rather than a definitive answer as to whether or not your training has had the desired impact.

Organisational review

Evaluating the impact on students and teachers directly is vital, but as a leader of CPD it is important to spend time considering the impact on your organisation as a whole. You may not be in charge of the organisation but reviewing where changes could take or have taken place in terms of policy, ethos and culture is important. This does not need to mean that changes are written in stone or that new policies are printed, but instead consider how, over time, the conversations and approaches might have changed. For example, do you hear policies and practices questioned more than they were previously? Do staff ask for justification for new policies or do you hear the terms 'research' and 'evidence' used on a more day-to-day level than previously and in what context and with what tone of voice?

If you find that over time there have been changes regarding the use of these terms then you will know that your changes, however small, have had an impact in the way you desired.

What now?

This is a long-term game! The next steps are up to you. I hope that you continue to question, read and discover the research that is yet to be written and the research that is yet to be released to the wider public. The whole journey is one of going round in circles – from finding an area to focus on to finding multiple solutions to trialling them then starting again. I think it is a journey made better by working with others and bringing them along with you. It is certainly a journey that will invite opinions but don't be deterred and don't be afraid to change your mind about things as you go along.

There will always be those who disagree with the evidence you cite and there will likely be evidence that disagrees with the evidence you have found – it isn't simple and this is just the start. You should see this as a journey that will not stop. You will require two to three years of embedding these ideas and training provision before you can create a culture of research-informed practice. Moreover, you will require support from a variety of colleagues, including senior leaders, teachers and support staff, to implement many of your ideas in the long term. This requires encouraging and adapting viewpoints, which is no slow process. Do not rush and do not panic – if you've got this far then you are clearly dedicated to your cause and are keen to continue improving.

Having the resources to explore educational research is a vital step – having the time to engage with it is key but having the confidence to approach it is even more important. Once you've built your confidence, learnt more and started on this journey, you will be the one inspiring others to do the same. Therefore, it is vital that you pass on your knowledge and advice to others and encourage teachers to find effective solutions to their questions without stumbling around in the dark for the next best thing only to find it doesn't work. Encourage others to become research informed so that decisions in classrooms near you are no longer based on well-intentioned yet ineffective guesses. Although evidence does not seem to suggest that quotations are in any way motivational, perhaps Dickens had the right idea when he said that 'My advice is, never do tomorrow what you can do today. Procrastination is the thief of time.' Time to plan your next steps.

Bibliography

Alexander, R. J. (2017), 'Developing dialogue: process, trial, outcomes', paper for the 17th International Conference of EARLI, Finland, www.robinalexander.org.uk/wp-content/uploads/2017/08/EARLI-2017-paper.pdf

Allison, S. and Tharby, A. (2015), *Making Every Lesson Count: Six principles to support great teaching and learning*. Carmarthen: Crown House.

Allison, S. and Tharby, A. (2017), 'Growing a culture of great teaching', https://classteaching.wordpress.com/2017/06/25/growing-a-culture-of-great-teaching

Ashman, G. (2015a), 'Minimal guidance', https://gregashman.wordpress.com/2015/03/16/minimal-guidance

Ashman, G. (2015b), 'Why students make silly mistakes in class (and what can be done)', www.theconversation.com/why-students-make-silly-mistakes-in-class-and-what-can-be-done-48826

Bartle, K. (2013), '*The Gruffalo* – an allegory for Trojan mice', https://dailygenius.wordpress.com/2013/10/20/the-gruffalo-an-allegory-for-trojan-mice

Benney, D. (2016), 'Optimal time for spacing gaps', www.mrbenney.wordpress.com/2016/11/03/optimal-time-for-spacing-gaps

Berger, R. (2003), *An Ethic of Excellence: Building a culture of craftsmanship with students*. Portsmouth, NH: Heinemann Educational.

Black, P. and Wiliam, D. (1998), 'Inside the black box: Raising standards through classroom assessment', www.rdc.udel.edu/wp-content/uploads/2015/04/InsideBlackBox.pdf

Brown, P., Roediger, H. and McDaniel, M. (2014), *Make It Stick: The science of successful learning*. Cambridge, MA: Harvard University Press.

Bruskill, J. (2016), 'Using knowledge organisers in primary', https://pedfed.wordpress.com/2016/12/30/using-knowledge-organisers-in-primary/#comment-398

Carlin, N. (2018), 'CPD: how our department is taking a DIY approach', *TES*, www.tes.com/news/cpd-how-our-department-taking-diy-approach

Carpenter, S. K. (2009), 'Cue strength as a moderator of the testing effect: The benefits of elaborative retrieval', *Journal of Experimental Psychology: Learning, Memory, and Cognition*, 35, 1563–1569.

Carvalho, P. F. and Goldstone, R. L. (2015), 'The benefits of interleaved and blocked study: Different tasks benefit from different schedules of study', *Psychonomic Bulletin and Review*, 22, (1), 281–288.

Centre for Education Statistics and Evaluation (2017), 'Cognitive load theory: Research that teachers really need to understand', www.cese.nsw.gov.au//images/stories/PDF/cognitive-load-theory-VR_AA3.pdf

Cepeda, N. J., Vul, E., Rohrer, D., Wixted, J. T. and Pashler, H. (2008), 'Spacing effects in learning: A temporal ridgeline of optimal retention', *Psychological Science*, 19, (11), 1095–1102.

Christodoulou, D. (2014), *Seven Myths About Education*. Abingdon: Routledge.

Christodoulou, D. (2016), *Making Good Progress*. Oxford: Oxford University Press.

Coane, J. and Minear, M. (2018), 'Who really benefits from retrieval practice?', www.learningscientists.org/blog/2018/11/6-1

Coe, R., Aloisi, C., Higgins, S. and Major, L. E. (2014), 'What makes great teaching? Review of the underpinning research', www.suttontrust.com/wp-content/uploads/2014/10/What-Makes-Great-Teaching-REPORT.pdf

Cohen, L., Manion, L. and Morrison, K. (2007), *Research Methods in Education*. Abingdon: Routledge.

Creemers, B. P. and Kyriakides, L. (2011), *Improving Quality in Education: Dynamic approaches to school improvement*. Abingdon: Routledge.

Danielson, C. (2007), *Enhancing Professional Practice: A framework for teaching*. Alexandria, VA: ASCD.

Deans for Impact (2015), *The Science of Learning*. Austin, TX: Deans for Impact.

De Bruyckere, P., Kirschner, P. A. and Hulshof, C. D. (2015), *Urban Myths About Learning and Education*. London: Academic Press.

Didau, D. (2015a), *What If Everything You Knew About Education Was Wrong?* Carmarthen: Crown House Publishing.

Didau, D. (2015b), 'Research vs evidence', *Learning Spy*, https://learningspy.co.uk/research/research-vs-evidence

Didau, D. (2017), 'Why do we forget stuff? Familiarity vs recall', *Learning Spy*, www.learningspy.co.uk/psychology/forget-stuff-familiarity-vs-recall

Didau, D. (2019), 'Three animated films about learning', *Learning Spy*, https://learningspy.co.uk/featured/three-animated-films-about-learning

Dunlosky, J., Rawson, K. A., Marsh, E. J., Nathan, M. J. and Willingham, D. T. (2013a), 'Improving students' learning with effective learning techniques: Promising directions from cognitive and educational psychology', *Psychological Science in the Public Interest*, 14, (1), 4–58.

Dunlosky, J., Rawson, K. A., Marsh, E. J., Nathan, M. J. and Willingham, D. T. (2013b), 'Psychologists identify the best ways to study', *Scientific American*, www.scientificamerican.com/article/psychologists-identify-best-ways-to-study

Education Endowment Foundation (2018a), 'Early Years Toolkit', https://educationendowmentfoundation.org.uk/public/files/Toolkit/complete/EEF-Early-Years-toolkit-July-2018.pdf

Education Endowment Foundation (2018b), 'Behaviour interventions', https://educationendowmentfoundation.org.uk/evidence-summaries/teaching-learning-toolkit/behaviour-interventions/

Education Endowment Foundation (2018c), 'Homework (secondary)', https://educationendowmentfoundation.org.uk/evidence-summaries/teaching-learning-toolkit/homework-secondary

Education Endowment Foundation (2018d), 'Homework (primary)', www.educationendowmentfoundation.org.uk/evidence-summaries/teaching-learning-toolkit/homework-primary

Education Endowment Foundation (2018e), 'Self-regulation strategies', www. educationendowmentfoundation.org.uk/evidence-summaries/early-years-toolkit/ self-regulation-strategies/

Elliott, V., Baird, J., Hopfenbeck, T., Ingram, J., Thompson, I., Usher, N., Zantout, M., Richardson, J. and Coleman, R. (2016), 'A marked improvement? A review of the evidence on written marking', Education Endowment Foundation, https:// educationendowmentfoundation.org.uk/evidence-summaries/evidence-reviews/ written-marking

Enser, M. (2017), 'In defense of being informed', *Teaching It Real*, https://teachreal. wordpress.com/2017/11/26/in-defense-of-being-informed

Enser, M. (2019a), *Making Every Geography Lesson Count: Six principles to support great geography teaching*. Carmarthen: Crown House.

Enser, M. (2019b), *Teach Like Nobody's Watching: The essential guide to effective and efficient teaching*. Carmarthen: Crown House.

Facer, J. (2016), 'Giving feedback the "Michaela" way', *Reading all the Books*, https:// readingallthebooks.com/2016/03/19/giving-feedback-the-michaela-way

Farme, R. J. (2016), 'Question: What's your preferred learning style?', http://blogs. northampton.ac.uk/learntech/2016/06/16/ question-whats-your-preferred-learning-style

Findlater, S. (2016), *Bloomsbury CPD Library: Marking and Feedback*. London: Bloomsbury Education.

Fletcher-Wood, H. (2013), 'Do they understand this well enough to move on? Introducing hinge questions', *Improving Teaching*, www.improvingteaching.co.uk/2013/08/17/ do-they-understand-this-well-enough-to-move-on-introducing-hinge-questions

Fletcher-Wood, H. (2016), *Ticked Off: Checklists for teachers, students, school leaders*. Carmarthen: Crown House.

Fletcher-Wood, H. (2018), *Responsive Teaching*. Abingdon: Routledge.

Goodall, J., Day, C., Lindsay, G., Muijs, D. and Harris, A. (2005), 'Evaluating the impact of continuing professional development', Research Report RR659, Department for Education.

Hendrick, C. and Macpherson, R. (2017), *What Does This Look Like In The Classroom? Bridging the gap between research and practice.* Woodbridge: John Catt Educational.

Hewett, V. (2017), 'Mrs Humanities shares... 5 whole class feedback examples', *Mrs Humanities*, www.mrshumanities.com/2017/10/15/ mrs-humanities-shares-5-whole-class-feedback-examples

Huntington Research School (2017), 'Homework: What does the evidence say?' https://researchschool.org.uk/huntington/blog/ homework-what-does-the-evidence-say

Jones, G. (2015), 'The school research lead and asking better questions – part one', *Evidence Based Educational Leadership*, http:// evidencebasededucationalleadership.blogspot.com/2015/01/the-school-research-lead-and-asking.html

Jones, G. (2016), *Evidence-Based Practice: A handbook for teachers and school leaders.* Amsterdam: Centre for Evidence-Based Management, https://drive.google. com/file/d/0B3LUp9PxnSZlZUVUSDJnUUE4M00/view

Jones, G. (2018), *Evidence-Based School Leadership and Management: A practical guide.* London: Sage.

Kirby, J. (2015), 'Knowledge organisers', *Pragmatic Reform*, https://pragmaticreform. wordpress.com/2015/03/28/knowledge-organisers

Kirschner, P. A., Sweller, J. and Clark, R. E. (2006), 'Why minimal guidance during instruction does not work: An analysis of the failure of constructivist, discovery, problem-based, experiential, and inquiry-based teaching', *Educational Psychologist*, 41, (2), 75–86.

Kotter, J. P. (2012), *Leading Change.* Brighton, MA: Harvard Business Review Press.

Lemov, D. (2014), 'The do now: A primer', *Doug Lemov's Field Notes*, www. teachlikeachampion.com/blog/now-primer

Lemov, D. (2015), *Teach Like A Champion 2.0.* San Francisco, CA: Jossey Bass.

Lemov, D. (2017), 'Bloom's taxonomy: that pyramid is a problem', *Teach Like a Champion*, http://teachlikeachampion.com/blog/blooms-taxonomy-pyramid-problem

Lolder, L. (2018), 'Ten testing strategies: A range of activities for varying retrieval practice', https://teachingtoptens.wordpress.com/2018/09/28/ten-testing-strategies-a-range-of-activities-for-varying-retrieval-practice

Ludgate, J. (2015a), 'Last night ResearchEd changed my life', *Little Miss Lud*, https://littlemisslud.wordpress.com/2015/09/06/last-night-researched-saved-my-life

Ludgate, J. (2015b), 'Research and revision', *Little Miss Lud*, https://littlemisslud.wordpress.com/2015/05/01/revision-and-research

Masic, I., Miokovic, M. and Muhamedagic, B. (2008), 'Evidence based medicine – new approaches and challenges', *Acta Informatica Medica*, 16, (4), 219–25.

Miller, E. (2017), 'Teachers on Twitter: Why you should join and how to get started', *Guardian*, www.theguardian.com/teacher-network/2017/apr/20/teachers-on-twitter-why-join-get-started-social-media

Nelson, J. and O'Beirne, C. (2014), 'Using evidence in the classroom: What works and why?', Slough: National Foundation for Educational Research, www.nfer.ac.uk/publications/IMPA01/IMPA01.pdf

Nevill, M. (2018), 'Action research in the classroom: A quick guide', *TES*, www.tes.com/news/action-research-classroom-quick-guide

Nuthall, G. (2007), *The Hidden Lives of Learners*. Wellington: NZCER Press.

Oxford Dictionaries (2010), 'Research', https://en.oxforddictionaries.com/definition/research

Pomerance, L., Greenberg, J. and Walsh, K. (2016), 'Learning about learning: What every new teacher needs to know', www.nctq.org/dmsView/Learning_About_Learning_Report

Quigley, A. (2016), 'Breaking beyond our old ideas', *The Confident Teacher*, www.theconfidentteacher.com/2016/03/escaping-the-tyranny-of-our-old-ideas

Quigley, A., Muijs, D. and Stringer, E. (2018), 'Metacognition and self-regulated learning', Education Endowment Foundation, https://educationendowmentfoundation.org.uk/tools/guidance-reports/metacognition-and-self-regulated-learning

Research Schools Network (2016), 'About us', https://researchschool.org.uk/about

Rose, N. (2018), 'Avoiding lethal mutations', www.ambition.org.uk/blog/avoiding-lethal-mutations

Rose, N. and Eriksson-Lee, S. (2017), 'Putting evidence to work: How can we help new teachers use research evidence to inform their teaching?', *TeachFirst*, www.teachfirst.org.uk/sites/default/files/2017-10/Putting_Evidence_to_work_2017.pdf

Rosenshine, B. (1997), 'The case for explicit, teacher-led, cognitive strategy instruction', http://citeseerx.ist.psu.edu/viewdoc/download?doi=10.1.1.468.1582&rep=rep1&type=pdf

Rosenshine, B. (2010), 'Principles of instruction', *Educational Practices*, 21. Brussels: International Academy of Education, www.ibe.unesco.org/fileadmin/user_upload/Publications/Educational_Practices/EdPractices_21.pdf

Rosenshine, B. (2012), 'Principles of instruction: Research-based strategies that all teachers should know', *American Educator*, https://files.eric.ed.gov/fulltext/EJ971753.pdf

Sadler, P. M., Sonnert, G., Coyle, H. P., Cook-Smith, N. and Miller, J. L. (2013), 'The influence of teachers' knowledge on student learning in middle school physical science classrooms', *American Educational Research Journal*, 50, (5), 1020–1049.

Sherrington, T. (2017), 'Teaching and learning research summaries: A collection for easy access', *Teacher Head*, www.teacherhead.com/2017/06/03/teaching-and-learning-research-summaries-a-collection-for-easy-access

Sherrington, T. (2019), *Rosenshine's Principles in Action*. Woodbridge: John Catt Educational.

Shibli, D. and West, R. (2018), 'Cognitive load theory and its application in the classroom', *Impact*, https://impact.chartered.college/article/shibli-cognitive-load-theory-classroom/

Simmonds, M. (2017), 'Is it really a low stakes quiz?', *Class Teaching*, https://classteaching.wordpress.com/2017/03/23/is-it-really-a-low-stakes-quiz

Smith, M. and Weinstein, Y. (2016), 'Learn how to study using... dual coding', *The Learning Scientists*, www.learningscientists.org/blog/2016/9/1-1

Stephens, K. (2014), 'Lesson starters: An outdated idea or a meaningful teaching tool?', *The Bridge Journal of Educational Research-Informed Practice*, 1, (1), 22–47.

Taylor, T. (2013), 'Using cognitive psychology in the classroom: Approach with caution', *Guardian*, www.theguardian.com/teacher-network/teacher-blog/2013/aug/20/cognitive-psychology-classroom-caution

Teaching How2, 'The principles of instruction', www.teachinghow2s.com/docs/HOW2_Poster_Principles_of_Instruction.pdf

Tharby, A. (2013), 'Modelling for excellence', *Class Teaching*, https://classteaching.wordpress.com/2013/11/24/modelling-for-excellence

Tharby, A. (2014), 'Spacing and interleaving', *Class Teaching*, www.classteaching.wordpress.com/2014/06/12/spacing-and-interleaving

The SUPER Blog (2018), 'Access to research', https://schooluniversitypartnership.wordpress.com/access-to-research

Thornton, G. (2016) 'Marking crib sheet and whole class feedback', *Mr Thornton Teach*, www.mrthorntonteach.com/2016/04/08/marking-crib-sheet

Tomsett, J. (2015), 'This much I know about... The Sutton Trust/EEF Toolkit and the Golden Thread from evidence to student outcomes, via deliberate intervention', https://johntomsett.com/2015/02/13/this-much-i-know-about-the-golden-thread-from-evidence-to-student-outcomes

Weinstein, Y. and Sumeracki, M. with Caviglioli, O. (2018), *Understanding How We Learn*. Abingdon: Routledge.

Wiliam, D. (2011), *Embedded Formative Assessment*. Bloomington, IN: Solution Tree Press.

Willingham, D. T. (2009), *Why Don't Students Like School?* San Francisco, CA: Jossey Bass.

Willingham, D. T. (2012), *When Can You Trust the Experts? How to tell good science from bad in education*. San Francisco, CA: Jossey Bass.

Websites

www.bestevidence.org.uk

www.diagnosticquestions.com

Bibliography

www.educationendowmentfoundation.org.uk

www.learningscientists.org

www.literacywagoll.com/resources.html

https://researchschool.org.uk/about

www.the-iee.org.uk/what-we-do/best-evidence-in-brief

Index